Learning Microsoft® Office PowerPoint® 2007

Catherine Skintik

PEARSON

Prentice Hall
DDC

1 2 3 4 5 6 7 8 9 10   11 10 09 08 07

ISBN-13: 978-0-13-365702-9
ISBN-10: 0-13-365702-7

Table of Contents

Introduction

Microsoft Office PowerPoint 2007 is Microsoft's tool for creating dynamic on-screen presentations. Use PowerPoint to build the exciting, changing, and interactive presentations that today's information-driven world demands from businesses, governments, schools, and virtually every organization that needs to communicate.

HOW THIS BOOK IS ORGANIZED

■ This book is organized into six lessons that begin with basic Microsoft Office skills:

- **Office 2007 Basics.** This lesson introduces essential Microsoft Office 2007 skills—including starting Microsoft Office, using the mouse and keyboard, working with the new Office 2007 screen elements, and getting help using the Help system. If you are completely new to PowerPoint 2007 or the Office 2007 suite, you should start with this lesson.

- **Lesson 1—PowerPoint Basics.** This lesson covers the most essential skills required to create a new presentation. You begin by working with the default blank presentation that displays when PowerPoint starts and learn to add slides with specific layouts; format the slides with themes, theme colors, and theme fonts; and work with PowerPoint's views. After this introduction to the basics, you move on to learn other ways to create a presentation, by working with a PowerPoint template and by working with a Word outline. You learn to insert, size, and position clip art on your slides, and you are introduced to skills such as copying, cutting, and pasting that enable you to duplicate or move text and slides. You learn different ways to view and print slide materials.

- **Lesson 2—Work with Text Elements.** In this lesson, you concentrate on improving and formatting text. Change text appearance and paragraph formatting by selecting new font, font size, font style, font color, and character spacing options as well as line spacing, alignment, indent, and tab options. Add text to a slide outside of a placeholder by inserting a text box and format the box by setting text in columns or applying an interesting fill. Another way to add text to a slide is to insert a WordArt graphic; you can modify the graphic in a number of ways to improve its appearance. You also fine-tune text using the Replace feature and the Thesaurus.

- **Lesson 3—Work with Tables, Charts, and Diagrams.** This lesson teaches you how to create eye-catching tables on a slide and insert Excel worksheets and other data files into a presentation to handle special types of information. You also learn how to add charts to a presentation and insert SmartArt diagrams, new in PowerPoint 2007, to graphically illustrate conceptual data. PowerPoint's contextual Table, Chart, and SmartArt tools make it a snap to modify and format these objects to make your presentations not only informative but visually striking.

- **Lesson 4—Work with Graphic Elements.** In this lesson, you go into more depth with PowerPoint's graphic elements. You learn how to customize a background; work with drawing shapes; insert pictures, movies, and sounds; and create a Photo Album. You also learn how to customize slide, notes, and handout masters to change formats throughout a presentation. At the end of the lesson, you learn how to create your own theme and template and apply custom themes and templates to new presentations.

- **Lesson 5—Prepare and Present a Slide Show.** This lesson introduces you to features and skills you need to finalize a presentation. You learn how to add transitions and animations that add visual interest, as well as how to rehearse a presentation and control slide advance. Add custom shows, links, and action settings to control the presentation of specific data, and add narration to take the place of a moderator's remarks. You learn to set up a show for different types of audiences, control the slides during a presentation, and mark on slides as you present them. PowerPoint 2007's robust protection options are covered, as are features that allow you to mark up slides and send them to team members via e-mail. You learn how to pack up a presentation for deliver elsewhere and save a presentation in other formats, such as shows, graphic files, and Web pages.

- Lessons are comprised of short exercises designed for using Microsoft Office PowerPoint 2007 in real-life business settings. Each exercise is made up of seven key elements:

  - **Software Skills.** Each exercise starts with a brief overview of the PowerPoint tools that you'll be working with in the exercise.

  - **Application Skills.** The objectives are then put into context by setting a scenario.

  - **Terms.** Key terms are included and defined at the start of each exercise, so you can quickly refer back to them. The terms are then highlighted in the text.

  - **Notes.** Concise notes for learning the computer concepts.

- **Procedures.** Hands-on mouse and keyboard procedures teach all necessary skills.

- **Application Exercise.** Step-by-step instructions put your skills to work.

- **On Your Own.** Each exercise concludes with a critical-thinking activity that you can work through on your own. In many of these exercises you need to create your own data. The On Your Own sections can be used as additional reinforcement, for practice, or to test skill proficiency.

- Each lesson ends with a **Critical Thinking Exercise** that, as with the *On Your Owns*, requires you to rely on your own skills to complete the task, and a **Curriculum Integration Exercise**, which incorporates Language Arts, Math, Science, or Social Studies content.

- Two or more **Curriculum Connections** appear in each lesson. These activities involve research on a topic and then using that data in PowerPoint. Below is a listing of the Curriculum Connections.

Directory of Curriculum Connections

WORKING WITH DATA AND SOLUTION FILES

As you work through the exercises in this book, you'll be creating, opening, and saving files. You should keep the following instructions in mind:

- For many of the exercises you can use the data files provided on the CD-ROM that comes with this book. The data files are used so that you can focus on the skills being introduced—not on keyboarding lengthy documents. The files are organized by application in the **Datafiles** folders on the CD-ROM.

- When the application exercise includes a file name and a CD icon 🔘, you can open the file provided on CD.

- Unless the book instructs otherwise, use the default settings for displaying Normal view and

Ribbon and Quick Access Toolbar settings. The appearance of your files may look different if the system is set to a screen resolution other than 800 x 600.

- All the exercises instruct you to save the files created or to save the exercise files under a new name.

- When you see _xx in any instructions in this book, it means that you should type an underscore followed by your own initials—not the actual text "_xx". This will help your instructor identify your work.

- You should verify the name of the hard disk or network folder to which files should be saved.

WHAT'S ON THE CD 🔘

The CD contains the following:

- **Data Files** for many of the exercises. This way you don't have to type lengthy documents from scratch.

- **Microsoft® Office 2007 Glossary** includes terms and definitions.

- **Glossary of Business and Financial Terms** used in the workplace, the financial arena, and Learning Microsoft Office PowerPoint 2007. Key business terms help you understand the work scenarios.

- **Keyboarding Course** teaches all the keys and includes skill-building drills.

- **Computer Literacy Basics.** These exercises include information on computer care, computer basics, and a brief history of computer.

To Access the Files Included on CD:

1. Insert the *Learning Microsoft Office PowerPoint 2007* CD in the CD-ROM drive.
2. Navigate to your CD-ROM drive; right-click **start** / and choose Explore from the shortcut menu.
3. Navigate to your CD-ROM drive.
4. Right-click the folder that you wish to copy.
5. Navigate to the location where you wish to place the folder.
6. Right-click and choose Paste from the Shortcut menu.

SUPPORT MATERIAL

A complete instructor support package is available with all the tools teachers need:

- **Teacher's Manual** includes teaching tips, hints, and pointers to help teachers maximize classroom presentation time. Includes solution files on CD. (ISBN: 0-13-365704-3)

- **Test Binder** includes both application and concept tests correlated to each lesson in the book. Also includes pretests, posttests, and final exams. (ISBN: 0-13-365705-1)

- **Solution Binder** includes printouts of exercise solutions to visually check students' results. Also includes solution files on CD. (ISBN: 0-13-365706-X)

Microsoft Office 2007 Basics

Skills Covered

- **About Business Technology**
- **About Microsoft Office 2007**
- **Use the Mouse**
- **Use the Keyboard**
- **Start and Exit Microsoft Office Programs**
- **Identify Common Screen Elements**
- **Conventions Used in This Book**

Software Skills Microsoft® Office 2007 contains a suite of programs that may be used independently or together to create simple documents, such as letters and memos, as well as complex reports, data tables, and budget spreadsheets. In addition, you can use the Microsoft Office programs to manage information and documents, collaborate with others, and communicate via e-mail. Many jobs in today's workplace require knowledge of this best-selling software suite.

Application Skills You have just been hired as the assistant to the president of Restoration Architecture, a firm that specializes in remodeling, redesign, and restoration of existing properties. He has asked you to become familiar with Microsoft Office 2007, since the company uses it throughout its business operations. In this exercise, you'll practice using the mouse and the keyboard to start and exit Microsoft Office 2007 programs, and you will review the screen elements common to the different programs.

TERMS

Elements Menus, icons, and other items that are part of an on-screen interface.

Hyperlink Text or graphics set up to provide a direct connection with a destination location. When you click a hyperlink, the destination is displayed.

I-beam A mouse pointer shape resembling the uppercase letter I.

Icon A picture used to identify an element on-screen, such as a toolbar button.

Insertion point The flashing vertical line that indicates where the next action will occur in a document or file on-screen.

Menu A list of commands or choices.

Mouse A device that allows you to select items on-screen by pointing at them with the mouse pointer.

Mouse pointer A marker on your computer screen that shows you where the next mouse action will occur. The mouse pointer changes shapes depending on the current action.

Ribbon A screen element that displays buttons for accessing Office features and commands.

Scroll wheel A wheel on some mouse devices (called a wheeled mouse) used to navigate through a document on-screen.

Toolbar A row of buttons used to select features and commands.

Window The area on-screen where a program or document is displayed.

NOTES

About Business Technology

- Businesses rely on technology of many types to make sure employees have the tools they need to complete assignments, tasks, and other responsibilities.

- Departments must evaluate the needs of each employee, research the available technologies, and then purchase and install the appropriate systems. They must also be sure employees know how to use the new systems.

- Technology purchases include hardware and software.

- Requirements vary from department to department and from company to company. For example, a large financial services company will have different technology needs from those of a small travel agency.

- At the very least, almost all businesses require a computer, a printer, a connection to the Internet, and software such as Microsoft Office for basic business applications, such as word processing, data management, and spreadsheet functions.

- When evaluating technology, consider the following:
  - Tasks you need to accomplish.
  - Cost.
  - Ease of use.
  - Compatibility with existing systems.

- You can learn more about hardware and software technology by using the Internet, by consulting a magazine or buyer's guide, or by visiting a retailer in your area to talk to a salesperson.

About Microsoft Office 2007

- Microsoft Office 2007 is the latest version of the popular Microsoft Office software suite.

- The new user interface is designed to make it easier to access the most commonly used commands. Key new features include the following.
  - The **Ribbon** replaces traditional menus and toolbars.
  - Galleries of preset formatting options let you preview how changes will affect your files and quickly apply the formatting with a single click.
  - The spelling checker provides consistent functionality across all Office 2007 programs.

- In addition, there are new default file formats based on Extensible Markup Language (XML) for some Office 2007 programs.
  - The new file formats result in smaller files, improved recovery of damaged files, improved security, and easier integration between different file types.
  - Microsoft Office 2007 programs are fully compatible with files created with previous versions.

- The Microsoft Office 2007 software suite is available in different editions.

- Most editions include the following core Microsoft Office System programs:
  - Word, a word processing program.
  - Excel, a spreadsheet program.
  - PowerPoint, a presentation graphics program.
  - Outlook, a personal information manager and communications program.

- Some editions may include the following additional programs:
  - Access, a database application.
  - Publisher, a desktop publishing program.
  - OneNote, a note-taking and management program.
  - InfoPath, an information gathering and management program.

- Microsoft Office 2007 can run with either the Microsoft Windows XP or the Microsoft Windows Vista operating system.

- There may be slight differences in the programs depending on the operating system you are using.

- For example, features that involve browsing for storage locations are different depending on the operating system. This includes opening and saving a file, and selecting a file to insert.

- In addition, there may be some minor visual differences in the way the programs look on-screen. For example, the colors may differ, and the program Close button may be larger under Windows Vista.

- The procedures in this book assume you are using Microsoft Windows XP.

Use the Mouse

- Use your **mouse** to point to and select commands and features of Microsoft Office 2007 programs.

- Traditional mouse devices work by sliding a tracking ball on your desk.

- Newer devices might work using light. Others may use a wireless connection.

    ✓ *Laptop and notebook computers may have a touchpad or trackball to move the pointer on the screen in place of a mouse.*

- When you move the mouse on your desk, the **mouse pointer** moves on-screen. For example, when you move the mouse to the left, the mouse pointer moves to the left.

- When you click a mouse button, the program executes a command. For example, when you move the mouse pointer to the Print button and then click, the program prints the current document or file.

- Clicking a mouse button can also be used to move the **insertion point** to a new location.

- A mouse may have one, two, or three buttons. Unless otherwise noted, references in this book are to the use of the left mouse button.

- Your mouse might have a **scroll wheel**. Spin the scroll wheel to move through the file open on your screen.

- The mouse pointer changes shape depending on the program in use, the object being pointed to, and the action being performed. Common mouse pointer shapes include an arrow (for selecting), an **I-beam** (which indicates location on-screen), and a hand with a pointing finger (to indicate a **hyperlink**).

- You should use a mouse on a mouse pad that is designed specifically to make it easy to slide the mouse.

    ✓ *You can move the mouse without moving the mouse pointer by picking it up. This is useful if you move the mouse too close to the edge of the mouse pad or desk.*

Use the Keyboard

- Use your keyboard to type characters, including letters, numbers, and symbols. The keyboard can also be used to access program commands and features.

- In addition to the regular text and number keys, computer keyboards have special keys used for shortcuts or for executing special commands.

    - Function keys (F1–F12) often appear in a row above the numbers at the top of the keyboard. They can be used as shortcut keys to perform certain tasks.

    - Modifier keys (Shift, Alt, Ctrl) are used in combination with other keys or mouse actions to select certain commands or perform actions. In this book, key combinations are shown as the modifier key followed by a plus sign followed by the other key or mouse action. For example, Ctrl + S is the key combination for saving the current file.

    - The Numeric keys are made up of the 17-key keypad to the right of the main group of keyboard keys on an enhanced keyboard.

        ✓ *Laptop and notebook computers integrate the numeric keys into the regular keyboard.*

    - When the Num Lock (number lock) feature is on, the keypad can be used to enter numbers. When the feature is off, the keys can be used as directional keys to move the insertion point in the current file.

    - The Escape key (Esc) is used to cancel a command.

    - Use the Enter key to execute a command or to start a new paragraph when typing text.

    - Directional keys are used to move the insertion point.

    - Editing keys (Insert, Delete, and Backspace) are used to insert or delete text.

    - The Windows key (sometimes called the *Winkey* or the *Windows Logo key*) is used alone to open the Windows Start **menu**, or in combination with other keys to execute certain Windows commands.

    - The Application key is used alone to open a shortcut menu, or in combination with other keys to execute certain application commands.

    - Some keyboards also have keys for opening shortcut menus, launching a Web browser, or opening an e-mail program.

Start and Exit Microsoft Office Programs

- To use a Microsoft Office 2007 program, you must first start it so it is running on your computer.
- Use Windows to start an Office program. Use any of these options, shown in the following illustration.
  - You can select the program you want to start from the Microsoft Office folder accessed from the Windows All Programs menu.

- If the program has been used recently, or pinned to the Windows Start menu, you can select it directly from the Windows Start menu.
- You can click a program shortcut **icon** on the desktop, if available.
- When you are done using a Microsoft Office program, close it to exit.

Start a Microsoft Office program using Windows XP

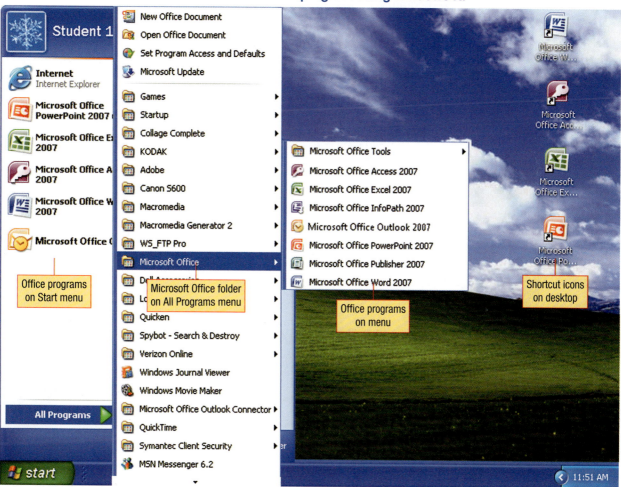

Identify Common Screen Elements

- When a program is running, it is displayed in a **window** on your screen.

- The program windows for each of the Microsoft Office applications contain many common **elements**.

  ✓ You will find more information about the PowerPoint window in Exercise 5 of Lesson 1.

- The following figure identifies the common elements you will find in the Office program windows.

- *Ribbon.* Displays buttons for accessing features and commands.

  ✓ Note that the way items display on the Ribbon may depend on the width of the program window. If your program window is wider than the one used in the figures, more or larger buttons may display. If your program window is narrower, fewer or smaller buttons may display. Refer to Exercise 2 for more information.

- *Ribbon tabs.* Used to change the commands displayed on the Ribbon.

Common elements in a PowerPoint window

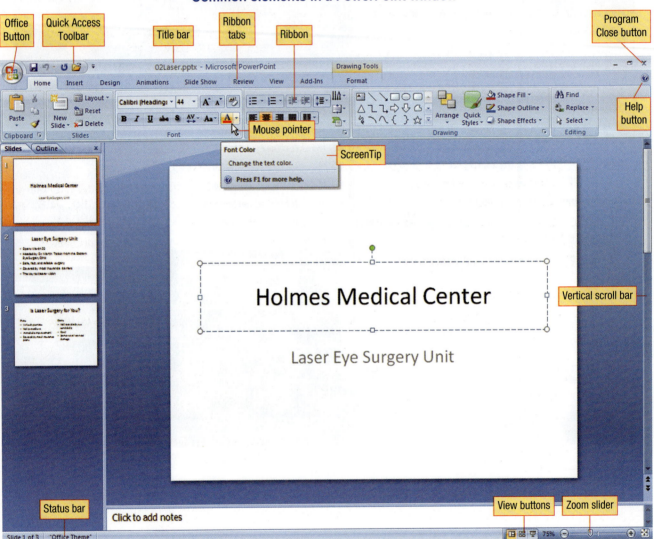

- *Quick Access Toolbar.* A **toolbar** that displays buttons for commonly used commands. You can customize the Quick Access Toolbar to display buttons you use frequently.

- *Office Button.* Click to display a menu of common commands for managing documents and files.

- *Program Close button.* Used to close the program window. It is one of three buttons used to control the size and position of the program window. Some Office applications also have a document Close button that closes the current document without closing the program.

  ✓ *Using the window control buttons is covered in Exercise 3.*

- *Mouse pointer.* Marks the location of the mouse on the screen.

  ✓ *The appearance of the mouse pointer changes depending on the program being used and the current action.*

- *Scroll bar.* Used with a mouse to shift the on-screen display up and down or left and right.

- *Status bar.* Displays information about the current document.

- *ScreenTip.* Displays information about the element on which the mouse pointer is resting.

- *Title bar.* Displays the program and file names.

- *Zoom slider.* Used to increase or decrease the size of the document on-screen.

- *Help button.* Used to start the program's Help system.

- *View buttons.* Used to change the document view.

Conventions Used in This Book

- Throughout this book, procedures for completing a task are documented as follows and as shown in the following illustration.

  - Keyboard shortcut keys (if available) are included next to the task heading.

  - Mouse actions including button icons are numbered on the left.

  - Keystrokes are listed on the right.

  - Keys pressed in sequence are separated by a comma.

  - Keys pressed in combination are separated by a plus sign.

  - The name of the Ribbon group precedes the steps where actions occur.

- As mentioned earlier, the width of the program window affects the way buttons and groups display on the Ribbon.

- If your screen is narrower than the one in this book, you may have to click a group button to display the commands in that group before you can complete the steps in the procedure.

- If your screen is wider, you may be able to skip a step for selecting a group button and go directly to the step for selecting a specific command.

  ✓ *Refer to Exercise 2 for more information on using the Ribbon.*

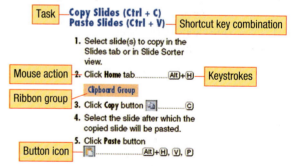

Sample of procedure conventions

Curriculum Connection: Language Arts

Office Applications

The Microsoft Office suite of applications provides the tools you need to prepare documents throughout a business organization. It offers sophisticated and easy-to-use programs that use a common interface and share many tools and features. Office programs are among the most widely used applications in the world.

Pitch Microsoft Office 2007

Prepare a presentation that you could deliver to a company that does not yet use Microsoft Office 2007. Write the main points you want to make in the form of titles and bulleted items that you can use to create PowerPoint slides. Your presentation should include information about the important features Office 2007 offers and how the company would benefit from using the Office applications.

PROCEDURES

Start an Office Program

1. Click **Start** button
   ........Ctrl+Esc
2. Click **All Programs**.......P, ↵Enter
3. Point to the Microsoft Office folder icon........↓, →
4. Click the name of the Office program........↓, ↵Enter

   OR

1. Click **Start** button
   ........Ctrl+Esc
2. Click the name of the Office program in the list of recently used programs........↓, ↵Enter

   OR

- Double-click a program short-cut icon on the desktop.

Exit an Office Program

- Click **Program Close** button ⊠ at the right end of the program's title bar.

   ✓ *If you are using Windows Vista, the Program Close button may look different.*

   OR

1. Click **Office Button** 🔵.......Alt+F
2. Click **Exit** *program name*........X
3. Click **Yes**........Y
   to save open documents.

   OR

   Click **No**........N
   to exit without saving.

Use the Mouse

Move the mouse pointer:

Right	Move mouse to right.
Left	Move mouse to left.
Up	Move mouse away from you.
Down	Move mouse toward you.

Mouse actions:

Point to	Move mouse pointer to touch specified element.
Click	Point to element then press and release left mouse button.
Right-click	Point to element then press and release right mouse button.
Double-click	Point to element then press and release left mouse button twice in rapid succession.
Drag	Point to element, hold down left mouse button, then move mouse pointer to new location.

   ✓ *Element, or icon representing element, moves with mouse pointer.*

Drop	Drag element to new location, then release mouse button.

IntelliMouse actions:

Scroll	Rotate center wheel backward to scroll down, or forward to scroll up.
Pan	Press center wheel and drag up or down.
Auto-Scroll	Click center wheel to scroll down; move pointer up to scroll up.
Zoom	Hold down Ctrl and rotate center wheel.

Use the Keyboard

- Press specified key on the keyboard.

For key combinations:

1. Press and hold modifier key(s).........Ctrl or Alt or ⬆Shift
2. Press combination key.

   ✓ *Remember, key combinations are written with a plus sign between each key. For example, Ctrl+Esc means press and hold Ctrl and then press Esc.*

EXERCISE DIRECTIONS

1. Start your computer if it is not already on.
2. Move the mouse pointer around the Windows desktop.
3. Point to the Start button.

   ✓ *A ScreenTip is displayed.*

4. Start Microsoft PowerPoint 2007.

   ✓ *You may use any method, or ask your instructor which method to use.*

5. Point to each button on the Quick Access Toolbar to see the ScreenTips.
6. Click the Insert tab above the Ribbon to display the Insert commands.
7. Point to the Chart button in the Illustrations group to see the ScreenTip. The window should look similar to Illustration A.

8. Move the mouse pointer over the *Click to add title* text on the blank slide. The pointer changes to an I-beam.
9. Press Alt+F, the shortcut key combination for opening the Office menu.

   ✓ *Notice the KeyTips that display letters over each command. You press the KeyTip letter to select the command with the keyboard. You learn more about KeyTips in Exercise 2.*

10. Press Esc to cancel the menu, and then press Esc again to hide the KeyTips.
11. Exit PowerPoint.
12. Click No if a box displays asking if you want to save the changes.

Illustration A

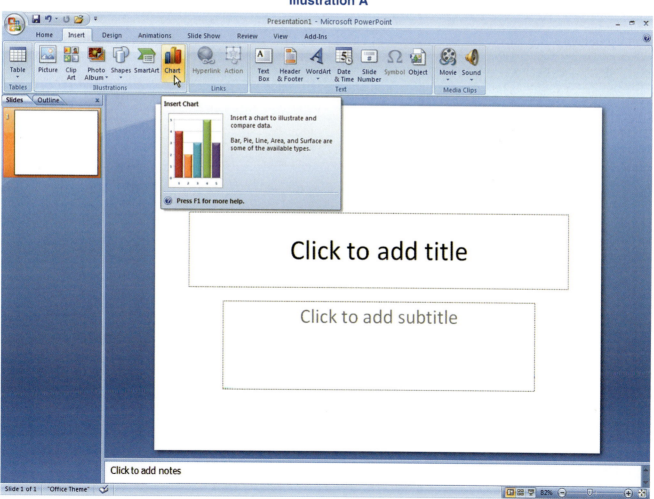

ON YOUR OWN

1. Working alone or in a team, research the types of technology required for at least two businesses. Try to pick businesses that are different. For example, you might select a bank and a doctor's office, or a public utility and a travel agent. Other possible businesses include your local government, a law firm, your school, or a printer.

2. Find out the types of hardware and software they use, and how they use them. For example, do they have a network so they can share data and resources, or do they use standalone computers?

Do they rely on laptops that employees can take away from the office? How many printers do they have? What software programs do they use? Do they use Microsoft Office?

3. You may conduct your research using the Internet, your school library, or by contacting local businesses to ask them what systems they use.

4. When you have gathered the information, organize it into an oral report and present it to your class.

Exercise | 2

Skills Covered

■ About Commands

■ About the Ribbon

■ Use the Ribbon

■ Use Access Keys

■ Use the Office Button

■ Use the Quick Access Toolbar

■ Use a Mini Toolbar

■ Use Shortcut Menus

■ Use Dialog Box Options

■ Use Task Panes

Software Skills   To accomplish a task in a Microsoft Office 2007 program, you must execute a command. You select the commands using buttons, menus, and toolbars. Once you learn to use these tools, you will be able to access the features you need to create documents in any Microsoft Office 2007 program.

Application Skills   To get up to speed using Microsoft Office 2007 programs, you want to spend more time exploring the user interface so that you know how to locate and use commands when you need them. In this exercise, you will practice using the Ribbon, the Office Button, and toolbars; selecting menu commands; and choosing options in dialog boxes.

TERMS

Access keys Keystrokes that can be used in place of mouse clicks to select any command.

Command Input that tells the computer which task to execute.

Contextual tab A Ribbon tab that is only available in a certain context or situation.

Dialog box A window in which you select options that affect the way the program executes a command.

Gallery A menu that displays pictures instead of plain text options. Often, the pictures indicate the effect that will result if you select the option.

KeyTip A pop-up letter that identifies the access key(s) for a command.

Live Preview A feature that displays the potential result of applying an editing or formatting change.

ScreenTip A balloon containing information that is displayed when you rest your mouse pointer on certain screen elements.

Shortcut menu A menu of relevant commands that displays when you right-click an item. Also called a context menu.

Submenu A menu that is displayed when you select a command on another menu.

Task pane A small window that displays additional options and commands for certain features in a Microsoft Office 2007 program.

Toggle A type of command that can be switched off or on.

NOTES

About Commands

- To accomplish a task in a Microsoft Office 2007 program, you execute **commands**. For example, Save is the command for saving a document.

- Most commands are available as buttons on the Ribbon.

- A few frequently-used commands such as Save are available on the Quick Access Toolbar.

- Some commands commonly used for file management are listed on the Office Button drop-down menu. For example, that's where you'll find the commands for creating a new file or opening an existing file.

- In some programs, a list of choices displays when you select a command. The list may be a standard menu, or it may be a **gallery**, which displays pictures instead of plain text descriptions.

- If a command requires that you select options to control specifications, a **dialog box** or **task pane** displays when you select the command.

- You use the mouse and/or the keyboard to select and execute commands.

About the Ribbon

- The Ribbon is the area where most commands are available.

- The Ribbon is organized into tabs based on activities, such as writing a document or inserting content.

- Each tab is organized into groups based on specific tasks, such as formatting text or applying slide transitions.

- In each group there are buttons representing specific commands and tasks.

- **Contextual tabs** are available only in certain situations. For example, if you select a picture, the Picture Tools Format tab becomes available. If you deselect the picture, the Picture Tools Format tab disappears.

- You can minimize the Ribbon to display only the tabs if you want to see more of the application's work area, as shown in the following illustration. When you click a tab, the Ribbon expands so you can select a command.

Microsoft PowerPoint with the Ribbon minimized

- Note that the way items display on the Ribbon may depend on the width of the program window, as shown in the following illustrations.

  - If the window is wide enough, groups expand to display all items.

  - If the window is not wide enough, groups collapse to a single group button. Click the button to display a menu of commands in the group.

  - The size of icons in a group may vary depending on the width of the window.

The View tab of the Ribbon in a wide PowerPoint window

The View tab of the Ribbon in a narrow PowerPoint window

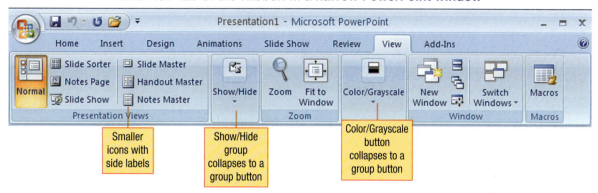

- If your program window is narrower or wider than the one used in this book, the Ribbon on your screen may look different from the one in the figures.
- In addition, the steps you must take to complete a procedure may vary slightly.
  - If your screen is narrower than the one in this book, you may have to click a group button to display the commands in that group before you can complete the steps in the procedure.
  - If your screen is wider, you may be able to skip a step for selecting a group button and go directly to the step for selecting a specific command.

Use the Ribbon

- When you point to a button on the Ribbon with the mouse, the button is highlighted, and a **ScreenTip** displays information about the command.
- Click the button to select the command.

- Buttons representing commands that are not currently available are dimmed.
- Some buttons are **toggles**; they appear highlighted when active, or "on."
- If there is an arrow on a button, it means that when you click that button, a menu or gallery displays so you can make a specific selection.
- Almost every Ribbon group has a dialog box launcher button.
- Click the dialog box launcher to display a dialog box, task pane, or window where you can select additional options, or multiple options at the same time.
- Sometimes, the entire first row of a gallery displays on the Ribbon.
- You can rest the mouse pointer on a gallery item to see a **Live Preview** of the way your document will look if you select that item.
- You can scroll a gallery on the Ribbon, or click the More button to view the entire gallery.

Ribbon elements on the Home tab in PowerPoint

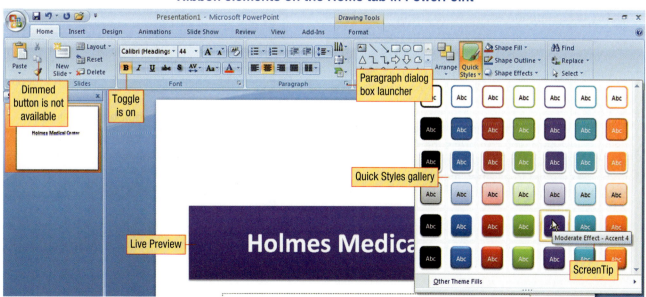

KeyTips on the Insert tab in PowerPoint

Use Access Keys

- Microsoft Office 2007 programs are designed primarily for use with a mouse.

- Many people prefer to select commands using the keyboard. In that case, you can press the Alt key to activate **access keys**.

- When access keys are active, **KeyTips** showing one or more keyboard letters display on the screen over any feature or command that can be selected using the keyboard, as shown in the above illustration.

- You press the letter(s) shown in the KeyTip to select the command or feature.

- If there is more than one access key for a command, you may press the keys in combination (at the same time) or consecutively (press the first key and then immediately press the next key).

- If a KeyTip is dimmed, the command is not available.

- The KeyTips remain active if you must press additional keys to complete a command.

- Once a command is executed, the KeyTips disappear.

- To continue using the keyboard, you must press the Alt key to activate the access keys again.

  ✓ *People accustomed to the shortcut key combinations in previous versions of Microsoft Office will be happy to know that they function in Microsoft Office 2007 programs as well. For example, you can still press Ctrl + Shift + F to open the Font dialog box.*

- If you just want to change the selected element using a keyboard, you can press the Alt key to activate the access keys, use the arrow keys to move from one element to another, and then press the Enter key to make a selection.

Use the Office Button

- Click the Office Button to display a menu of common file management commands, shown in the following illustration.

  ✓ *If you are familiar with previous versions of Microsoft Office, you may see the similarity between the Office menu and the old File menu.*

The Office Button menu in PowerPoint

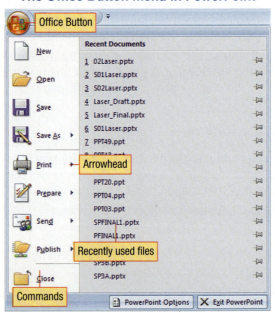

- Commands are listed on the left side of the menu next to their icons.

- Recently used files are listed on the right side of the menu, providing easy access.

  ✓ *Hint: You can click the pushpin icon to the right of an item on the recently-used files list to keep that item on the list. Click the icon again when you no longer need the item on the list.*

- An arrowhead to the right of the command indicates that the command opens a **submenu** or gallery.

Use the Quick Access Toolbar

- The Quick Access Toolbar is always available in the upper left corner of the program window, no matter which tab displays on the Ribbon.

- To select a command from the Quick Access Toolbar, click its button.

- The Quick Access Toolbar is the only screen element that can be customized in Microsoft Office 2007 programs.

- By default, there are three buttons on the Quick Access Toolbar: Save, Undo, and Repeat, shown in the following illustration. The Repeat button changes to Redo once you use the Undo command.

The default Quick Access Toolbar

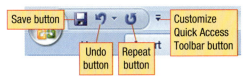

- Use the Customize Quick Access Toolbar button to select or deselect the commands you want on the toolbar.

Use a Mini Toolbar

- A Mini toolbar displays when the mouse pointer rests on selected text or data that can be formatted.

- At first, the Mini toolbar is semi-transparent, as shown in the following illustration, so you can ignore it if you want.

Transparent Mini toolbar

- When you move the mouse pointer over the Mini toolbar, it becomes opaque, as shown in the following illustration.

Opaque Mini toolbar

- Select a command from a Mini toolbar the same way you select a command from the Ribbon.

Use Shortcut Menus

- When you right-click almost any element on the screen in any Microsoft Office 2007 program, a **shortcut menu** displays.

- Shortcut menus include options relevant to the current item.

    ✓ *Shortcut menus are sometimes called context menus.*

- Click an option on the shortcut menu to select it.

- If you right-click selected data, a Mini toolbar may display in addition to the shortcut menu, as shown in the following illustration. The Mini toolbar disappears when you select an option on the menu.

Shortcut menu and Mini toolbar display when you right-click in a placeholder

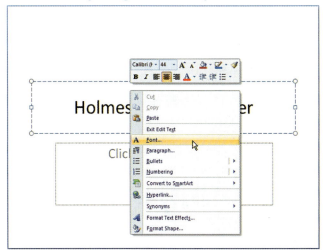

Use Dialog Box Options

- Although many commands are available directly from the Ribbon, when you must provide additional information before executing a command, a dialog box will display. For example, in the Print dialog box, you can specify which slides to print.

- You enter information in a dialog box using a variety of elements.

- To move from one element to another in a dialog box you can click the element with the mouse, or press Tab.

- Some dialog box elements have access keys that are underlined in the element name. Press Alt and the access key to select the element.

- Common dialog box elements include the following. Some of these elements are shown on the figures below.

  - *Drop-down list box:* A combination of text box and list box; type your selection in the box or click the drop-down arrow to display the list.

  - *Palette:* A display, such as colors or shapes, from which you can select an option.

    ✓ *Some Ribbon buttons also open palettes.*

  - *Check box:* A square that you click to select or deselect an option. A check mark in the box indicates that the option is selected.

  - *Command button:* A button used to execute a command. An ellipsis on a command button means that clicking the button opens another dialog box.

- *Tabs:* Markers across the top of the dialog box that, when clicked, display additional pages of options within the dialog box.

- *Increment box:* A space where you type a value, such as inches or numbers. Increment arrows beside the box are used to increase or decrease the value with a mouse. Sometimes called a spin box.

- *Preview area:* An area where you can preview the results of your selections before executing the commands.

- *Text box:* A space where you type variable information, such as a file name.

- *Option buttons:* A series of circles, only one of which can be selected at a time. Click the circle you want to select one item or one control in the series.

Font dialog box in PowerPoint

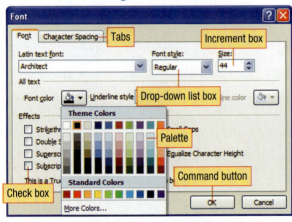

Print dialog box in PowerPoint

Use Task Panes

- Some commands open a task pane instead of a dialog box. For example, if you select to insert a clip art picture, the Clip Art task pane displays.

- Task panes have some features in common with dialog boxes. For example, some have text boxes in which you type text as well as drop-down list boxes, check boxes, and options buttons. The following illustration shows PowerPoint's Reuse Slides task pane.

The Reuse Slides task pane

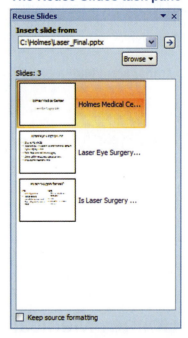

- You can leave a task pane open while you work, or you can close it to get it out of the way.

PROCEDURES

Select a Command on the Ribbon

1. Click a tab on the Ribbon............ `Alt`, access key
2. Click command......access key

   ✓ *If the button you want is not displayed, click the Group button arrow to display additional buttons, and then click the button you want.*

3. If necessary, click option on drop-down menu or gallery ....access key

Hide KeyTips

■ Press `Esc`.

Select Screen Elements with the Keyboard

1. Press `Alt`.
2. Press arrow keys to move from one element to another.................. `↑`, `↓`, `←`, `→`
3. Press `↵Enter` to select a command.

Use the Office Menu

1. Click the **Office Button** [icon] ....`Alt`+`F`
2. Click desired command................access key

   OR

   a. Click the **Office Button** [icon] ....`Alt`+`F`
   b. Click or point to command's submenu arrow...................access key
   c. Click option on submenu...........access key

Select a Command from the Quick Access Toolbar

1. Point to a button ....`Alt`
2. Click button to select................access key

Add a Command Button to the Quick Access Toolbar

1. Click the **Customize Quick Access Toolbar** button [icon] ....`Alt`, `↑`, `→`, `↵Enter`
2. Click command to add................`↓`, `↵Enter`

   ✓ *A check mark next to command name indicates it is already on the Quick Access Toolbar.*

   OR

1. Right-click command button to add on Ribbon.
2. Click **Add to Quick Access Toolbar** ....`A`

Minimize/Expand the Ribbon *(Ctrl+F1)*

■ Double-click the active tab.

   OR

1. Click the **Customize Quick Access Toolbar** button [icon] ....`Alt`, `↑`, `→`, `↵Enter`
2. Click **Minimize the Ribbon** ....`N`

   ✓ *A check mark next to command indicates it is already selected.*

Use a Mini Toolbar

1. Select text or data to format.
2. Move mouse pointer over Mini toolbar.
3. Select option on Mini toolbar.

Use a Shortcut Menu

1. Right-click **element** on screen ....`⇧Shift`+`F10`
2. Click **command**...........access key

   ✓ *If no access keys are available, use arrow keys to select command, then press Enter.*

Use a Dialog Box

1. Click group's **dialog box launcher** button [icon].

   ✓ *Some dialog boxes open when you select a command.*

2. Make selections or type text entries in dialog box.

   ✓ *See procedures below.*

3. Click **OK** ....`↵Enter`

   ✓ *Sometimes button displays Close, Add, Insert, or Yes in place of OK.*

   OR

   Click **Cancel** to close dialog box without making changes....`Esc`

Use Dialog Box Options

To move from one option to the next:

■ Click desired option.

   OR

■ Press **Tab** key................`Tab`

   OR

■ Press option's access keys.................`Alt`+access key

To select from a list box:

■ Click desired item ....`↑`, `↓`, `↵Enter`

To select from a drop-down list box:

1. Click **drop-down arrow** .... Alt +access key
2. Click desired **item** .... ↑, ↓, ↵Enter

To select/deselect check box:

■ Click **check box** .... Alt +access key

✓ *A check mark indicates box is selected. Repeat action to remove check mark and deselect box.*

To display tabbed pages:

■ Click desired **tab** .... Alt +access key

✓ *If no access key is displayed, press Ctrl + Tab⇆ .*

To use a text box:

1. Click in **text box** .... Alt +access key
2. Type **data**.

To use an increment box:

1. Click in **increment box** .... Alt +access key
2. Type **value**.

   OR

■ Click **increment arrows** to change value.

To select option button:

■ Click **option button** .... Alt +access key

To select palette option:

1. Click **palette** drop-down arrow .... Alt +access key

✓ *Some palettes are always open. If the palette is open, skip to step 2.*

2. Click desired **option** .... ↑, ↓, ←, →, ↵Enter

Close a Task Pane

■ Click **Close** button ⊠ on task pane title bar.

EXERCISE DIRECTIONS

1. Start PowerPoint and click in the *Click to add title* placeholder.
2. Click the Office Button 🔘 to open the Office menu using the mouse, and then take note of the available commands.
3. Click the Print submenu arrow to display the submenu.
4. Click the Office Button or press Esc to close the menu without making a selection.
5. Press Alt and then press W to display the View tab using the keyboard.
6. Press Esc twice to hide the access key KeyTips.
7. Use the mouse to display the Home tab.
8. Click the Font group dialog box launcher 🔳 to display the Font dialog box.
9. Select Bold in the Font style list box.
10. Select the Superscript check box.
11. Select the Character Spacing tab to show another page of options.
12. Select the Font tab.
13. Open the Underline style drop-down list.
14. Cancel the dialog box without making any of the selected changes.
15. Click the Clipboard group dialog box launcher 🔳 to display the Clipboard task pane.

    ✓ *The Clipboard is a temporary storage area that you use when copying and moving selections.*

16. Close the task pane.
17. Click the Customize Quick Access Toolbar button and then click Minimize the Ribbon to minimize the Ribbon so that only the tabs show.
18. Make the Design tab active.
19. Right-click in the *Click to add title* placeholder to display a shortcut menu and a Mini toolbar.
20. Select the Paragraph command on the shortcut menu

    ✓ *Note that the Paragraph dialog box includes increment boxes and drop-down lists.*

21. Cancel the dialog box without making any changes.
22. Click the Customize Quick Access Toolbar button and then click Minimize the Ribbon to expand the Ribbon.
23. Click the More button in the Themes group to display the Themes gallery.
24. Move the mouse pointer across the themes. A live preview displays each theme on the current slide.

25. Click the Apex theme to apply it to the presentation slide.

26. Click the Customize Quick Access Toolbar button and then click Print Preview to add the Print Preview button to the Quick Access Toolbar. The program window should look similar to Illustration A.

27. Repeat step 26 to remove the Print Preview button from the Quick Access Toolbar.

28. Exit PowerPoint. Do not save changes.

✓ *In the confirmation dialog box, select No.*

Illustration A

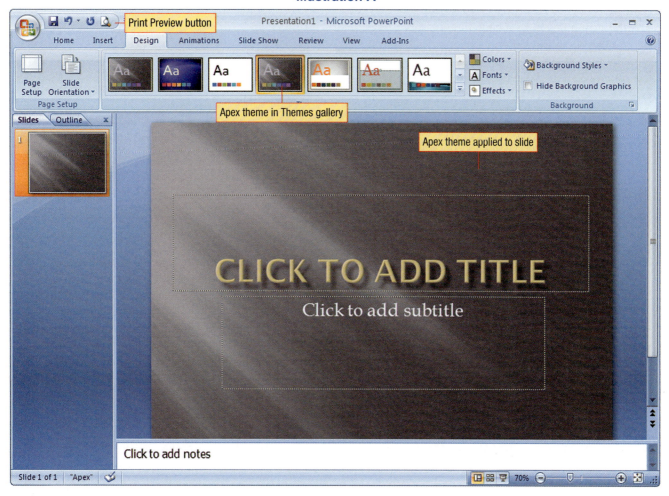

ON YOUR OWN

1. Start PowerPoint and explore the Ribbon tabs.

2. Look to see which commands are on each tab, and use ScreenTips to identify commands.

3. Determine if any commands open dialog boxes or galleries.

4. Use any group's dialog box launcher, such as the Page Setup group on the Page Layout tab.

5. If the dialog box has multiple tabbed pages, click each tab. Note the different options available on each tab.

6. Add buttons to the Quick Access Toolbar.

7. Remove the added buttons from the Quick Access Toolbar.

8. Exit PowerPoint without saving any changes.

9. Repeat these steps using any other Office application.

Skills Covered

- **Use Window Controls**
- **Zoom**
- **Scroll**
- **Use Multiple Windows**

Software Skills Controlling the way Microsoft Office 2007 programs and documents are displayed on your computer monitor is a vital part of using the programs successfully. For example, you can control the size and position of the program window on-screen, and you can control the size a document is displayed. In addition, you can open more than one window on-screen at the same time, so that you can work with multiple documents and even multiple programs at once.

Application Skills As you spend more time working with Microsoft Office 2007 programs, you'll find that there are many tools that help you do your job more efficiently. In this exercise, you will learn how to maximize, minimize, and restore windows on your screen, and you will experiment with the zoom level. You'll also practice scrolling through a document and opening more than one window at the same time.

TERMS

Active window The window in which you are currently working.

Cascade Arrange windows so they overlap, with the active window in front. Only the title bars of the non-active windows are visible.

Default A standard setting or mode of operation.

Group button A taskbar button that represents all open windows for one application.

Maximize Enlarge a window so it fills the entire screen.

Minimize Hide a window so it appears only as a button on the Windows taskbar.

Restore Return a minimized window to its previous size and position on the screen.

Restore down Return a maximized window to its previous size and position on the screen.

Scroll Shift the displayed area of the document up, down, left, or right.

Tile Arrange windows so they do not overlap.

Zoom in Increase the size of the document as it is displayed on-screen. This does not affect the actual size of the printed document.

Zoom out Decrease the size of the document as it is displayed on-screen. This does not affect the actual size of the printed document.

NOTES

Use Window Controls

- When you start a Microsoft Office 2007 program, it opens in a program window using **default** settings.
- You can control the size and position of the program window.
  - You can **maximize** the window to fill the screen.
  - You can **minimize** the window to a taskbar button.
  - You can **restore** a minimized window to its previous size and position.
  - You can **restore down** a maximized window to its previous size and position.
- There are three ways to control a program window:
  - Use the Control buttons located on the right end of the title bar.
    - ▭ Minimize
    - ▭ Maximize
    - ▭ Restore Down
    - ✓ *Restore Down is available only in a maximized window.*
  - Use the Windows' taskbar button shortcut menu.
  - Use the program's control menu.

Taskbar button shortcut menu

Zoom

- In Word, Excel, and PowerPoint, you can adjust the zoom magnification setting to increase or decrease the size a program uses to display a file on-screen.
  - ✓ *The Zoom options may differ depending on the program you are using.*

- There are three ways to set the zoom:
  - The Zoom slider on the right end of the program's status bar.

Zoom slider

  - The commands in the Zoom group of the View tab on the Ribbon.

Zoom group in PowerPoint

  - The Zoom dialog box.

Zoom dialog box in Word

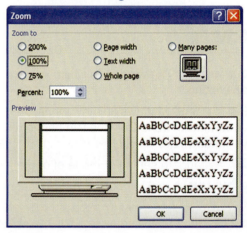

- **Zoom in** to make the file contents appear larger on screen. This is useful for getting a close look at graphics, text, or data.
  - ✓ *When you zoom in, only a small portion of the file will be visible on-screen at a time.*

- **Zoom out** to make the document contents appear smaller on-screen. This is useful for getting an overall look at a document, slide, or worksheet.

- You can set the zoom magnification as a percentage of a document's actual size. For example, if you set the zoom to 50%, the program displays the document half as large as the actual, printed document would appear. If you set the zoom to 200%, the program displays the document twice as large as the actual printed file would appear.

- Other options may be available depending on your program.

  - In Word, you can select from the following preset sizes:

    Page width. Word automatically sizes the document so that the width of the page matches the width of the screen. You see the left and right margins of the page.

    Text width. Word automatically sizes the document so that the width of the text on the page matches the width of the screen. The left and right margins may be hidden.

    Whole page. Word automatically sizes the document so that one page is visible on the screen.

    Many pages. Word automatically sizes the document so that the number of pages you select can all be seen on-screen.

    ✓ *Some options may not be available, depending on the current view. Options that are not available will appear dimmed.*

  - In Excel you can Zoom to Selection, which adjusts the size of selected cells to fill the entire window.

  - In PowerPoint you can Fit to Window, which adjusts the size of the current slide to fill the entire window.

Scroll

- When there is more data in a window or dialog box than can be displayed on-screen at one time, you must **scroll** to see the hidden parts.

- You can scroll up, down, left, or right.

- You can scroll using the directional keys on the keyboard, or using the arrows and boxes on the scroll bar.

  ✓ *Some mouse devices have scroll wheels that are used to scroll.*

- The sizes of the scroll boxes change to represent the percentage of the file visible on the screen.

- For example, in a very long document, the scroll boxes will be small, indicating that a small percentage of the document is visible. In a short document, the scroll boxes will be large, indicating that a large percentage of the document is visible.

Tools for scrolling in a document

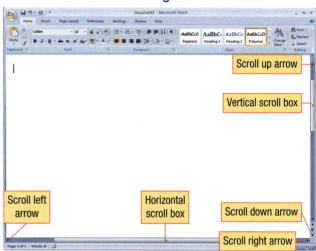

Use Multiple Windows

- You can open multiple program windows at the same time.

- Each open window is represented by a button on the Windows taskbar.

  ✓ *If you are using a version of Windows Vista that supports the Aero interface, you see a live preview of a taskbar button in its ScreenTip.*

- If there is not room on the taskbar to display buttons for each open window, Windows displays a **group button**.

  ✓ *The taskbar may not be visible on-screen if Windows is set to hide the taskbar, or to display windows on top of the taskbar. To see the taskbar, move the mouse pointer to the edge of the screen where it usually displays, or press Ctrl + Esc.*

- Only one window can be active—or current—at a time.

- The **active window** is displayed on top of other open windows. Its title bar is darker than the title bars of other open windows, and its taskbar button appears pressed in.

- You can switch among open windows to make a different window active.
- You can **tile** windows if you want to see all of them at the same time, as shown in the following illustration. Tiled windows do not overlap.

  ✓ *You can tile windows horizontally or vertically.*

Windows tiled horizontally

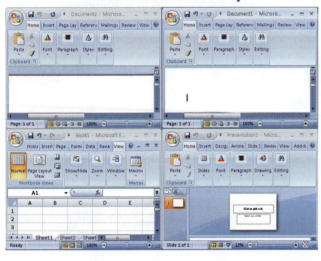

- The more windows you have open, the smaller they display when tiled.
  - If necessary in smaller windows, the program may hide common screen elements such as the Office Button, Quick Access Toolbar, and Ribbon and display only a program icon on the left end of the title bar.
  - You can click the program icon to display a shortcut menu of commands including Maximize, Minimize, and Close.
- You can **cascade** windows if you want to see the active window in its entirety, as shown in the following illustration, with the title bars of all open windows displayed behind it.

Cascading windows

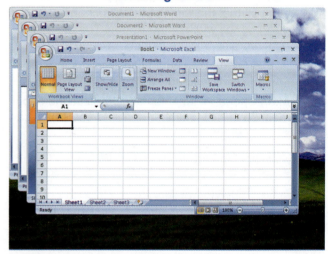

Curriculum Connection: Mathematics

The Cost of Starting a Business

A new business must spend money before it can start earning money. There are overhead costs such as rent and electricity, costs of office supplies, costs of technology, and salaries that must be paid. Smart business owners develop a business plan that itemizes start-up costs. This helps avoid surprises and gives everyone a blueprint to use to meet common goals.

Technology Budget

Imagine you are responsible for purchasing the technology for a new small business and have been asked to prepare a presentation to communicate the business's technology expenditures. Create a list of items you think you need and how much each item costs. Break the expenditures into sections that might be presented on individual slides, such as telecommunications equipment, computers and peripherals, network needs, copying and printing equipment, and so on. Create a final summary of all costs that could appear on the final slide of the presentation.

PROCEDURES

Control Windows

To minimize a window (Alt+Spacebar, N):

- Click the **Minimize** button ⬓.

    OR

1. Right-click the taskbar button.
2. Click **Minimize** .... Ⓝ

    OR

1. Press Ⓐⓛⓣ+Ⓢⓟⓐⓒⓔⓑⓐⓡ.
2. Click **Minimize** .... Ⓝ

To restore a window (Alt+F5):

- Click the **Restore Down** button ⬒.

    OR

1. Right-click the taskbar button.
2. Click **Restore** .... Ⓡ

    OR

1. Press Ⓐⓛⓣ+Ⓢⓟⓐⓒⓔⓑⓐⓡ.
2. Click **Restore** .... Ⓡ

To maximize a window (Ctrl+F10):

- Click the **Maximize** button ⬜.

    OR

1. Right-click the taskbar button.
2. Click **Maximize** .... Ⓧ

    OR

1. Press Ⓐⓛⓣ+Ⓢⓟⓐⓒⓔⓑⓐⓡ.
2. Click **Maximize** .... Ⓧ

Adjust Zoom

To use zoom slider to zoom out:

- Drag the slider to the left.

    OR

- Click the **Zoom Out** button ⊖.

To use zoom slider to zoom in:

- Drag the slider to the right.

    OR

- Click the **Zoom In** button ⊕.

To use Zoom group:

1. Click **View** tab .... Ⓐⓛⓣ+Ⓦ

    Zoom Group

2. Click desired zoom option button.

    ✓ *Available options depend on the program you are using.*

To use Zoom dialog box:

1. Click **View** tab .... Ⓐⓛⓣ+Ⓦ

    Zoom Group

2. Click **Zoom** button 🔍 .... Ⓠ
3. Click desired zoom option.

    OR

    a. Click **Percent** increment box .... Ⓐⓛⓣ+Ⓔ

    ✓ *In Excel, click the Custom box.*

    b. Type percentage.

4. Click **OK** .... ↵Enter

Scroll

To scroll down:

- Click **scroll down arrow** 🔽 .... ↓

    OR

- Click in **Vertical scroll bar** below Scroll box.

    OR

- Drag **Scroll box** down.

    OR

- Press ⓅⓖⒹⓝ.

    OR

- Spin scroll wheel on mouse toward your palm.

To scroll up:

- Click **scroll up arrow** 🔼 .... ↑

    OR

- Click in **Vertical scroll bar** above Scroll box.

    OR

- Drag Scroll box up.

    OR

- Press ⓅⓖⓊⓟ.

    OR

- Spin scroll wheel on mouse away from your palm.

To scroll left:

- Click **scroll left arrow** ◀ .... ←

    OR

- Click in **Horizontal scroll bar** to left of Scroll box.

    OR

- Drag **Scroll box** left.

To scroll right:

- Click **scroll right arrow** ▶ ...... →

    OR

- Click in **Horizontal scroll bar** to right of Scroll box.

    OR

- Drag **Scroll box** right.

Start Multiple Programs

1. Start first program.

    ✓ *Refer to Exercise 1 for information on starting Microsoft Office 2007 programs.*

2. Start additional program(s).

Arrange Program Windows

1. Right-click on blank area of Windows taskbar.
2. Select desired option:
   - **Cascade Windows** ...... S, ↵Enter
   - **Tile Windows Horizontally** ...... H
   - **Tile Windows Vertically** ...... E

   ✓ *Maximize active window to display active window only.*

To arrange Word document windows:

1. Click **View** tab .... Alt + W

   Window Group

2. Click **Arrange All** 🗐 .... A

To arrange Excel workbook windows:

1. Click **View** tab .... Alt + W

   Window Group

2. Click **Arrange All** 🗐 .... A
3. Select desired option:
   - **Tiled** .... T
   - **Horizontal** .... O
   - **Vertical** V
   - **Cascade** C
4. Click **OK** .... ↵Enter

To arrange PowerPoint presentation windows:

1. Click **View** tab .... Alt + W

   Window Group

2. Click **Arrange All** 🗐 .... A
   to tile windows vertically.

   OR

   Click **Cascade** 🗗 .... E
   to cascade windows.

Switch Between Open Windows

- Click taskbar button of desired window.

   OR

- Click in desired window.

   OR

1. Click group taskbar button.
2. Click name of window.

   OR

1. Press and hold Alt.
2. Press Tab⇆ to cycle through open windows.
3. Release both keys when desired window is selected.

EXERCISE DIRECTIONS

1. Start Word
2. Minimize the Word window.
3. Maximize the Word window.
4. Restore Down the Word window.
5. Start PowerPoint.
6. Cascade the open windows on-screen.

   ✓ *Right-click on a blank area of the Windows taskbar and select Cascade Windows.*

7. Tile the windows horizontally.
8. Tile the windows vertically.
9. Make the Word window active.
10. Maximize the Word window.
11. Click in the document window and type **Restoration Architecture**.

    ✓ *Do not worry about making errors while you type. This is just a practice exercise, and you will not save the document.*

12. Press ↵Enter.
13. Type **12345 Main Street**.
14. Press ↵Enter.
15. Type **Hometown, City 12345**.
16. Set the Zoom to 25%.
17. Set the Zoom to 500%.
18. Scroll the window so that all lines of the address are visible. It should look similar to the document shown in Illustration A.
19. Scroll down to the bottom of the document.
20. Scroll up to the top of the document.
21. Scroll to the right margin.
22. Scroll to the left margin.
23. Set the Zoom to Page Width.
24. Make PowerPoint active.
25. Maximize the PowerPoint window.
26. Exit PowerPoint.
27. Exit Word.
28. When Word prompts you to save the changes, select No.

Illustration A

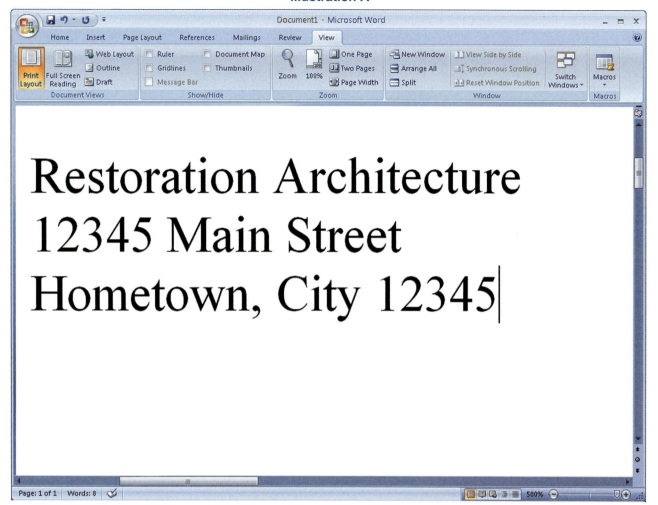

ON YOUR OWN

1. Start more than one Microsoft Office 2007 program, including PowerPoint.
2. Practice maximizing, minimizing, and restoring the windows, using all available methods.
3. Practice arranging the windows on-screen.
4. Type some text in the PowerPoint window.
5. Click the mouse pointer anywhere in the document window and start typing.
6. Try different zoom magnifications to see how they affect the display.
7. Set the zoom very high so you have to scroll down to see the end of the document.
8. Exit all programs without saving any documents.

Exercise | 4

Skills Covered

- **Use the Help Program**
- **Search for Help**
- **Use the Help Table of Contents**
- **Recover a File**

Software Skills   Each Microsoft Office 2007 program comes with Help information that you can access and display in a window while you work. You can search for help on a particular topic, or browse through the Help Table of Contents to find the information you need. The Help programs are linked to the Microsoft Office Web site, making it easy to locate and access the most current information available.

Application Skills   As a new employee at Restoration Architecture, you know it's important to learn how to solve problems on your own. In this exercise, you will learn how to use the Help system to answer the questions you may have while working with Microsoft Office 2007 programs.

TERMS

AutoRecover A feature in some Microsoft Office 2007 programs that automatically saves files at a set interval so that in the event of a system failure the files may be recovered.

Internet A worldwide network of computers.

NOTES

Use the Help Program

- Use the Help program to search for help topics, access the Help table of contents, or link to additional resources on the Microsoft Office Web site.
- Each Microsoft Office program has its own Help.
- To start Help in any Microsoft Office 2007 program, click the Help button 🌐 or press F1.
  - Some dialog boxes have a Help button ⍰ that you can click to go directly to a relevant Help topic.
  - Some command button ScreenTips prompt you to press F1 to go directly to a relevant Help topic.

- Help opens in a window that you can keep open while you work.
- By default, the Help Home page displays, listing links to Help categories, as shown in the following illustration.
- When the mouse pointer touches a link, it changes to a hand with a pointing finger.

- Click a link to display subcategories or topics in a category, and then click a topic to display the specific Help information.

  ✓ *If a list of subcategories displays, click a subcategory and then click a topic.*

The PowerPoint Help Home page

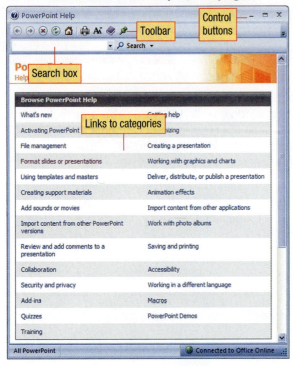

- Under the heading *What do you want to do?*, most Help topic pages list links to content on the page, as shown in the following illustration.

- Other links might go to related content on different pages.

- The links are formatted in blue so they stand out from the surrounding text.

- Some words or phrases link to definitions or explanations. These links are formatted in dark red.

  ✓ *Click Show All at the top of a page to display all definitions and explanations within the page text.*

- You can use buttons on the Help window toolbar to control the Help display.

  - At the bottom of most Help pages there is a question asking if you found the information helpful. If you are connected to the Internet click Yes, No, or I don't know to display a text box where you can type information that you want to submit to Microsoft.

- The Help window has control buttons so you can minimize, maximize, restore down, or close it at any time.

Help topic page

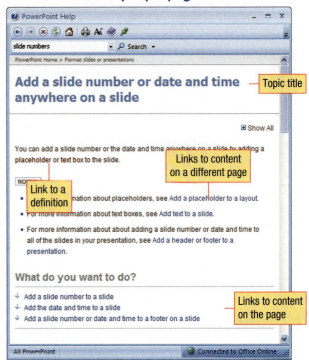

Search for Help

- You can search for a Help topic at any time.

- Simply type the term or phrase for which you want to search in the Search box, and then click the Search button (see the following illustration).

- A list of topics that contain the term or phrase displays in the Help window.

- Click a topic to display the Help information.

- If you have access to the **Internet**, Help automatically includes information from the Microsoft Office Web site in all searches.

- You can control where Help searches by selecting an option from the Search drop-down list.

Search for Help

Use the Help Table of Contents

- The Table of Contents is an alternative to the Help Home page.

- In the Table of Contents, each Help category displays in a list.

- You can click a category to expand the list to show categories, subcategories, and topics at the same time.

    ✓ *Categories have book icons; topics have help button icons.*

- Click a topic to display its Help page in the Help window.

- The Help Table of Contents opens in a separate pane on the left side of the Help window.

- Close the Table of Contents pane to display only the Help window.

Use the Help Table of Contents

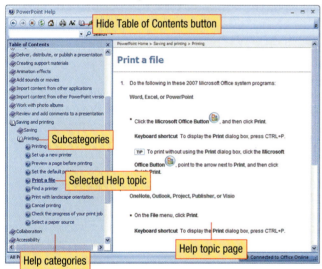

Recover a File

- By default Word, Excel, and PowerPoint are set to save **AutoRecover** information every ten minutes.

- In the event of a system failure, these programs will attempt to recover your files based on the most recently saved AutoRecover information.

- If any damage was done to the file data during the crash, the program will attempt to repair it.

- When you open the program again, the Document Recovery task pane displays, listing original files, recovered files (if any), and repaired files (if any), as shown in the following illustration.

Document Recovery task pane

- Click the drop-down arrow beside a file name to display a list of options for opening the file, saving it with a new name, deleting it, or showing repairs.

- In addition, in the event of a program crash the Microsoft Office programs will ask if you want to send a report to Microsoft. If you agree to send a report, your computer will log on to the Internet and transmit the information.

PROCEDURES

Display Help (F1)

1. Click **Microsoft Office** *program name* **Help** button 🔵.
2. Click Help category.
3. Click Help topic.
4. Use links as necessary.

Search for Help

1. Display Help window.
2. Click in **Search** box.
3. Type keyword, topic, or question.
4. Click **Search** button drop-down arrow 🔍 Search.
5. Click location to search.
6. Click **Search** button
   🔍 Search .... ⏎Enter
7. Click topic in Search Results task pane.
8. Use links as necessary.

Use the Help Table of Contents

1. Display Help window.
2. Click **Show Table of Contents** button 🔷.
3. Click Help category.
4. Click Help topic.
5. Use links as necessary.
6. Click **Hide Table of Contents** button 🔷 to close pane.

Use the Help Toolbar

- Click a button on the toolbar to select that command or feature:
  - Click the **Back** button ⬅ to display the previously viewed page.
  - Click the **Forward** button ➡ to return to a viewed page.
  - Click the **Home** button 🏠 to display the Help Home page.
  - Click the **Show Table of Contents** button 🔷 to display the Help table of contents page.
  - Click the **Stop** button ⊗ to cancel a search.
  - Click the **Refresh** button 🔄 to update the current page.
  - Click the **Print** button 🖨 to print the current page.
  - Click the **Change Font Size** button 🅰 to select an option to change the size of the characters in the Help window.
  - Click the **Keep on Top button** 🔷 to set the Help window to always display on top of other open windows.

Get Help from a Dialog Box

- In the dialog box, click **Help** button ❓.

Get Help for a Command

1. Rest mouse pointer on command button on Ribbon.
2. Press **F1**.
3. If necessary, use Help tools to locate specific Help information.

Close Help

- Click **Close** button ✖ on Help title bar .... Alt+F4

Recover a File

1. Click drop-down arrow beside desired file in Document Recovery task pane.
2. Click desired option to open, save, or delete file.

   ✓ *Steps for saving files are covered later in this book.*

   ✓ *If you save a repaired file, the program will prompt you to review the repairs before continuing.*

EXERCISE DIRECTIONS

1. Start PowerPoint.
2. Display the Help window.
3. Search for help topics about changing the zoom.
   - Type **Zoom** in the Search box and then click the Search button.
4. Read the available topics.
5. Click the topic *Zoom in or out of a document, presentation, or worksheet*.
6. Under the heading *What do you want to do?*, click the link to *Choose a particular zoom setting*.
7. Read the Help topic.
8. Display the Help Home page.
   - Click the Home button on the Help window toolbar.
9. Click the category *Creating a presentation*.
10. Click the subcategory *Create a basic presentation in PowerPoint 2007*.
11. Click the topic *Familiarize yourself with the PowerPoint workspace*.
12. Display the Table of Contents, if necessary.
   - Click the Show Table of Contents button on the Help window toolbar.
13. Click the category *Getting help* to expand it to show topics and subcategories. It should look similar to Illustration A.
14. Click the topic *Work with the Help window*.
15. Close the Table of Contents and then close the Help window.
16. Click on the *Click to add title* placeholder text to activate the placeholder. Click the dialog box launcher in the Font group on the Home tab of the Ribbon to display the Font dialog box.
17. Click the Help button in the dialog box to display the related Help topic.
18. Minimize the Help window and cancel the Font dialog box.
19. Click the Home tab on the Ribbon if it is not already displayed.
20. Rest the mouse pointer on the New Slide button to display a ScreenTip.
21. Press F1 to display the related Help topic.
22. Close the Help window.
23. Exit PowerPoint. Do not save any changes.

Illustration A

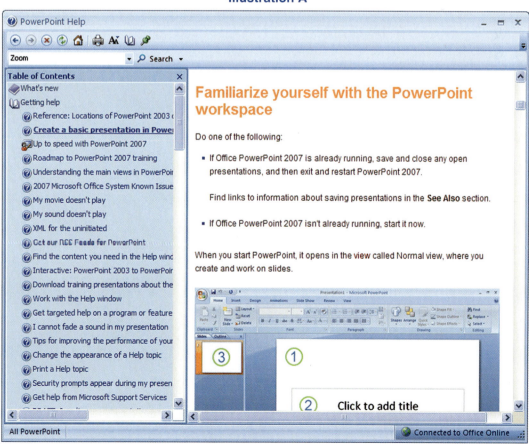

ON YOUR OWN

1. Start PowerPoint and display Help.
2. Search for help topics related to saving.
3. Open any topic that sounds interesting.
4. Go back to the Home page.
5. Open the Table of Contents and explore the topics.
6. Open any topic that sounds interesting.
7. Close the Table of Contents and then close the Help window.
8. Use ScreenTips to identify the Format Painter button in the Clipboard group on the Home tab.
9. With the ScreenTip displayed, press F1 to display the relevant Help topic.
10. Continue to explore the help topics as long as you want. When you are done, close the Help window and exit PowerPoint. Do not save the presentation.
11. If you want, explore the Help programs for the other Microsoft Office programs.

Lesson | 1

PowerPoint Basics

Skills Covered

- **About Microsoft Office PowerPoint 2007**
- **The PowerPoint Window**
- **Create a Presentation from a Blank Presentation**
- **Work with Placeholders**

- **Add Slides to a Presentation**
- **Select a Slide Layout**
- **Save a Presentation**
- **Add Presentation Properties**

Software Skills PowerPoint's many features make it easy to create both simple and sophisticated presentations. One way to create a new slide show is to start with the default blank presentation that displays when PowerPoint opens.

Application Skills Holmes Medical Center has contacted you about preparing a presentation announcing their new laser eye surgery unit. In this exercise, you start a new presentation and explore basic features such as placeholders and layouts.

TERMS

Active slide The slide currently selected or displayed.

Normal view PowerPoint's default view that displays the Slide pane, the Notes pane, and the Slides/Outline pane.

Placeholders Designated areas in PowerPoint layouts that can be used to easily insert text, graphics, or multimedia objects.

Presentation A set of slides or handouts that contains information you want to convey to an audience.

Properties Details about a presentation (or any document) that describe or identify the file.

Slide layout Prearranged sets of placeholders for various types of slide content.

NOTES

About Microsoft Office PowerPoint 2007

- PowerPoint is a presentation graphics program that lets you create slide shows you can present by showing the slides on a computer or projection screen or by publishing the slides as interactive Web pages.

- A **presentation** can include handouts, outlines, and speaker notes as well as slides.

- PowerPoint slides may contain text and various other types of content, such as clip art, pictures, movies, tables, or charts.

- You can create all the slide content in PowerPoint, or import data from other Microsoft Office programs such as Word and Excel to create slide content.

The PowerPoint Window

■ After you start PowerPoint, you see a screen such as the one shown in the following illustration.

The PowerPoint window

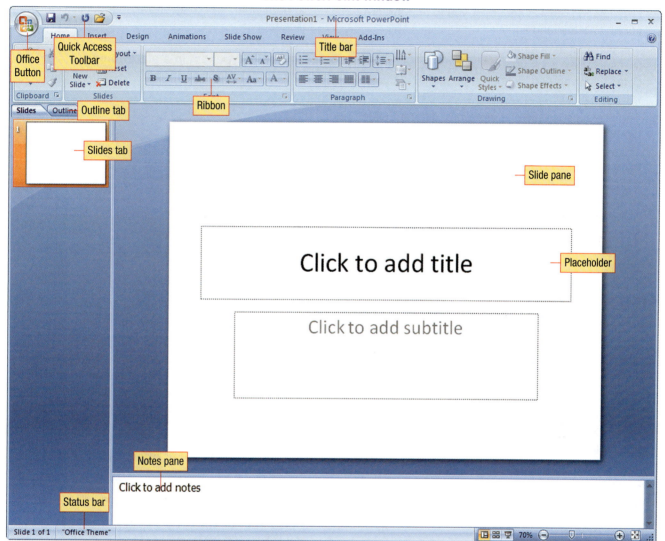

■ PowerPoint supplies the default title *Presentation* and a number (for example, *Presentation1*) in the title bar of each new presentation. You should change this default title to a more descriptive title when you save a new presentation.

■ PowerPoint, like other Microsoft Office 2007 applications, displays the new Ribbon interface that groups commands on tabs across the top of the window below the title bar.

■ The status bar displays information about the presentation, such as the slide number and theme name.

■ A presentation opens by default in **Normal view**, which displays the Slide pane, the Notes pane, and the Slides/Outline pane. You will learn more about these panes in a later exercise.

Create a Presentation from a Blank Presentation

- When PowerPoint starts, it displays a single blank slide you can use to start a new presentation. The default slide is intended to be the first slide of the presentation, so it is set up for you to add the presentation's title and subtitle.

- The blank slide does not include any graphic content such as a background. You can change the default appearance by applying a theme, as you will learn in Exercise 6.

- The title slide is only one of several different slide types you can use to create a new presentation. You will learn more about slide layouts later in this exercise.

- If you are already working in PowerPoint and need to create a new blank presentation, you can do so using the New command to open the New Presentation dialog box (see the following illustration).

The New Presentation dialog box

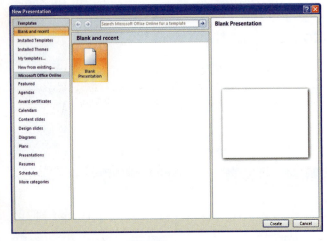

Work with Placeholders

- PowerPoint displays **placeholders** to define the arrangement and location of text and other objects you can add to slides.

- The title slide you see when creating a new presentation has two placeholders: one for the title and one for the subtitle.

- To insert text in a placeholder, click inside the placeholder and begin typing. When you click the placeholder, PowerPoint selects the box with a dashed outline, displays sizing handles you can use to resize the placeholder, and displays a blinking insertion point that shows where text will appear when typed, as shown in the following illustration.

Type text in a placeholder

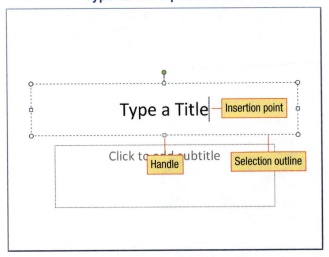

- Different types of slides in a presentation have different types of placeholders. In the following illustration, the slide offers a title placeholder and a content placeholder in which you can insert a bulleted list or other type of content such as a table, a chart, or a picture.

Title and Content layout offers two placeholders

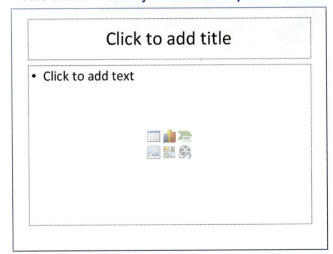

Add Slides to a Presentation

- Most presentations consist of a number of slides. Use the New Slide button on the Home tab to add a slide to a presentation.

- If you simply click the New Slide button, PowerPoint adds the kind of slide you are most likely to need. With the default title slide displayed, for example, PowerPoint will assume the next slide should be a Title and Content slide.

- If the **active slide**—the currently displayed slide— uses a layout other than Title Slide, PowerPoint inserts a new slide with the same layout as the one currently displayed.

- A new slide is inserted immediately after the active slide.

Select a Slide Layout

- To specify a particular layout for a slide, click the down arrow on the New Slide button to display a gallery of **slide layout** choices, as shown in the following illustration.

New Slide gallery

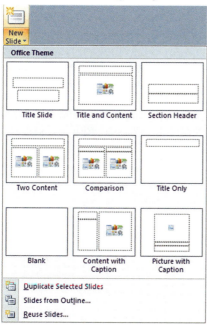

- A slide layout arranges the standard objects of a presentation—titles, charts, text, clip art—on the slide to make it attractive. Each layout provides placeholders for specific types of content.

- PowerPoint 2007 has many fewer layout choices than previous versions of PowerPoint offered, but layouts are multifunctional. Rather than having a layout that offers side-by-side text and a layout that offers side-by-side content, for example, PowerPoint 2007 has one layout that allows you to insert side-by-side content of any type, including text, graphics, charts, or movies.

Save a Presentation

- Save a new presentation so that you can work on it again later. By default, a new presentation is saved in XML format, the standard for Office 2007 applications, giving the file an extension of .pptx.

- If you wish to use a presentation with earlier versions of PowerPoint, you can save the file in PowerPoint 97-2003 Presentation format. You can also save the presentation in several other formats, such as PDF or XPS, or as a template or show.

  ✓ *You will save presentations as templates and shows in later lessons.*

- To save in a version different from the default, select an option from the Save As dialog box's Save as type list, as shown in the following illustration.

Save As dialog box

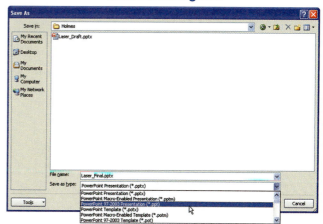

Add Presentation Properties

- When you create a presentation, you can store information about the presentation called **properties**. Properties can include the author of the presentation, its title, and keywords to help you quickly identify the presentation.

- You add properties using the Document Information Panel, shown in the following illustration.

Document Information Panel

- The Document Information Panel shows information that PowerPoint collects for you, such as the file location, as well as standard properties you supply yourself, such as the author, title, status, and any comments you want to add.

- Document properties, which are sometimes referred to as *metadata*, not only allow you to provide information about a presentation but also make it easy to organize and locate files that have the same kinds of information. When searching for files, for example, you can use document properties as criteria in the search.

- You can see more properties for a document by clicking the down arrow next to Document Properties in the Document Information Panel and selecting Advanced Properties to open the Properties dialog box shown in the following illustration.

Properties dialog box

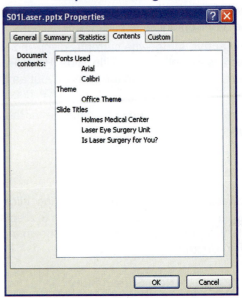

- The tabs in the Properties dialog box allow you to view general file information, a summary of current properties, statistics about the presentation such as when it was created and how many slides it has, and the contents of all slides in the presentation (shown in the previous illustration). You can use the Custom tab to create your own categories of properties.

- You can view or edit properties at any time by displaying the Document Information Panel or the Properties dialog box.

- After you have added properties to a presentation, you can view them when you save or open the file by changing the View in the Save As or Open dialog box.

PROCEDURES

Start PowerPoint

1. Click [start] / [icon] on the Windows taskbar .... Ctrl + Esc
2. Click **All Programs** .... P , ↵Enter
3. Click **Microsoft Office**.
4. Click **Microsoft Office PowerPoint 2007**.

Start a New Presentation

1. Start PowerPoint.
2. Begin creating the presentation using the default blank title slide.

   OR
1. Click **Office Button** [icon] ..... Alt + F
2. Click **New** .... N
3. Click [Create] .... ↵Enter

Work with Placeholders

1. Click once in a placeholder to select it and position an insertion point.
2. Begin typing text.

To type a bulleted list in a placeholder:

1. Click the *Click to add text* prompt and begin typing the first item.
2. Press ↵Enter to move to the next line.
3. Type the next bullet item.

Add a Slide (Ctrl + M)

To add the default next slide:

1. Click **Home** tab .... Alt + H

   Slides Group
2. Click **New Slide** button [icon] .

   ✓ *Adds a Title and Content slide after a Title slide or a slide with the same layout as the currently active slide.*

To add a slide and select a slide layout:

1. Click **Home** tab .... Alt + H

   Slides Group
2. Click **New Slide** button [icon] down arrow. I
3. Click the desired slide layout from the gallery.

Save a Presentation (Ctrl + S)

1. Click **Office Button** [icon] .... Alt + F
2. Click **Save** .... S

   OR

   Click **Save** button [icon] on the Quick Access Toolbar .. Alt + 1
3. Click **Save in** down arrow .... Alt + I
4. Select drive and folder.
5. Double-click **File name** box .... Alt + N
6. Type file name.
7. Click [Save] . ... ↵Enter

Add Document Properties

1. Click **Office Button** [icon] .... Alt + F
2. Point to **Prepare** .... E
3. Click **Properties** .... P
4. Type properties in supplied text boxes.
5. Click [x] to close the Document Information Panel.

To view advanced properties:

1. Click down arrow to right of Document Properties heading in Document Information Panel.
2. Click **Advanced Properties**.
3. Click Properties dialog box close button [x] when finished viewing properties.

EXERCISE DIRECTIONS

1. Start PowerPoint.
2. Save the default blank presentation as **05Laser_xx**, where *xx* stands for your initials.
3. Type the title and subtitle as shown in Illustration A.
4. Insert a new slide and accept the Title and Content layout for the second slide.
5. Type the title and bulleted list as shown in Illustration B.
6. Add a third slide that uses the Comparison slide layout.
7. Type the title and bulleted lists as shown in Illustration C.
8. Open the Document Information Panel and add the following properties to the presentation:
   Author: **Your name**
   Title: **Holmes Medical Center**
   Subject: **Laser Eye Surgery**
   Keywords: **laser surgery**
   Status: **Draft**
   Comments: **First draft of the Laser Eye Surgery Unit presentation.**
9. Close the Document Information Panel.
10. Save your changes, close the presentation, and exit PowerPoint.

Illustration A

Holmes Medical Center

Laser Eye Surgery Unit

Illustration B

Laser Eye Surgery Unit

- Opens March 22
- Headed by Dr. Martin Talbot from the Eastern Eye Surgery Clinic
- Safe, fast, and reliable surgery
- Covered by most insurance carriers
- The key to clearer vision

Illustration C

Is Laser Surgery for You?

Pros
- Virtually painless
- Fast procedure
- Immediate improvement
- Covered by most insurance plans

Cons
- Not everybody is a candidate
- Cost
- Some risk of corneal damage

ON YOUR OWN

1. Start PowerPoint.

2. Save the blank presentation as **OPP05_xx**, where *xx* stands for your initials.

3. Create a presentation about yourself beginning with the title slide. Type a title such as **My Life** or **All About Me**. Enter your name as the subtitle.

4. Insert a second slide using the default Title and Content slide layout.

5. Type a title on the second slide, and then type at least three items describing what the presentation will be about. For example, the first item might be **The Early Years**, the second item might be **A Budding Athlete**, and so on.

6. Insert one slide for each of the items on slide 2, using appropriate slide layouts. The title of each slide should be one of the bullet items on slide 2. Type at least three bulleted items on each of these slides. The illustrations below show several sample slides.

7. Add appropriate properties to the presentation if desired.

8. Save your changes, close the presentation, and exit PowerPoint.

Illustration A

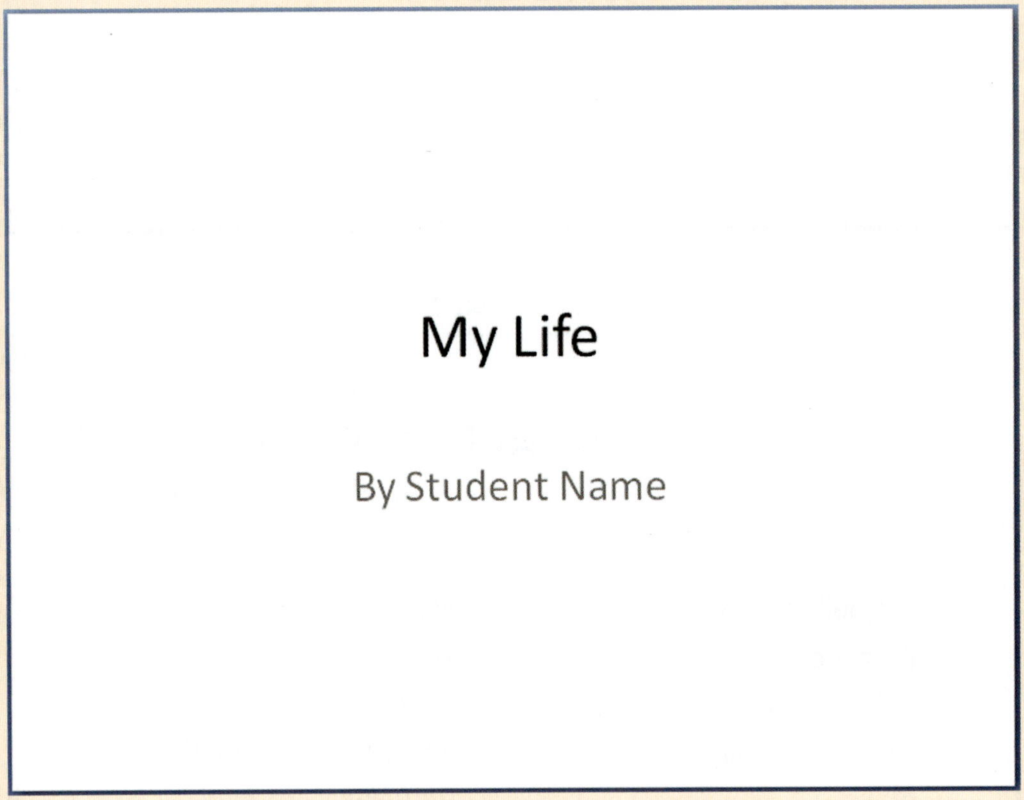

My Life

By Student Name

Illustration B

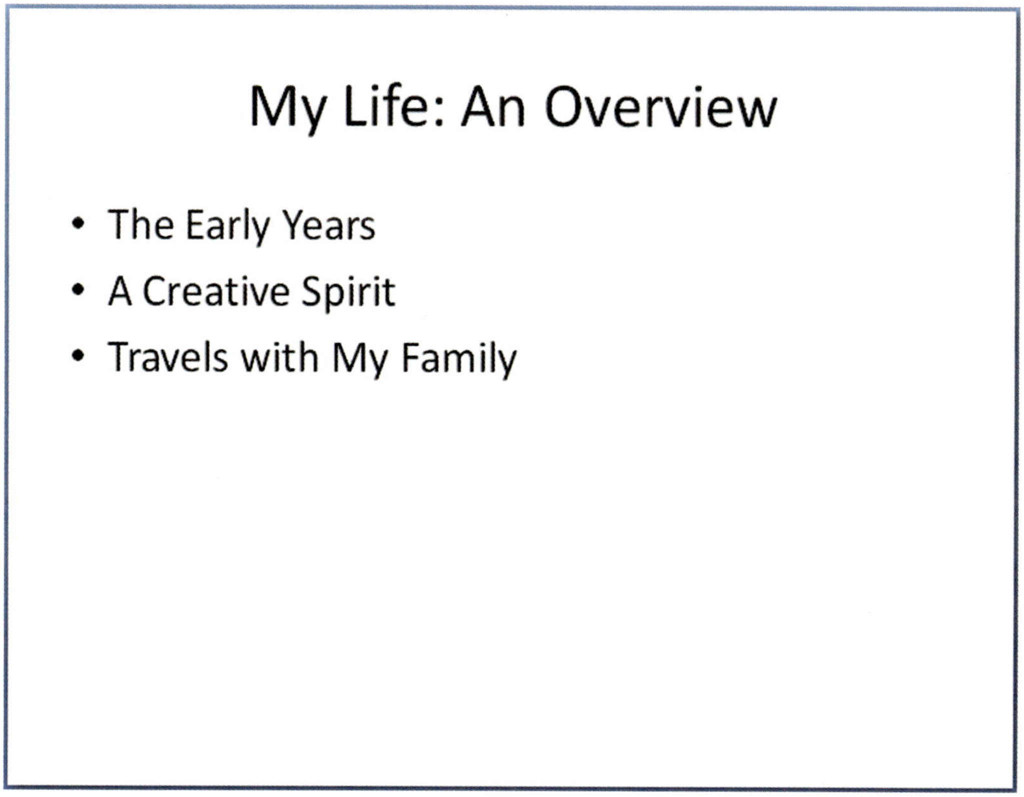

My Life: An Overview

- The Early Years
- A Creative Spirit
- Travels with My Family

Illustration C

The Early Years

- Born in Connecticut
- Two sisters
- Piano lessons
- Good student

Skills Covered

- **Open an Existing Presentation**
- **Move from Slide to Slide**
- **Apply a Theme**

Software Skills Open existing presentations to continue to work on them. You can use several methods to move from slide to slide in a presentation. Features such as themes make it easy to improve the look of a presentation.

Application Skills In this exercise, you continue to work with the Holmes Medical Center presentation. After you open the presentation, you will add a slide and apply a theme for visual interest.

TERMS

Theme Formatting feature that applies a background, colors, fonts, and effects to all slides in a presentation.

NOTES

Open an Existing Presentation

- Open an existing presentation to modify, add, or delete material.
- PowerPoint makes it easy to open presentations on which you have recently worked by listing them in the Recent Documents list that you access using the Office Button.
- Click any of the presentations in the Recent Documents list to open the presentation.
- If you do not see the presentation on this list, you can use the Open command and the Open dialog box to navigate to the presentation you want to open.

- You can click the View button in the Open dialog box to display files in different ways; for example, as thumbnails, in a list, or as icons. You can also display the properties for a file or see a preview of its first slide, as shown in the following illustration.

Adjust the view in the Open dialog box to see a preview of the presentation

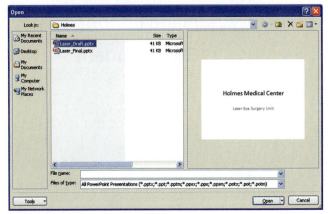

Move from Slide to Slide

- Most presentations include multiple slides. You will need to move from slide to slide in Normal view to enter text and modify the presentation.

- PowerPoint offers a variety of ways to select and display slides. Click in the scroll bar or drag the scroll box to display slides, or use the Previous Slide and Next Slide buttons at the bottom of the scroll bar to move through the slides.

- As you drag the scroll box in the scroll bar, a ScreenTip shows the current slide number and slide title, as shown in the following illustration.

Scrolling options in Normal view Slide pane

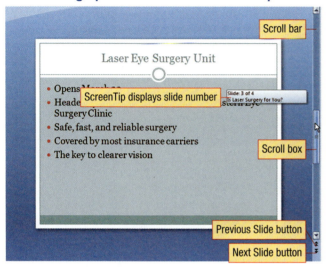

- You can also select slides by clicking them in the Slides tab. You learn more about this tab in the next exercise.

Apply a Theme

- In PowerPoint 2007, **themes** replace slide designs as a means of supplying graphical interest for a presentation.

- A theme provides a background, a color palette, a selection of fonts for titles and text, distinctive bullets, and a range of special effects that can be applied to shapes. The theme also controls the layout of placeholders on slides.

- Themes are located in the Themes group on the Design tab, as shown in the following illustration. The size of the PowerPoint window determines how many theme thumbnails display in the group.

The Themes group on the Design tab

- When you rest the pointer on a theme thumbnail, the slide in the Slide pane immediately displays the theme elements. This Live Preview feature makes it easy to choose a graphic look for slides—if you don't like the look of the theme, simply move the pointer off the theme to return to the previous appearance or point at a different theme to try another appearance.

- Themes have names that you can see if you rest the pointer on a theme thumbnail.

- By default, the Themes group shows only a few of the available themes. To see all themes, click the More button in the theme scroll bar to display a gallery of themes, as shown in the following illustration.

The Themes gallery

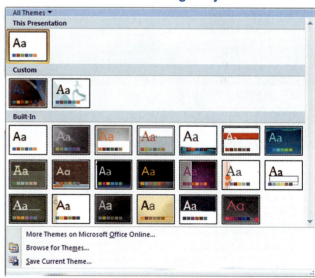

- The gallery shows the theme (or themes) currently used in a presentation in the This Presentation area. Options at the bottom of the gallery allow you to search for other themes or save the current theme for future use.

✓ *You will learn how to save a theme in Exercise 40.*

- When choosing a theme, consider the subject and audience of your presentation. As the illustration below shows, different themes can provide quite different looks for the same content.

Different themes convey different moods

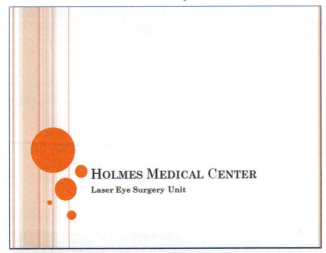

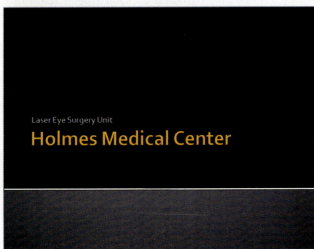

- Clicking a theme thumbnail applies it to all slides in the presentation. You can also choose to apply the theme to one or more selected slides in the presentation.

- To apply a theme to only a few slides, select the slides in the Slides tab by clicking the first, holding down Shift, and clicking additional slides. Then right-click a theme and select Apply to Selected Slides.

- Using more than one theme in a presentation is a good way to emphasize certain slides in the presentation, such as slides used to start sections.

- As shown in the previous illustration of the Theme gallery, PowerPoint supplies a limited number of themes. Although they can be customized by modifying background, colors, and fonts, you may eventually want more variety.

- You can find other presentation themes by clicking the More Themes on Microsoft Office Online link at the bottom of the Themes gallery.

- The link opens the Templates page at Microsoft Office Online with a selection of themes that can be downloaded, as shown in the following illustration.

Themes available to download from Microsoft Office Online

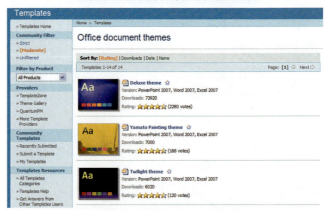

- Themes you download from Microsoft Office Online display in the Theme gallery's Custom section and are available for use in any presentation.

  ✓ *Microsoft will check to make sure you are using authentic Microsoft software before allowing you to download a theme.*

- You can delete custom themes you download or themes you create yourself by right-clicking the theme thumbnail and selecting Delete.

  ✓ *You cannot delete built-in themes this way.*

Curriculum Connection: Science

Global Warming

Global warming has developed into a major environmental concern. Scientists estimate that the Earth has warmed by about 1 degree Fahrenheit in the last 100 years, which may not seem like a lot at first, but has had a significant impact on our habitat. There are many different theories about what causes global warming; some people say it is a natural occurrence while others say it is because of pollution.

Illustrate the Causes of Global Warming

Create a PowerPoint presentation that explains the major causes of global warming and what people might be able to do to stop it. For example, you might include information about the greenhouse effect and the ozone hole. Try to vary the layout from slide to slide. Apply a theme that supports the mood of your presentation.

PROCEDURES

Open an Existing Presentation

1. Click **Office Button** ..... Alt+F
2. Click the name of a previous opened presentation in the Recent Documents list, or press the presentation's shortcut number.

   OR

   a. Click **Open** .... O
   b. Navigate to the location of the file to open and click the file name.
   c. Click [Open ▾] .... ↵Enter

Move from Slide to Slide

1. Press PgDn to display next slide.
2. Press PgUp to display previous slide.

   OR

1. Click **Next Slide** button ⬇ on Slide pane scroll bar.
2. Click **Previous Slide** button ⬆ on Slide pane scroll bar.

   OR

   ■ Click on a slide in the Slides or Outline tab.

Apply a Theme

1. Click **Design** tab .... Alt+G

   Themes Group

2. Click a theme thumbnail to apply it to all slides.

To view all available themes:

1. Click **Design** tab .... Alt+G

   Themes Group

2. Click **More** button ▾ .... H
3. Click a theme thumbnail to apply it to all slides.

To apply a theme to one or more slides in a presentation:

1. Click **Design** tab .... Alt+G
2. Select a slide or slides in the Slides tab.

   Themes Group

3. Right-click the theme thumbnail.
4. Click **Apply to Selected Slides** .... S, ↵Enter

EXERCISE DIRECTIONS

1. Start PowerPoint and open **05Laser_xx** or ⊙**06Laser**.
2. Save the file as **06Laser_xx**.
3. Move to slide 3 and insert a new slide that uses the Two Content slide layout.
4. Type the title **Laser Eye Surgery Facts**.
5. In the left placeholder, type the first bullet item, **LASIK is most common refractive surgery**.

6. Type the remaining bullet items as follows, pressing ⏎Enter to start each new item:
   Relative lack of pain
   Almost immediate results (within 24 hours)
   Both nearsighted and farsighted can benefit
7. Apply the Civic theme to all slides, and then move through the slides to see how the new theme has changed the appearance of slides. Slide 4 should look like Illustration A.
8. Save your changes, close the presentation, and exit PowerPoint.

Illustration A

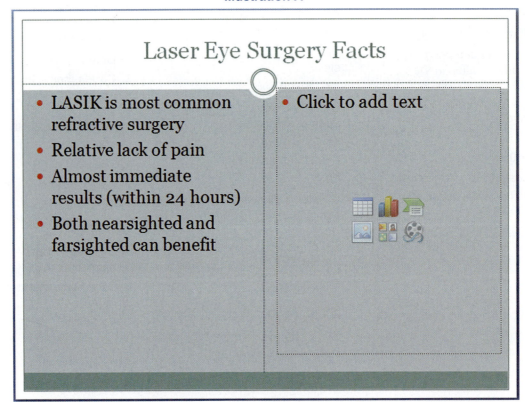

ON YOUR OWN

1. Start PowerPoint and open the **OPP05_xx** presentation you created in the On Your Own section of Exercise 5, or open 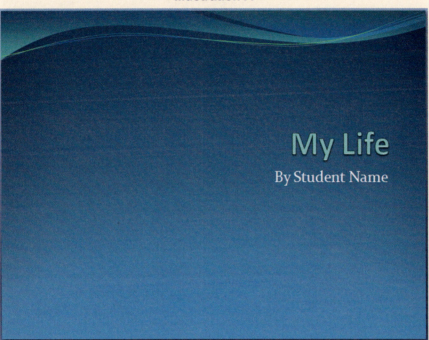 **OPP06**.

2. Save the file as **OPP06_xx**.

3. Download a theme from Office Online that you think will suit your presentation, or choose one of the built-in themes.

4. Scroll through the slides to see the changes.

5. If your presentation includes slides that fall into natural groups, try applying a different theme to a group of selected slides, or apply a different theme to the title slide, as shown in Illustrations A and B.

6. Save your changes, close the presentation, and exit PowerPoint.

Illustration A

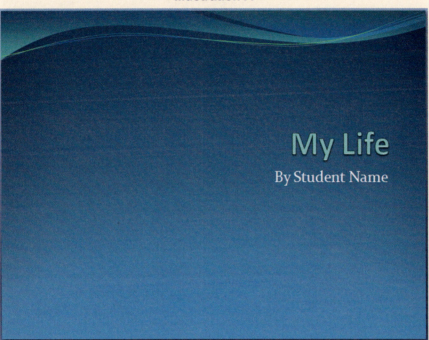

My Life
By Student Name

Illustration B

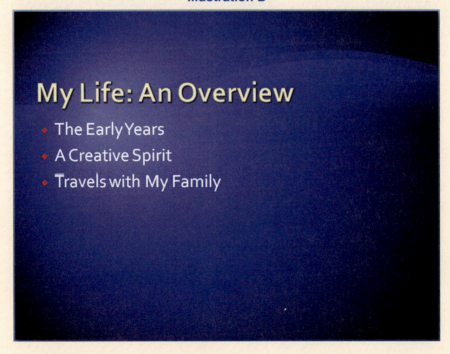

My Life: An Overview

- The Early Years
- A Creative Spirit
- Travels with My Family

Skills Covered

- **Change Slide Layout**
- **Work with the Normal View Panes**
- **Use the PowerPoint Zoom Controls**
- **Spell Check a Presentation**

Software Skills   You can change a slide layout at any time without losing content or having to re-enter it. The Normal view panes allow you to work with slides in several ways. Zoom controls make it easy to change the view size. Be sure to spell check a presentation to avoid embarrassing errors.

Application Skills   In this exercise, you continue to work with the Holmes Medical Center presentation. You will insert another slide and enter content in the Outline tab, and then you will check spelling.

TERMS

No new terms in this exercise.

NOTES

Change Slide Layout

- You may need to change a slide's layout as you work. Use the Layout button on the Home tab to apply a new slide layout.

- Clicking the Layout button displays a gallery of the standard slide layouts. Click any layout to apply it to the current slide or selected slides. If you have already added content to a slide, it may move into a new location to follow the new slide layout.

- If you have more than one theme applied in a presentation, the Layout gallery allows you to choose layouts according to theme, as shown in the illustration at right.

- If you have made changes to a slide layout by moving placeholders or adjusting text formats, you can restore the original formatting of the layout by clicking the Reset button in the Slides group on the Home tab.

  ✓ *You will use the Reset option in Exercise 11 to restore layout formats after creating slides from a Word outline.*

Choose a new layout with a specific theme

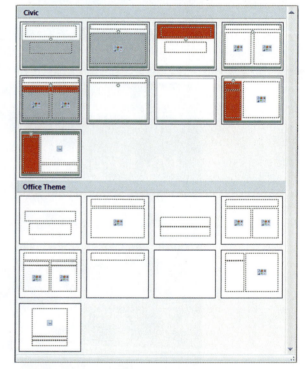

Work with the Normal View Panes

- Normal view, the default view, allows you to work with slides in several ways.

- The three panes in Normal view—the Slide pane, the Notes pane, and the Slides/Outline pane—are separated by borders that you can drag to increase the size of a pane.

- Use the Slide pane to insert and modify slide content. This pane provides the largest view of the current slide, making it easy to work with text and graphics.

- Use the Notes pane, shown in the illustration below, to add text for personal reference, such as material you want to remember to cover during the presentation. Notes recorded in the Notes pane can also be printed along with the slide to use as audience handouts.

Inserting text in the Notes pane

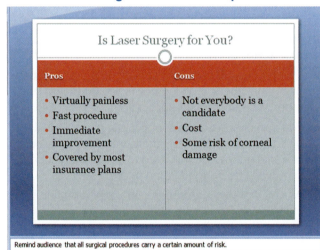

- To insert text in the Notes pane, click the placeholder text and begin typing.

- You can format the text in the Notes pane to some extent: If you highlight the notes text, you can use some options on the Mini toolbar that appears to change the look of the text. You can add bold or italic formatting, for example, adjust alignment, or apply bullet or number formats.

  ✓ *You learn more about changing text formats in the next lesson.*

- The Slides tab in the Slides/Outline pane shows a small version of all slides in the presentation and can be used to quickly select slides or reorganize them.

- The Outline tab, behind the Slides tab in the Slides/Outline pane, lets you view all slide content in outline format, as shown in the following illustration.

The Outline tab shows slide content in outline form

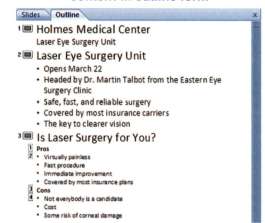

- Many PowerPoint users prefer to create presentation text in the Outline tab because they can concentrate on the text and move quickly from slide to slide.

- To begin a new presentation in the Outline tab, click next to the first slide icon and type the text that will become the slide title. As you type the text in the Outline tab, it appears on the current slide in the Slide pane.

- Press ↵Enter to start a new slide in the Outline pane. If you do not want a new slide but want to insert a subtitle or bulleted content, press Tab↹ to "back up" to the previous slide and insert the subordinate text. You can then press ⬆Shift+Tab↹ to return to the first level of the outline and create the next slide title.

Use the PowerPoint Zoom Controls

- You were introduced to zoom controls for Office 2007 in the Basics lesson. In this section, you learn how these tools work in PowerPoint to allow you to change the size of the slide in the Slide pane.

- You can adjust the size of the slide in the Slide pane using the zoom controls in the lower-right corner of the PowerPoint window, shown in the following illustration.

Zoom control

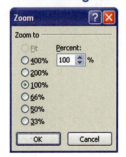

- Drag the Zoom slider to adjust the zoom to any percentage. The current percentage displays at the left end of the zoom controls.

- Clicking the Zoom Out or Zoom In button adjusts the zoom by 10% with each click.

- Click the Fit slide to current window button to automatically resize the slide to fill the current Slide pane window.

- To specify an exact zoom percentage, click the current zoom percentage to open the Zoom dialog box, where you can click spin arrows to set the percentage.

- You can also adjust the zoom using tools in the Zoom group on the View tab. Click the Fit to Window button to fit the slide in the current window size. Click the Zoom button to open the Zoom dialog box shown in the following illustration, where you can select a preset zoom percentage or use spin arrows to set a specific percentage.

Zoom dialog box

Spell Check a Presentation

- PowerPoint provides two methods of spell checking in your presentation: automatic and manual.

- Automatic spell checking works while you're typing, displaying a wavy red line under words PowerPoint doesn't recognize. Right-click a wavy underline to see a list of possible correctly spelled replacements, as shown in the following illustration.

Correcting a spelling error

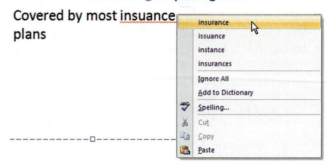

- To check spelling manually, use the Spelling button on the Review tab.

- The process of checking spelling in a presentation using the Spelling dialog box is similar to that in other Microsoft Office applications.

- You can change a misspelling to a correct spelling by choosing from a list, ignore one or all instances of the word, or add the word to a custom dictionary so it won't be flagged in the future.

- As you work with a presentation, pay attention to the spelling icon in the status bar to the right of the current theme name. It will alert you if the presentation contains possible spelling errors. You can click the icon to open the Spelling dialog box.

PROCEDURES

Change Slide Layout

1. Click **Home** tab .... Alt + H

   Slides Group

2. Click **Layout** button ⊞ L
3. Select the desired layout.

Work with the Normal View Panes

To adjust the size of any Normal view pane:

- Drag the pane's border to increase or decrease the size of the pane.

To insert text in the Notes pane:

- Click the *Click to add notes* prompt and begin typing.

To select slides in the Slides tab:

- Click a slide thumbnail to select that slide.

   OR

1. Click the first slide of a selection.
2. Hold down Ctrl while selecting additional slides.

To enter text in the Outline tab:

1. Click **Outline** tab.
2. In a new presentation, click to the right of the slide 1 symbol and type the presentation title.
3. Press ↵Enter, press Tab↹, and then type the presentation subtitle.
4. Press ↵Enter, press ⬆Shift + Tab↹ to start a new slide, and then type the slide title.
5. Press ↵Enter, press Tab↹, and then type the first bullet item.

Change the Zoom Setting

To zoom out:

- Drag the zoom slider to the left.

   OR

- Click the **Zoom Out** button ⊖.

To zoom in:

- Drag the zoom slider to the right.

   OR

- Click the **Zoom In** button ⊕.

To specify an exact zoom percentage:

1. Click the current zoom percentage in the zoom controls at lower-right of PowerPoint window.
2. Type desired percentage.

   OR

   Click spin arrows to set percentage.

3. Click [OK] .... ↵Enter

To adjust zoom using the Zoom group:

1. Click **View** tab .... Alt + W

   Zoom Group

2. Click **Zoom** button .... Q
3. Click desired zoom option.

   OR

   a. Click **Percent** increment box .... Alt + E
   b. Type **percentage**.

4. Click [OK] .... ↵Enter

To fit slide to current window:

- Click **Fit slide to current window** button ▣.

   OR

1. Click **View** tab .... Alt + W

   Zoom Group

2. Click **Fit to Window** button ▣ .... F

Spell Check a Presentation

To respond to automatic spell check errors:

1. Right-click a word identified as an error by a wavy red underline.
2. Select one of the options on the shortcut menu.

To manually check spelling:

1. Click **Review** tab .... Alt + R

   Proofing Group

2. Click **Spelling** button ✓ᴬᴮᶜ .... S
3. Proceed from slide to slide, choosing new words to replace those flagged as errors or ignoring words that are not errors.
4. When the spell check is complete, click [OK] .... ↵Enter

EXERCISE DIRECTIONS

1. Start PowerPoint and open **06Laser_xx** or ⊙**07Laser**.

2. Save the file as **07Laser_xx**.

3. Move to slide 4 and change the layout to Title and Content.

4. Add a new slide in the Outline tab as follows:

   ■ Activate the Outline tab and click just to the right of the last word of slide 4 (*benefit*).

   ■ Press ⏎Enter, then press ⬆Shift+Tab⇄ to create a new slide.

   ■ Type the title **Glossary**.

   ■ Press ⏎Enter, then Tab⇄ and type the following bullet item exactly as shown.

   Astigmatism: a distortion of the imge on the retina caused by irregularities in the corena or lens

   ■ Press ⏎Enter and then type the remaining bullet items below, pressing ⏎Enter after the first two.

   Hyperopia: farsightedness

   Myopia: nearsightedness

   Presbyopia: inability to maintain a clear image as objects are moved closer

5. Hide the Outline tab by displaying the Slides tab. Adjust the size of the Slides/Outline pane so that the slides in the Slides tab are larger.

6. Move to slide 4 and enter the following text in the Notes pane:

   Discuss issues for patients who have astigmatism.

7. Change the zoom to fit the slide in the current window size, then change the zoom to 70% (or a size that will fit comfortably in the current window).

8. Check the presentation for spelling errors. You can ignore *Hyperopia* and *Presbyopia* if you typed them exactly as shown in step 4. Your slide 5 should look like Illustration A.

9. Save your changes, close the presentation, and exit PowerPoint.

Illustration A

Glossary

- Astigmatism: a distortion of the image on the retina caused by irregularities in the cornea or lens
- Hyperopia: farsightedness
- Myopia: nearsightedness
- Presbyopia: inability to maintain a clear image as objects are moved closer

ON YOUR OWN

1. Start PowerPoint and open the **OPP06_xx** presentation, or open 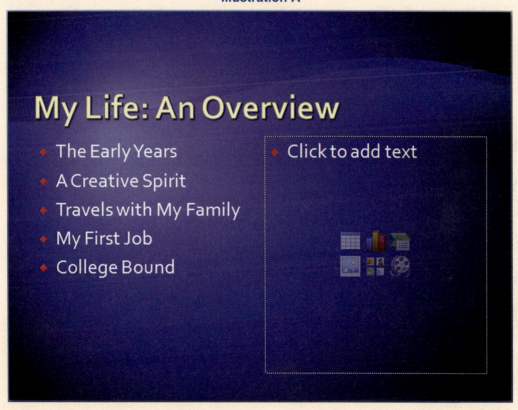**OPP07**.

2. Save the file as **OPP07_xx**.

3. Check the spelling in the presentation.

4. Change the layout of slide 2 to Two Content so you can add a picture to this slide later. Illustration A shows a sample slide after the new layout has been applied.

5. Use the Outline tab to add several bullet items to one or more of your slides.

6. Save your changes, close the presentation, and exit PowerPoint.

Illustration A

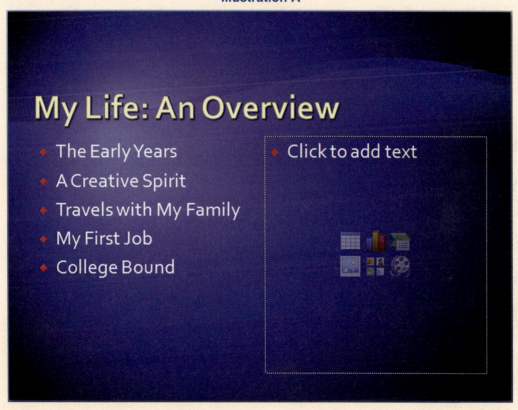

57

Skills Covered

- **Insert Clip Art**
- **Resize and Position Clip Art**
- **Use Undo, Redo, and Repeat**

Software Skills Use clip art to provide more graphic interest on slides. You can resize and move clip art to improve its appearance on the slide. If you make a mistake, you can undo it, and you can repeat actions to save time.

Application Skills In this exercise, you continue to work with the Holmes Medical Center presentation. Your client has asked you to add clip art to make it more interesting.

TERMS

Clip art Predrawn artwork, photos, animations, and sound clips that you can insert into your files.

NOTES

Insert Clip Art

- Most PowerPoint slide layouts offer a content placeholder that allows you to insert a variety of types of content. Using the icons shown in the following illustration, you can insert a table, chart, SmartArt graphic, picture, clip art graphic, or media clip.

  ✓ *You will work with all these content types in later exercises.*

The icons let you add different types of content

- **Clip art** images are pictures in a variety of styles that you can use to add graphic interest to a slide. Though the term *clip art* is generally used to refer to cartoon-like line art, Microsoft Office includes in its clip art files photographs, sounds and music, and animated graphics.

- To search for and select clip art objects, click the Clip Art icon in a content placeholder to open the Clip Art task pane. You can also click the Clip Art button on the Insert tab.

- Clip art objects are identified by keywords that allow you to search for objects by subject. For example, if you want to add an image of a giraffe to a presentation, you type the word *giraffe* in the Search for box in the Clip Art task pane, as shown in the following illustration.

- You can choose what kind of clip art objects the search will display by clicking the Results should be list arrow to display the list of media types shown in the following illustration.

Set up a search for clip art in the Clip Art task pane

■ You can select more than one media type if desired to find objects of different media types that match your keyword.

■ By default, PowerPoint searches everywhere it can: collections on your computer and collections on the Web. You can specify what collections to search by clicking the Search in list arrow to display available collections and then selecting or deselecting them.

■ After you have entered the appropriate keyword and selected a media type, clicking the Go button displays the results of the search, as shown in the following illustration. To insert a clip art object, click it in the task pane.

Results of a search for giraffe clip art images

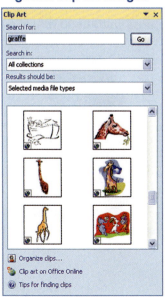

■ Pointing to an image in the task pane displays a list arrow you can click to show a menu of other options, such as Copy, Edit Keywords, and Preview/Properties.

■ If you opened the Clip Art task pane by clicking Clip Art in a content placeholder, clicking an image in the task pane inserts it into the content placeholder at the most appropriate size for the placeholder.

■ Finding an appropriate clip art image using the Clip Art task pane can sometimes require a number of searches, particularly if you do not have a specific subject in mind. Searching for images that denote *business*, for example, may result in many images you have to look at to find one that meets your needs.

■ You can sometimes minimize the amount of searching you have to do by using the Clip Organizer or Office Online. The links at the bottom of the Clip Art task pane give you access to these options.

■ The Clip Organizer categorizes images on your computer by subject so that you can easily scroll through all images in a particular category or easily move to a different category without having to run a new search. The following illustration shows images in the Buildings category.

The Clip Organizer groups images by category

- You may have noticed in the earlier illustration of the giraffe clip art results that all of the images displayed a small symbol in the lower-left corner of the image.

- This symbol indicates that the image is being downloaded from Office Online. By default, a clip art search looks not only for images on your computer but also images and objects on Microsoft's Office Online Web site.

- You can go directly to this Web site by clicking the Clip art on Office Online link at the bottom of the Clip Art task pane.

- On the Clip Art page, you can type a search keyword and select a media type as in the Clip Art task pane. Clips that match the keyword display on the page, as shown in the following illustration. It can be easier to page through these results than to view them in the Clip Art task pane.

Search results on the Clip Art page at Office Online

- If you find clips you like, you can download them to your computer to be available the next time you search.

- Click the check box of a clip and then click the Download link to start the process of downloading.

- Downloaded clips are stored in the Clip Organizer.

Resize and Position Clip Art

- Although a clip art image usually fills the placeholder into which it is inserted, some images will not use up the entire placeholder dimensions.

- Also, if you do not have the content placeholder selected, or if you launch the Clip Art task pane by clicking the Clip Art button on the Insert tab, images you insert will display in the middle of the slide, as shown in the following illustration.

Image inserted in the middle of the slide

- If the inserted image is not the right size or in the right location, you can move and resize the image.

- Move the image where you want it by dragging it with the mouse. You can also use the mouse to resize a graphic by dragging a corner handle as shown in the following illustration.

Drag a corner handle to resize a graphic

- When you click an image to select it, PowerPoint displays one of its *contextual tabs*, the Picture Tools Format tab. You can use the Height and Width options in the Size group on this tab to set precise dimensions for a clip.

  ✓ *You'll learn more about the Picture Tools Format tab options in a later exercise.*

Use Undo, Redo, and Repeat

- PowerPoint contains an Undo feature, as in other Microsoft Office applications, which reverses the most recent action or a whole series of previous actions.

- The Undo button displays on the Quick Access Toolbar. Click the button once to reverse the most recent change, or click the button's down arrow to see a list of changes. Clicking any item on the list will undo that action as well as all the actions above it on the list.

- The Quick Access Toolbar also displays a Repeat button that allows you to easily repeat the last action, such as applying a format or inserting an object.

- If you have used the Undo button, the Repeat button changes to the Redo button.

- The Redo button allows you to redo actions after you undo them, if you change your mind.

PROCEDURES

Insert Clip Art

1. Click **Clip Art** button 🖼 in any content placeholder.

   OR

   a. Click **Insert** tab........... Alt + N

   Illustrations Group

   b. Click **Clip Art** button 🖼..... F

2. Type a keyword in the Search for box in the Clip Art task pane.

3. Click the Search in down arrow and select collections to search, if desired.

4. Click the Results should be down arrow and choose the type(s) of results to display.

5. Click Go ....↵Enter to begin search.

6. Click an image from the search results to insert the image on the slide.

To view and insert images in the Clip Organizer:

1. Display the Clip Art task pane by clicking a Clip Art button.

2. Click the **Organize Clips** link at the bottom of the Clip Art task pane.

3. Click a category in the left pane of the Microsoft Clip Organizer dialog box to view images in that category.

4. To insert an image:

   a. Right-click the image and click **Copy**........................... C

   b. Display the slide on which you want the image to appear, making sure no placeholder is selected.

   c. Click **Home** tab.......... Alt + H

   Clipboard Group

   d. Click **Paste** button 📋........ V

To view and download images from Office Online:

1. Display the Clip Art task pane by clicking a Clip Art button.

2. Click the **Clip art on Office Online** link at the bottom of the Clip Art task pane.

3. Click in the Clip Art text box and type a keyword.

4. Click the Search button's down arrow and select media type.

5. Page through results if necessary to locate a clip you want.

6. Click the check box below the clip to select it.

7. In the left pane in the Selection Basket group, click **Download [number] item[s]** link.

8. Click Download Now on the Download page.

9. Click Open to open the Clip Organizer and store the downloaded image.

Resize and Position Clip Art

To resize an image:

1. Click the clip art image if necessary to select it.

2. Position the pointer over a sizing handle.

3. Hold down the mouse button and drag the handle toward the image to reduce in size or away from the image to enlarge in size.

To position an image:

1. Click on the image and hold down the mouse button.

2. Drag the image to the desired location.

Use Undo (Ctrl + Z), Redo (Ctrl + Y), and Repeat (Ctrl + Y)

To undo a single action:

- Click **Undo** button 🔄 on the Quick Access Toolbar.

To undo multiple actions:

1. Click **Undo** button 🔄 down arrow .... Alt + 2 to display a list of recent actions.
2. Click any action on the list .... ↓, ↵Enter

   ✓ *All actions above the one you select will also be reversed.*

To redo the previous Undo action:

- Click **Redo** button ↷ on the Quick Access Toolbar .... Alt + 3

   ✓ *The Redo button does not become active until after you use the Undo button.*

To repeat an action:

- Click **Repeat** button ↻ on the Quick Access Toolbar .... Alt + 3 immediately after the action you want to repeat.

EXERCISE DIRECTIONS

1. Start PowerPoint and open **07Laser_xx** or 💿**08Laser**.
2. Save the file as **08Laser_xx**.
3. Move to slide 4 and insert a new slide that uses the Two Content slide layout.
4. Type the title and text as shown in Illustration A.
5. Insert a relevant clip art image in the right content placeholder.

   ✓ *For best results, use the keyword "eye" and choose to search the Microsoft Office Online Web Collection.*

6. Move the clip art image to center it horizontally in the right content placeholder and resize it to be about twice as large.
7. Add another new slide using the Content with Caption slide layout.
8. Insert the title and text shown in Illustration B.
9. Use the keyword "sun" to search for an attractive clip art photograph and insert it in the right content placeholder. Resize the photo as necessary to fit in the placeholder.

   ✓ *For best results, choose a picture in landscape orientation—wider than it is tall.*

10. Close the Clip Art task pane.
11. Display slide 4 and select the word *nearsighted* in the last bullet item.
12. Apply bold formatting to the word, then click Undo to remove the formatting.
13. With the word still selected, apply italic formatting to the word. Then select the word *farsighted* and click the Repeat button to apply the same italic formatting.
14. Save your changes, close the presentation, and exit PowerPoint.

Illustration A

The Cost of Laser Surgery

- Typically as low as $499 per eye
- Custom options can add significantly to costs
- Financing is available for some candidates

Illustration B

Clear Vision in a Day

In most cases, vision clears immediately, or within 24 hours of surgery. The patient should be able to return to normal activities in a day and feel no discomfort or side effects from the surgery.

ON YOUR OWN

1. Start PowerPoint and open the **OPP07_xx** presentation or open 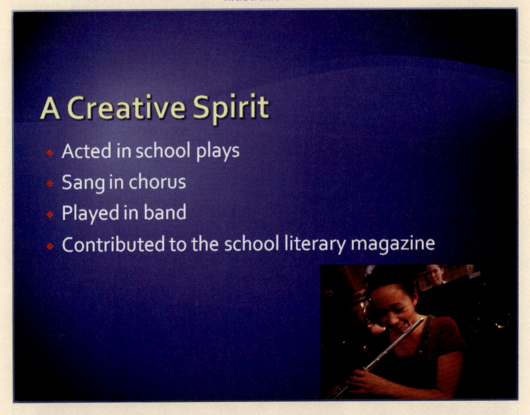**OPP08**.

2. Save the file as **OPP08_xx**.

3. Insert a clip art graphic or photograph on slide 2. Try to select a picture that is somehow related to the text on the slide.

4. Resize and position the image as desired.

5. Insert a clip art graphic or photograph on slide 4, using the Insert tab to insert the clip art. Try locating a clip on Office Online and then download it to your Clip Organizer and insert it on the slide. Illustration A shows a sample slide.

6. Resize and reposition the image as desired.

7. Save your changes, close the presentation, and exit PowerPoint.

Illustration A

Skills Covered

- **Change Theme Colors**
- **Change Theme Fonts**
- **Change Background Style**

Software Skills   You can change theme colors, theme fonts, and backgrounds to customize a presentation. Making these types of changes can freshen a presentation's look and make it more appropriate for a specific audience.

Application Skills   In this exercise, you continue to work with the Holmes Medical Center presentation. You want to explore how changing theme elements such as colors, fonts, and background style might impact the presentation's appearance.

TERMS

Font A set of characters with a specific size and style.

NOTES

Change Theme Colors

- Each PowerPoint theme uses a palette of colors selected to work well together. These colors are applied to various elements in the presentation, such as the slide background, text, shape fills, and hyperlink text.

- You can see the color palettes for each theme by clicking the Theme Colors button in the Themes group on the Design tab, as shown in the illustration at right.

Theme Colors gallery

- PowerPoint offers several ways to adjust theme colors:
  - If you like the layout and fonts of a particular theme but not its colors, you can choose to use the color palette of a different theme. All theme elements stay the same, but colors used for those elements change to those of the chosen theme.
  - You can change one or more colors in the current theme to customize the theme's colors.
- To use the color palette of a different theme, click the palette in the Theme Colors gallery. Clicking the color palette applies colors to all slides in the presentation.
- You can also apply a different theme's colors to a selection of slides by choosing them, then right-clicking the color palette you want to use and selecting Apply to Selected Slides.
- You modify theme colors in the Create New Theme Colors dialog box, shown in the following illustration.

Choose new colors for a theme

- Change a color by clicking the down arrow for a particular color to display a palette like the one shown in the following illustration. Select a different tint or hue of a theme color, choose one of ten standard colors, or click More Colors to open the Colors dialog box and pick from all available colors.

Theme Colors palette

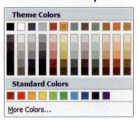

- As soon as you change a theme color, the preview in the Create New Theme Colors dialog box also changes to show you how your new color coordinates with the others in the theme.
- You can name a new color scheme and save it. It then displays in the Custom area at the top of the Theme Colors gallery. Custom colors are available to use with any theme.

Change Theme Fonts

- As a theme offers a palette of specific colors, it also offers a set of two specific **fonts**, one font for all titles and the other for body text such as the text in bullet lists.
- You can apply the fonts of another theme by choosing a set from the Theme Fonts gallery shown in the following illustration.

Theme Fonts gallery

- You can create your own theme fonts if desired, or you can change the font of text in any placeholder using the tools in the Font group on the Home tab.

  ✓ *You'll work more extensively with fonts in Lesson 2.*

Change Background Style

- Each theme has a specific background color, and some have background graphics or other effects such as gradients—gradations from one color to another.

- To customize a theme, you can change the background style to one of the choices offered by the current theme, such as those in the Background Styles gallery shown in the following illustration.

Background Styles gallery

- Background styles use the current theme colors. You can apply a new style to all slides or to selected slides.

- As you rest your pointer on different background styles, the current slide shows that background.

- If you want to make a more radical change to the background, click the Format Background link on the Background Styles gallery to open a dialog box where you can create a new background using a solid color, a gradient, a texture, or even a picture.

  ✓ *You'll work more extensively with backgrounds in Lesson 4.*

PROCEDURES

Change Theme Colors

1. Click **Design** tab .... Alt+G

   Themes Group

2. Click **Theme Colors** button 🔳 .... T, C

3. Select a different theme's color palette if desired.

To change theme colors for selected slides:

1. In the Slides tab, select slides to which you will apply different theme colors.

2. Click **Design** tab ..... Alt+G

   Themes Group

3. Click **Theme Colors** button 🔳 .... T, C

4. Right-click a different theme's color palette.

5. Click **Apply to Selected Slides** ..... S

To change one or more theme colors:

1. Click **Design** tab .... Alt+G

   Themes Group

2. Click **Theme Colors** button 🔳 .... T, C

3. Click **Create New Theme Colors** C

4. Click the down arrow of the color to be changed.

5. Select a new color from the palette.

   OR

   Click one of the Standard colors.

   OR

   a. Click **More Colors** .... M

   b. Create or select a color from the Colors dialog box.

   c. Click [OK] .... ↵Enter

6. Click **Name** .... N and type a name for the new color scheme if desired.

7. Click [Save] .... Alt+S

Change Theme Fonts

1. Click **Design** tab .... Alt + G

2. Click **Theme Fonts** button A .... T, F
3. Click a different theme's font combination to apply it.

Change Background Style

1. Click **Design** tab .... Alt + G

2. Click **Background Styles** button .... B
3. Click a background style to select and apply it.

To apply the style to one or more slides:

1. Select a slide or slides in the Slides tab.
2. Right-click the background style thumbnail.
3. Click **Apply to Selected Slides** ..... S

EXERCISE DIRECTIONS

1. Start PowerPoint and open **08Laser_xx** or **09Laser**.
2. Save the file as **09Laser_xx**.
3. Change the theme colors to those from the Equity theme.
4. Change the theme fonts to those for the Trek theme (Franklin Gothic Medium and Franklin Gothic Book).
5. Display slide 1 and apply background style 10 to all slides.
6. Undo this change and then apply background style 10 to slide 1 only. Your slide should look like Illustration A.
7. Save your changes, close the presentation, and exit PowerPoint.

Illustration A

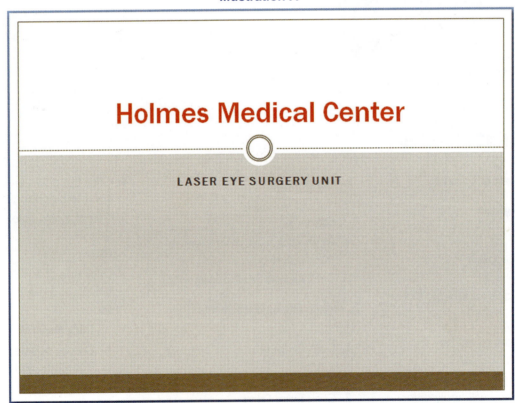

ON YOUR OWN

1. Start PowerPoint and open the **OPP08_xx** presentation or open **OPP09**.

2. Save the file as **OPP09_xx**.

3. Apply a different set of theme fonts to all slides.

4. Change at least one of the theme colors for your current theme, using the Create New Theme Colors dialog box. Save the theme colors with a new name.

5. Apply a different background style to one or more slides in the presentation. Illustration A shows a new background on slide 1.

6. Save your changes, close the presentation, and exit PowerPoint.

Illustration A

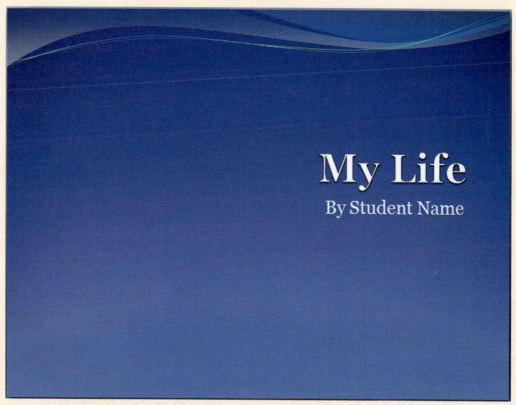

Exercise | 10

Skills Covered

- **Create a Presentation from a Template or Existing Presentation**
- **PowerPoint Views**
- **Copy, Duplicate, and Delete Slides**
- **Rearrange Slides**

Software Skills PowerPoint provides a number of templates you can use to format a presentation or help you create a specific kind of presentation. As you work on a presentation, you often need to copy, delete, or rearrange slides. Use PowerPoint views to work with slides and view a finished presentation.

Application Skills The owners of Harriet's Place have asked you to create a presentation to show at a staff strategy session. You will use a template as the basis for the strategy presentation. You will then work with the slides to adjust content and order.

TERMS

Template A presentation that is already formatted with a theme and may also include sample text to guide you in completing the presentation.

NOTES

Create a Presentation from a Template or Existing Presentation

- So far you have created presentations by starting from the default blank presentation. PowerPoint offers several other methods for creating a presentation, including creating slides from an outline (covered in the next exercise), creating a presentation from one of PowerPoint's many **templates**, and creating a presentation based on an existing presentation.

- You can find PowerPoint templates in the New Presentation dialog box shown in the following illustration. This dialog box allows you to browse templates installed on your system or templates available from Microsoft Office Online in a number of categories.

Choose a template from the New Presentation dialog box

- Some templates provide a number of slides with sample text and graphics as well as slide layouts specifically designed for the template. Other templates provide only a single slide with specific content or a design.

- If you choose a template from one of the Microsoft Office Online categories, you must have an active Internet connection to download it. The downloaded template opens in PowerPoint with a default title such as Presentation1.

- Some presentations shown in the Microsoft Office Online galleries have been supplied to Microsoft by outside vendors and are available for download only to computers running genuine Microsoft software. You may be required to validate your software before you can download one of these templates.

- The New Presentation dialog box also allows you to create a new presentation based on an existing one.

- Selecting the New from existing link in the New Presentation dialog box opens the New from Existing Presentation dialog box, shown in the following illustration.

Navigate to the location of the existing presentation

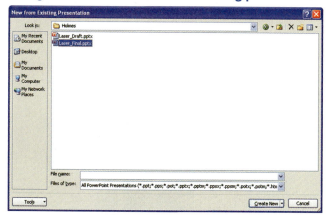

- Use this dialog box to navigate to the location of the existing presentation.

- After you select the existing presentation, PowerPoint opens a copy of it with a default title such as Presentation1.

- Your existing presentation remains unchanged as you modify the new version of it.

PowerPoint Views

- You have worked so far in Normal view, the view necessary for adding and modifying slide content. PowerPoint offers two additional views to help you finalize a presentation:

  - Slide Sorter view displays the entire presentation in large thumbnails so you can easily identify slides to add, delete, and rearrange. This view is also useful for adding transitions to a number of slides at once. You cannot edit content in this view.

    ✓ *To move quickly from Slide Sorter view to Normal view, double-click a slide.*

  - Slide Show view displays one slide at a time using the full monitor size, displaying the slide as it would be displayed if projected in a slide show. This view is useful for checking slide elements and making sure animations work as desired.

- To switch to either of these views, use the View buttons toward the right side of the status bar, shown in the following illustration.

View buttons let you quickly change views

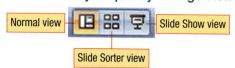

- You can also switch views using options in the Presentation Views group on the View tab, shown in the following illustration.

View options on the View tab

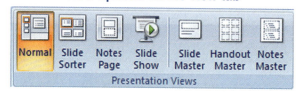

- The Presentation Views group gives you access to another view: Notes Page view.

- This view shows a full-size portrait-orientation page with the current slide in the top half of the page and a space for slide notes in the bottom half of the page.

- While viewing slides in Notes Page view, you can add notes just as you do in the Notes pane in Normal view.

  ✓ *You will work with Notes Page view in Exercise 12.*

Copy, Duplicate, and Delete Slides

- In the course of working with a presentation, you may often need to create slides similar to one another. You can simplify this process by copying or duplicating slides.
  - Copy a slide if you want to paste the copy some distance from the original or in another presentation.
  - Duplicate a slide to create an identical version immediately after the original slide. This process can be very helpful if you want to retain the same title for the next slide or want to create another slide very like the current slide.
- To remove a slide from the presentation, display it in the Slide pane or select it in the Slides tab or the Slide Sorter view and then delete it using the Delete button ⊠ on the Home tab.
- Note that PowerPoint does not ask you if you're sure you want to delete a slide—the slide is immediately deleted. If you change your mind about the deletion, use Undo to restore the slide.

Rearrange Slides

- Another task you must frequently undertake when working with slides is to rearrange them. Slide Sorter view is your best option for moving slides from one place in a presentation to another.
- You can rearrange slides in Slide Sorter view by simply dragging a slide to a new location, as shown in the following illustration.

Rearrange slides in Slide Sorter view by dragging

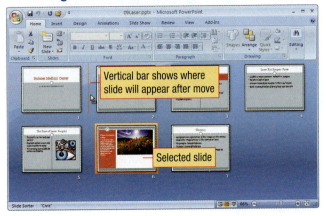

- If the presentation has a large number of slides, it can be a challenge to drag a slide from one location to another. In this situation, you can move a slide by cutting it from one location and pasting it in another location.
- You may also want to copy slides to a new location so that you have two versions of a slide in the presentation. This can be an effective way to mark the beginnings of sections of slides.
- Copy slides in Slide Sorter view by holding down Ctrl while dragging or by using the Copy and Paste commands.
- Although Slide Sorter view gives you the best overall view of the slides in a presentation, you can also rearrange slides in the Slides tab in Normal view, using the slide thumbnails in the Slides tab.
- Drag a slide up or down in the Slides tab, as shown in the following illustration, to move or copy it.

Rearrange slides in the Slides tab by dragging

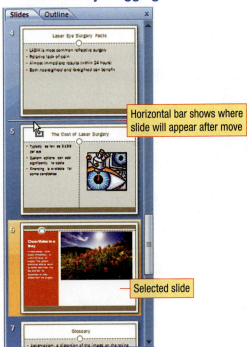

- You can use Copy and Paste or Cut and Paste to move slides in the Slides tab just as in Slide Sorter view.

Curriculum Connection: Mathematics

Mathematicians

Frenchman Rene Descartes was a mathematician and philosopher who wrote a book called *La Géométrie*, in which he explained his application of algebra to geometry. That is how modern Cartesian geometry developed. He is also famous for his quote, "I think, therefore I am."

Find Your Own Mathematician

Research another mathematician and create a PowerPoint presentation about him or her. You might include information such as birth date, hometown, and contributions to modern-day mathematics. Find a picture of your mathematician and insert it into one of your slides. Customize your presentation by downloading a new theme or template from Office Online and modifying theme colors and fonts.

PROCEDURES

Create a Presentation from a Template

1. Click **Office Button** ..... Alt + F
2. Click **N**ew ..... N
3. Click a template category.
4. Select the desired template.
5. Click [Create] ..... ↵Enter

To download a presentation from Microsoft Office Online:

1. Click **Office Button** ..... Alt + F
2. Click **N**ew ..... N
3. Click a category in the Microsoft Office Online list.
4. Select a category if necessary.
5. Select the desired template.
6. Click [Download] ..... ↵Enter
7. Click [Continue] ..... ↵Enter

Create a Presentation from an Existing Presentation

1. Click **Office Button** ..... Alt + F
2. Click **N**ew ..... N
3. Click **New from existing**.
4. Navigate to the location of the existing presentation and select it.
5. Click [Create New ▾] ..... ↵Enter

Change Views

■ To change to Slide Sorter view or Slide Show view, click the appropriate button on the status bar.

OR

1. Click **View** tab ..... Alt + W

Presentation Views Group

2. Click one of the following:
   ■ **Normal** button L
   ■ **Slide Sorter** button I
   ■ **Notes Page** button ..... T
   ■ **Slide Show** button ..... S

OR

■ Press F5 to start the slide show from slide 1 no matter what the current slide is.

Copy Slides (Ctrl + C)/ Paste Slides (Ctrl + V)

1. Select slide(s) to copy in the Slides tab or in Slide Sorter view.
2. Click **Home** tab ..... Alt + H

Clipboard Group

3. Click **Copy** button C
4. Select the slide after which the copied slide will be pasted.
5. Click **Paste** button ..... Alt + H, V, P

   ✓ *Click the Paste button's down arrow for other pasting options, such as Paste Special.*

Duplicate Slides

1. Select slide(s) to duplicate in the Slides tab or in Slide Sorter view.
2. Click **Home** tab ..... Alt + H

Slides Group

3. Click **New Slide** button down arrow I
4. Click **Duplicate Selected Slides** ..... D

OR

Clipboard Group

a. Click **Paste** button down arrow V
b. Click **Duplicate** I

Delete Slides

1. Select slide(s) to delete in the Slides tab or in Slide Sorter view.
2. Click **Home** tab .... Alt + H

3. Click **Delete** button ⊠ .... D

Rearrange Slides

To rearrange using drag-and-drop:

1. Select slide(s) to move in Slides tab or Slide Sorter view.
2. Drag to the desired location. Vertical bar in Slide Sorter view or horizontal bar in Slides tab shows where the slide will appear when the mouse button is released.

   ✓ To copy a slide from one location to another using drag-and-drop, hold down Ctrl while dragging.

To rearrange by cutting and pasting:

1. Select slide(s) to move in Slides tab or Slide Sorter view.
2. Click **Home** tab .... Alt + H

3. Click **Cut** button ✂ X
4. Click at the location in Slide Sorter view or Slides tab where the moved slide should display. A vertical or horizontal line appears where you clicked.
5. Click **Paste** button 📋 .... Alt + H, V, P

   ✓ To copy a slide from one location to another, click the Copy button rather than the Cut button.

EXERCISE DIRECTIONS

1. Start PowerPoint.
2. Create a new presentation using a template:
   - In the New Presentation dialog box, click the Presentations category under the Microsoft Office Online section.
   - Choose the Business category.
   - Select the Presentation for strategy recommendation template with the blue background.

     ✓ If you do not have a live Internet connection, choose to create a new presentation from the existing presentation ◉ 10Crunch.

   - Click Download, and then click Continue to download and open the template.
3. If the Help window displays, close it. Save the file as **10Crunch_xx**.
4. On slide 1, select the title *Recommending a Strategy* and type **Resolving the "Lunch Crunch"**.
5. Select the subtitle and type **Harriet's Place Strategy Session**.
6. Delete slides 2 and 3.
7. On the new slide 2, replace the existing text with the text shown in Illustration A.
8. On slide 3, replace the existing text with the text shown in Illustration B.
9. Insert the following note for slide 3:

   The "crunch" is particularly pressing from 12:00 to 1:00 p.m.

10. On slide 4, insert the text shown in Illustration C. Then insert the following note for this slide:

    Enlarging the dining room could make it possible for us to open Harriet's Place for dinner as well as breakfast and lunch.

11. Change to Slide Sorter view.
12. Move slide 2 to follow slide 3.
13. Duplicate slide 4. Double-click slide 5 to return to Normal view and change the title of slide 5 to **Additional Options**. (You will add the additional options at a later time.)
14. Open ◉ 10Slide. This file is one of the content templates from Microsoft Office Online.
15. Copy the slide and then paste it after the currently active slide in **10Crunch_xx**.
16. Remove the notes in the Notes pane, and then move the slide to the end of the presentation by dragging it in the Slides tab.
17. Display slide 1 and then change to Notes Page view (on the View tab). Scroll through the slides to see how the slides and notes are presented in this view.
18. Display slide 1 again and select Slide Show view. Move through the presentation by clicking the mouse button to display each new slide.
19. Save your changes, close both presentations, and exit PowerPoint.

Illustration A

How Did This Happen?

- Our location makes us an ideal lunch venue for students and hospital staff
- Our organic and vegetarian specialties have become popular alternatives to fast food
- Our reputation for good, inexpensive meals has spread throughout the community

Illustration B

Today's Situation

- Harriet's Place is currently experiencing a "lunch crunch"
- Customers are waiting too long for tables
- The wait staff is overburdened
- How can we improve lunch operations?

Illustration C

Available Options

- Increase space in the dining room by building out into patio area
- Hire additional wait staff for lunch service
- Market and improve carryout service for customers who just want the food fast

ON YOUR OWN

1. Start PowerPoint and create a new presentation file using one of the design slide templates from Microsoft Office Online. If you do not have an active Internet connection, you may want to create a new presentation from the existing presentation ⊙ **OPP10**.

2. Save the file as **OPP10_xx**. In this presentation, create slides that briefly summarize some of the park or recreation facilities in your city or town.

3. Insert an appropriate title and subtitle on the Title slide.

4. Add at least four slides to the presentation, duplicating as desired to make content entry easier. Create several bullets on each slide to describe park and/or recreation facilities. You may also add notes that give further information about programs or special events.

5. Insert a clip art graphic on at least one slide. (Use clip art photos if desired.)

6. Rearrange slides as desired.

7. Add another new slide, then add a final slide with a clip art image of a runner, walker, or biker.

8. Delete any unused slides.

9. View the slides in Notes Page view, and then view the slides in Slide Show view. The illustrations below show several sample slides.

10. Save your changes, close the presentation, and exit PowerPoint.

Illustration A

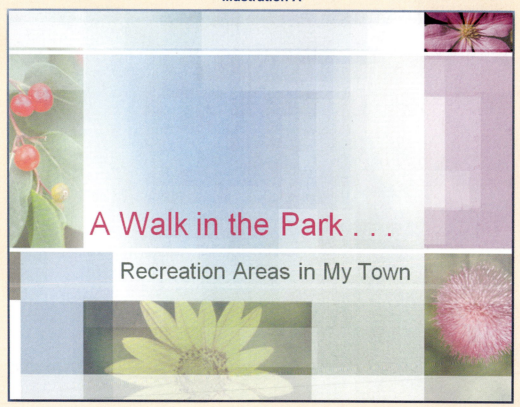

Central City

- City parks
  - Rawson Woods
  - Burnet Woods
  - Ault Park
  - Sawyer Point
  - Mt. Storm Park

Skills Covered

- **Create Slides from an Outline**
- **Reuse Slides from Other Presentations**
- **Insert Header/Footer, Date, and Slide Numbers**
- **Hide Background Graphics**

Software Skills   Use data created in other programs or in other presentations to save time when creating a presentation. Word outlines can be readily imported to create slides. Footers, dates, and numbers provide additional information on slides. In some instances, you may want to hide the background graphics created as part of a theme.

Application Skills   Your client, Voyager Travel Adventures, has supplied you with files they want you to use in the presentation you're creating for them. You'll also add information on each slide to help identify and organize the slides.

TERMS

Footer   An area at the bottom of a slide in which you can enter a date, slide number, or other information.

Header   An area at the top of a slide in which you can enter a date or other information that repeats for each page.

NOTES

Create Slides from an Outline

- You can use text created in other programs, such as Word, in your PowerPoint presentation. One reason to do this is so that you don't have to retype the text. You might also prefer organizing the contents of the presentation in Word.

- To use a Word outline to create slides, text in the Word document must be formatted with heading styles that clearly indicate text levels. Text formatted with the Word Heading 1 style become slide titles. Text styled as Heading 2 or Heading 3 becomes bulleted items, as shown in the illustration at right.

PowerPoint can convert Word outlines to slides

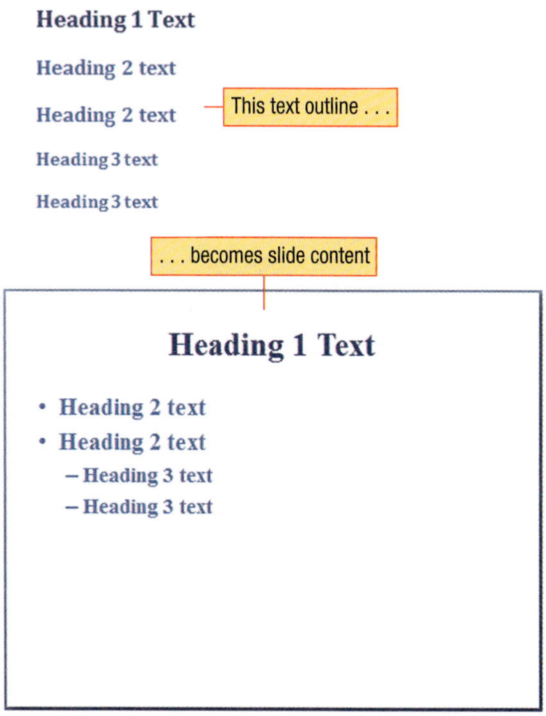

Heading 1 Text

Heading 2 text

Heading 2 text   ⟶ This text outline . . .

Heading 3 text

Heading 3 text

. . . becomes slide content

Heading 1 Text

- Heading 2 text
- Heading 2 text
  - Heading 3 text
  - Heading 3 text

- You have two options for using a Word outline to create slides:
  - You can simply open the Word document in PowerPoint to create the slides. This is the option to use when you want to create a new presentation from outline content.
  - You can use the Slides from Outline command on the New Slide drop-down list to add slides to an existing presentation. (You cannot use this command unless a presentation is already open.)
- Note from the previous illustration that when a Word document is used to create a presentation, the slides will display the same fonts and styles used in the document, and they do not change even if a new theme or theme fonts are applied.
- To make sure the slides use the fonts you want them to, you can use the Reset button to restore the theme defaults for colors, fonts, and effects. This command is also useful if you want to reverse changes you have made to slide layout or themes.

Reuse Slides from Other Presentations

- You will find that preparing presentations can be a time-consuming process, especially as you venture into more complex formatting and content. It makes sense to reuse slides whenever you can to save time.
- Borrowing slides from other presentations can also help to ensure consistency among presentations, an important consideration when you are working with a number of presentations for a company or organization.
- You can find the Reuse Slides command on the New Slide drop-down list. This command opens the Reuse Slides task pane shown in the following illustration.

Choose slides to reuse

- You specify the presentation file to open, and the slides are then displayed in the task pane. To see the content more clearly, rest the pointer on a slide in the current presentation. To insert a slide, simply click it.
- By default, slides you insert this way are formatted by the slide masters of the presentation they're inserted into (the destination presentation). If you want to retain the original formatting of the inserted slides, click the Keep source formatting check box at the bottom of the Reuse Slides task pane.

  ✓ *You will learn about slide masters in Lesson 4.*

Insert Header/Footer, Date, and Slide Numbers

- You can add several types of information that repeat for each slide to help organize or identify slides.
  - Use a slide **footer** to identify a presentation's topic, author, client, or other information.
  - Add the date and time to a slide footer so you can tell when the presentation was created or updated.
  - Include a slide number in the footer to identify the slide's position in the presentation.
- The locations of the slide footer, date and time, and slide number are controlled by the presentation's *slide master*. The slide master provides placeholders for these elements, as shown in the following illustration.

Slide master showing placeholders for footer, date, and slide number

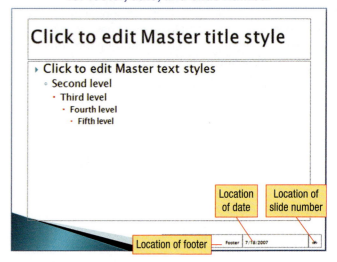

■ Even though these placeholders are provided by default on the slide master, the footer, date, and slide number will not display on slides unless you select these options in the Header and Footer dialog box, shown in the following illustration.

Specify slide footer, date, and slide number

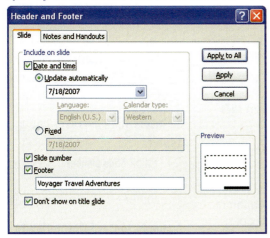

■ Note that you can choose a fixed date or a date that updates each time the presentation is opened. You can also choose to not display the information on the title slide, apply the information only to the current slide, or apply it to all slides.

■ If you are working with notes pages or handouts, you can use the options on the Notes and Handouts tab of the Header and Footer dialog box to add a **header** in addition to date and time, slide number, and footer.

✓ *You will work with notes pages and handouts in the next exercise.*

Hide Background Graphics

■ Many themes include some type of graphics such as lines or shapes that form a part of the slide background. You cannot select these graphics in Normal view because they are included on the slide masters, which control the layout and appearance of each type of slide in a presentation.

✓ *You will learn how to create and manipulate background graphics on slide masters in Lesson 4.*

■ You may find these graphics obtrusive or inappropriate in some situations. If you don't want to take the trouble to modify the slide masters, you can still remove the background graphics from view using the Hide Background Graphics option on the Design tab.

■ The following illustrations show a slide with the background graphics displayed (the default slide appearance) and hidden.

Background graphics displayed (top) and hidden (bottom)

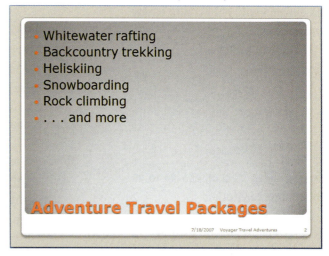

■ Be careful when you hide background graphics. Sometimes text colors are chosen to contrast with the graphic background, and when it is removed, the text color blends into the background, making it seem to disappear. You may need to change text color to make it visible again.

PROCEDURES

Create Slides from an Outline

To open an outline to create a new presentation:

1. Click **Office Button** 📇 ...... `Alt`+`F`
2. Click **Open** .... `O`
3. In **Files of type** list, click **All Files**.
4. Navigate to the location of the outline file and select the file.
5. Click [**Open** ▾] .... `↵Enter`

To add slides from an outline to an existing presentation:

1. Select the slide after which the new slides will be inserted.
2. Click **Home** tab .... `Alt`+`H`

   Slides Group

3. Click **New Slide** button 📧 down arrow .... `I`
4. Click **Slides from Outline** .... `L`
5. Navigate to the location of the outline file and select the file.
6. Click [**Insert**] .... `↵Enter`

Reset Slides

1. Click **Home** tab .... `Alt`+`H`

   Slides Group

2. Click the **Reset** button 📧 ...... `Q`

Reuse Slides from Other Presentations

1. Click **Home** tab .... `Alt`+`H`

   Slides Group

2. Click **New Slide** button 📧 down arrow .... `I`
3. Click **Reuse Slides** .... `R`
4. Type the path to the desired presentation in the **Insert slide from** box.

   OR

   a. Click [Browse ▾].
   b. Click **Browse File**.
   c. Navigate to the location of the presentation to open and select the file.
   d. Click [**Open** ▾] .... `↵Enter`

5. Take any of the following actions:

   - Point to a slide in the task pane to see an enlarged version.
   - Click a slide to insert it in the current presentation after the current slide.
   - To keep the formatting of the source presentation, click in **Keep source formatting** in Reuse Slides task pane.

Insert a Header/Footer, Date, and Slide Numbers

1. Click **Insert** tab .... `Alt`+`N`

   Text Group

2. Click **Header & Footer** button 📄 .... `H`
3. Click **Date and time** .... `Alt`+`D`

4. Choose a date option:

   - Click **Update automatically** .... `Alt`+`U` and select a date format that updates when the presentation is opened.

   OR

   - Click **Fixed** .... `Alt`+`X` and type a date that will not change.

To insert slide numbers and a footer:

1. Click **Slide number** .... `Alt`+`N`
2. Click **Footer** and type footer .... `Alt`+`F`

To apply footer information to some or all slides:

- Click **Don't show on title slide** .... `Alt`+`S` to suppress date, slide number, and footer on title slide.
- Click [**Apply**] .... `A` to apply changes to the current slide only.
- Click [**Apply to All**] .... `↵Enter` to apply changes to all slides in the presentation.

Hide Background Graphics

1. Click **Design** tab .... `Alt`+`G`

   Background Group

2. Click **Hide Background Graphics** .... `M`

EXERCISE DIRECTIONS

1. Start PowerPoint.

2. Open the Word document 🔘 **11Travels.docx** in PowerPoint to create slides.

   ✓ *You will need to select All Files from the Files of type drop-down list in the Open dialog box.*

3. Save the file as **11Travels_xx**.

4. Reset each slide to restore default formatting and placeholders. Change the layout of slide 1 to Title Slide.

5. Apply the Concourse theme to the entire presentation.

6. Hide the background graphics on the first slide only. Change the background style on slide 1 to Style 7.

7. On slide 2, add the text shown in Illustration A.

8. Choose to reuse slides and browse to the 🔘 **11Slides.pptx** file.

9. Point to each of the three slides in the task pane to see their content.

10. Click the second slide in the task pane to insert it in the current presentation as slide 3. Note that the inserted slide takes on the theme of the current presentation.

11. Display slide 5 in the current presentation and then insert the third slide in the task pane to become slide 6. Close the task pane.

12. Insert a date that updates automatically, slide numbers, and the following footer: **Voyager Travel Adventures**. Do not show this information on the title slide, but apply it to all other slides.

13. Save your changes, close the presentation, and exit PowerPoint.

Illustration A

Adventure Travel Packages

▸ Whitewater rafting
▸ Backcountry trekking
▸ Heliskiing
▸ Snowboarding
▸ Rock climbing
▸ . . . and more

Voyager Travel Adventures   7/31/2007   2

ON YOUR OWN

1. Start PowerPoint and create a new presentation using the outline in ◉ **OPP11A.docx**.

2. Save the file as **OPP11_xx**.

3. Reset all slides, and change the layout of slide 1 from Title to Title and Content.

4. Choose a new theme for the presentation and change background style if desired.

5. On slide 1, edit the text to refer to a particular cause or organization. You can select any organization or cause you want and modify the text as necessary. Illustration A shows a sample slide.

6. Choose to reuse the slides in ◉ **OPP11B.pptx**.

7. Insert the first slide from the task pane, and then move it up in the Slides tab to become the first slide in the presentation.

8. Add the remaining two slides from the task pane to become the last two slides in the presentation.

9. Review the slides, and then choose to hide background graphics on one or more of the slides.

10. Modify the clip art on the last slide if desired to better reflect the charity or organization you chose.

11. Add a date, slide numbers, and a suitable footer to all slides except the first one.

12. Save your changes, close the presentation, and exit PowerPoint.

Illustration A

Help the Homeless
- Many of our citizens are currently living on the streets
- Help our homeless citizens by donating your time, money, or goods
- Improve the quality of life for those who don't have a stable home

The Power of Giving   7/18/2007

Skills Covered

- **View Notes Pages**
- **Preview Handouts**
- **Change Slide Size and Orientation**

Software Skills Notes pages allow you to easily refer to slide notes during a presentation, while handouts can give the audience a helpful reference of what has been covered in the presentation.

Application Skills You have a draft of the laser surgery information to show your client, Holmes Medical Center. In this exercise, you will prepare notes pages and handouts to present to the client.

TERMS

Aspect ratio The ratio of the width of an image to the height of an image.

Handouts Printed copies of the presentation for the audience to refer to during and after the slide show.

Landscape orientation A slide or printout that is wider than it is tall.

Portrait orientation A slide or printout that is taller than it is wide.

NOTES

View Notes Pages

- You learned in an earlier exercise that Notes Page view is one of PowerPoint's four available views.

- Notes Page view allows you to view each slide on a page with a large area for notes beneath the slide, as shown in the following illustration.

Notes Page view

- You use this view to easily see the notes you have inserted for a particular slide. You can choose to print your presentation as notes pages so that you have a copy of the notes you will be delivering to your audience.

  ✓ *For this reason, this printing option was called Speaker Notes in earlier versions of PowerPoint.*

- If you need to add a number of notes to a slide, Notes Page view can be more convenient than using the Notes pane in Normal view. You can see all your notes without having to scroll, and you have access to text formatting options that are unavailable in the Notes pane.

- For example, you can change the font, font style (such as bold or italic), font size, or font color for the notes text.

- If you enter more text than will fit in the text placeholder on the page, PowerPoint will adjust the font size to fit the text.

  ✓ *You will learn more about how this AutoFit feature adjusts text size on slides in the next lesson.*

- You can increase the zoom to make it easier to enter and edit notes, if you do not change the default text size.

- You can scroll through the pages in Notes Page view using the scrolling options you use in Normal view. The scroll bar, the Next Slide button, and the Previous Slide button work the same way in this view as in Normal view.

- You may find that you want to adjust the layout of Notes Page view to provide more space for notes or to change the direction that the information on the page prints. To make these types of layout changes, you can adjust the notes master.

  ✓ *You learn how to work with the notes master in Exercise 39.*

- By default, notes pages display a page number in the lower-right corner. If you wish to display a header and/or the date and time, you can select these options on the Notes and Handouts tab of the Header and Footer dialog box.

Preview Handouts

- Like notes pages, **handouts** are simply another way to view existing slide content. Handouts show you a given number of slides per page, as shown in the following illustration.

A handout with two slides per page

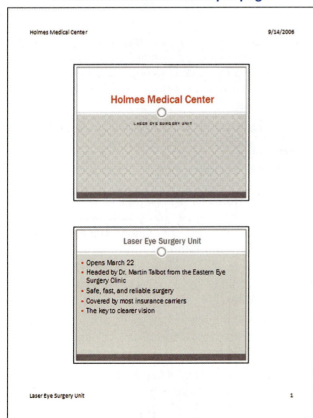

- As the name suggests, handouts are generally printed to hand out to an audience so that they have a hard copy of the slides for note taking or later review.

- You decide how many slides to place on each handout page in the Print dialog box, covered in the next exercise. You can see what your handouts will look like, however, by using the Print Preview feature.

- Use the Print What list in Print Preview, shown in the following illustration, to select the desired handout option. The preview changes to show the handout option you selected.

Preview handouts in Print Preview

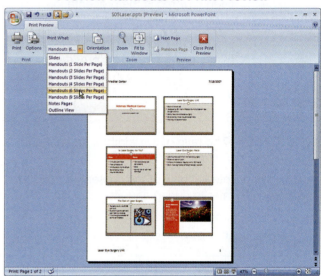

- By default, handouts display the current date and a page number. You can add a header and/or a footer to each handout page by supplying that information on the Notes and Handouts tab of the Header and Footer dialog box.

  ✓ *You will learn more about working in Print Preview in the next exercise.*

Change Slide Size and Orientation

- By default, slides are displayed in **landscape orientation**—they are wider than they are tall—and notes pages and handouts are displayed in **portrait orientation**—they are taller than they are wide.

- In some instances, you may want to reverse the usual orientation of slides to display them in portrait orientation. You can use the new Slide Orientation button on the Design tab to quickly switch from one orientation to another.

  ✓ *If your presentation includes graphics, they may become distorted when orientation is changed.*

■ For more control over orientation and slide size, use the Page Setup dialog box shown in the following illustration.

**Modify slide size and orientation
in the Page Setup dialog box**

■ Slides are initially sized for an on-screen show on a screen that uses a standard 4:3 **aspect ratio**. You can change slide sizes to better fit the type of output device, such as a wide-screen display with a 16:9 aspect ratio.

■ You can also select a size that will work best for a particular paper size, for 35mm slides, for overheads, or even for a custom size that you specify in the Width and Height boxes.

PROCEDURES

View Notes Pages

1. Click **View** tab .... Alt+W

   Presentation Views Group

2. Click **Notes Page** button 🖻 ..... T

Preview Handouts

1. Click **Office Button** 🖻 ..... Alt+F
2. Point to **Print** right-pointing arrow .... W
3. Click **Print Preview** V

   Page Setup Group

4. Click **Print What** list .. Alt+P, W
5. Select a handout option .... ↓, ↵Enter

To close Print Preview:

   Preview Group

■ Click **Close Print Preview** button ❌ .... Alt+P, C

Add Headers/Footers to Notes Pages and Handouts

1. Click **Insert** tab .... Alt+N

   Text Group

2. Click **Header & Footer** button 🖻 .... H
3. Click **Notes and Handouts** tab in the Header and Footer dialog box.

To insert a date on pages:

1. Click **Date and time** .... Alt+D
2. Choose a date option:

   ■ Click **Update automatically** .... Alt+U and select a date format that updates when the presentation is opened.

   OR

   ■ Click **Fixed** .... Alt+X and type a date that will not change.

To insert header, page numbers, and a footer:

1. Click **Header** and type header .... Alt+H
2. Click **Page number** .... Alt+P
3. Click **Footer** and type footer .... Alt+F

To apply header and footer to all slides:

■ Click Apply to All .... ↵Enter to apply changes to all slides in the presentation.

Change Slide Size and Orientation

1. Click **Design** tab .... Alt+G

   Page Setup Group

2. Click **Slide Orientation** button 🖻 .... O
3. Select desired orientation .... ↑ or ↓, ↵Enter

To change page setup options:

1. Click **Design** tab .... Alt+G

   Page Setup Group

2. Click **Page Setup** button 🖻 ..... S
3. Select slide size and orientation option for slides, notes, handouts, and outlines.
4. Click OK .... ↵Enter

EXERCISE DIRECTIONS

1. Start PowerPoint and open 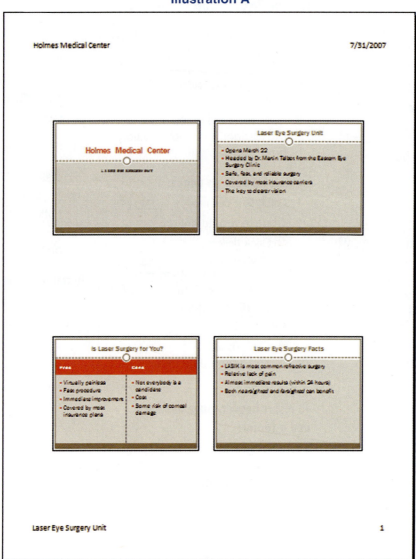12Laser.

2. Save the file as 12Laser_xx.

3. Switch to Notes Page view and type the following note for slide 1:

   Welcome to Holmes Medical Center!

4. Return to Normal view and change the orientation to Portrait. Note what happens to the graphics on slides 5 and 6.

5. Open the Page Setup dialog box and change the slide orientation back to landscape. Change the slide size to the size for On-Screen Show (16:9). Close the dialog box to see how the shape of the slides changes.

6. Undo the size change, and then apply landscape orientation again to restore the slides to their original appearance.

7. Open the Header and Footer dialog box to make changes for notes and handouts.

8. Choose to display an automatically updating date, the header **Holmes Medical Center**, page numbers, and the footer **Laser Eye Surgery Unit**. Apply these formats to all slides.

9. Preview the presentation and view each handout option in the Print What list. Illustration A shows the handout with 4 slides per page.

10. Close Print Preview

11. Save your changes, close the presentation, and exit PowerPoint.

Illustration A

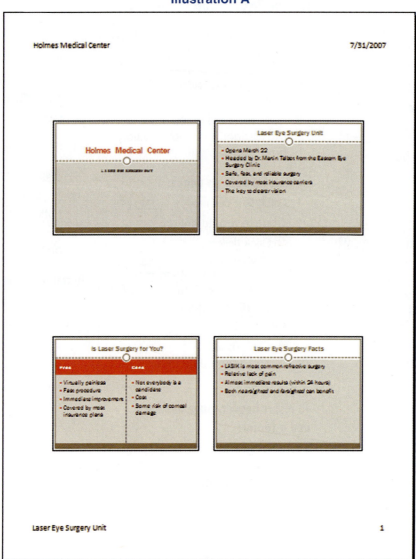

ON YOUR OWN

1. Start PowerPoint and open the **OPP11_xx** presentation you created in the previous On Your Own Exercise, or open  **OPP12**. You have been asked to deliver your presentation at a "Make a Difference Day" event that encourages community activity and charitable contributions.

2. Save the file as **OPP12_xx**.

3. In Notes Page view, add notes for some or all of the slides in the presentation.

4. Supply a suitable header and footer for notes and handouts.

5. View the presentation as handouts with four slides per page. Your handout should look similar to Illustration A.

6. Save your changes, close the presentation, and exit PowerPoint.

Illustration A

Skills Covered

- ■ View Slides in Grayscale or Black and White
- ■ Other Preview Options
- ■ Print Presentation Materials
- ■ Send Presentation Materials to Microsoft Office Word

Software Skills   You can view slides in grayscale or black and white to see how they will look if printed on a non-color printer. Use options in Print Preview to view slides before printing. When printing a presentation, you can choose to output notes pages, handouts, slides, or even the presentation outline. Send presentation materials to Microsoft Word to take advantage of Word's formatting options.

Application Skills   You are ready to print materials for the Holmes Medical Center presentation. You will first view the slides in grayscale and black and white, then create handouts in Word, and finally you will print the presentation in various ways.

TERMS

No new terms in this exercise.

NOTES

View Slides in Grayscale or Black and White

- ■ You can view a color presentation in grayscale or in black and white.
- ■ When you view or print a presentation in grayscale, the colors change to varying tones of gray, as shown in the illustration at right. When you view a presentation from the pure black and white view, all colors are converted to either black or white.

Presentation displayed in grayscale

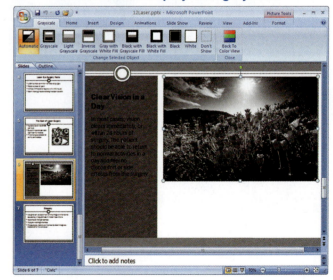

- Switching to grayscale or black and white view allows you to concentrate on the slide's text and layout rather than its color design elements. If you intend to print your slide materials in grayscale or black and white, this view can show you how your printed materials will look.

- Use the settings in the Color/Grayscale group on the View tab to switch to Grayscale or Pure Black and White view.

- Selecting one of these options displays the presentation in the chosen view, with options for the view on a tab such as the Grayscale tab in the previous illustration.

- Options in the Change Selected Object group will be dimmed until you select an object on the slide. In the previous illustration, the picture is selected, activating buttons for viewing the picture with a variety of grayscale options.

- Applying a grayscale or pure black and white view does not change the presentation permanently to that view. You can return to color view at any time by clicking the Back to Color View button.

Other Preview Options

- You learned in the last exercise about previewing handouts in Print Preview. You can also use Print Preview to view slides, notes pages, and the slide outline before printing any of these items.

- Print Preview has its own tab, shown in the following illustration. You can use buttons on this tab to:
  - Print the current display.
  - Set printing options such as whether the pages are displayed and printed in color, grayscale, or black and white.
  - Determine what is printed: slides, handouts, notes pages, or outline.
  - Change the display orientation or zoom.
  - Page forward and back through the presentation.

Print Preview tab

Print Presentation Materials

- A presentation can be printed in various formats: as slides, notes pages, handouts, or as an outline.

- You choose the settings for these formats in the Print dialog box, shown in the following illustration.

Print dialog box

- Among the options you can choose are:
  - Which printer to use.
  - Which slides to print, number of copies to print, and whether multiple copies should be collated.
  - What material (slides, notes pages, handouts, or outline) to print.
  - Whether to print in grayscale, color, or black and white.
  - If handouts are to be printed, how many slides per page and the order in which the slides display on the page.
  - Whether the material should be scaled (sized) to fit the page or framed by a box.
  - Whether comments and markup annotations should be printed.
  - Whether hidden slides should be printed and whether the material should be printed at a high quality that will show shadow effects.

- If you do not need to adjust settings and simply want to print the presentation in the current view, as full-page slides, for example, you can use the Quick Print option on the Print submenu.

Send Presentation Materials to Microsoft Office Word

- You have another option for outputting presentation materials: you can export the presentation to Microsoft Word as handouts or as an outline.

- Exporting a presentation to Microsoft Word gives you the option of using Word's tools to format the handouts.

- Use the Create Handouts in Microsoft Office Word command on the Office menu's Publish submenu to begin the process of sending materials to Word.

- The Send To Microsoft Office Word dialog box, shown in the following illustration, opens to allow you to select an export option.

Send To Microsoft Office Word dialog box

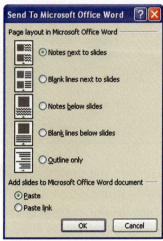

- You have two options for positioning slide notes relative to the slide pictures and two options for placing blank lines that your audience can use to take their own notes. You can also choose to send only the outline.

- One advantage to sending the outline to Word over simply printing the outline from PowerPoint is that you can easily format the outline in Word using outline styles.

- Note that you can choose either to paste the presentation materials in a Word document or paste link them. When you choose the Paste link option, you create a link between the Word document and the PowerPoint presentation. Any changes you save to the slides in PowerPoint will appear in the Word document.

- Exported slides display in a Word table similar to the one shown in the following illustration.

Slides display in a Microsoft Word table

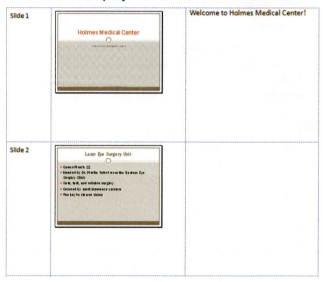

- You can modify the size of the slide images, format text, and add new text as desired to customize your handouts.

- Save the Word document as you would any other document.

Curriculum Connection: Social Studies

State Government

Like the federal government, state governments in this country consist of executive, judicial, and legislative branches that work together to govern the state. All states have governors, a court system, and representatives, though the members of the legislative branch may have different names in different states.

Explore Your State Government

Research your state government, identifying the current governor (the executive branch), the state's courts (the judicial branch), and the system of representatives (the legislative branch). Find out what legislative district you are in and who represents your district. Create a slide show to present this material.

PROCEDURES

View Slides in Grayscale or Black and White

1. Click **View** tab .... Alt + W

   Color/Grayscale Group

2. Click **Grayscale** button ▣ ...... O

   OR

   Click **Pure Black and White** button ▣ .... B

3. Click an element on any slide to activate buttons on the Change Selected Object group.

To return to color view:

- Click **Back to Color View** button ▣ .... Alt + W, C

Use Print Preview Options

1. Click **Office Button** ▣ ..... Alt + F
2. Point to **Print** right-pointing arrow .... W
3. Click **Print Preview** V

To change color display:

Print Group

1. Click **Options** button ▣ .... Alt + P, N
2. Click **Color/Grayscale** C
3. Choose a color option:
   - **Color** C
   - **Grayscale** .... G
   - **Pure Black and White** .... U

To choose what to preview:

Page Setup Group

1. Click **Print What** list .. Alt + P, W
2. Select a view .... ↓, ↵Enter

To close Print Preview:

Preview Group

- Click **Close Print Preview** button ▣ .... Alt + P, C

Print Presentation Materials (Ctrl + P)

To quick-print all slides:

1. Click **Office Button** ▣ ...... Alt + F
2. Point to **Print** right-pointing arrow .... W
3. Click **Quick Print** .... Q

To choose print options:

1. Click **Office Button** ▣ ..... Alt + F
2. Click **Print**. .... P
3. Choose desired options in the Print dialog box.
4. Click [OK] .... ↵Enter

Send Presentation Materials to Microsoft Word

1. Click **Office Button** ▣ ..... Alt + F
2. Point to **Publish** right-pointing arrow .... U
3. Click **Create Handouts in Microsoft Office Word** .... H
4. Select a page layout option:
   - **Notes next to slides** ...... Alt + N
   - **Blank lines next to slides** .... Alt + A
   - **Notes below slides** .... Alt + B
   - **Blank lines below slides** .... Alt + K
   - **Outline only** .... Alt + O
5. Select an option for adding slides to a Word document:
   - **Paste** .... Alt + P
   - **Paste link** .... Alt + I
6. Click [OK] .... ↵Enter

EXERCISE DIRECTIONS

1. Start PowerPoint and open ⊙ **13Laser**.
2. Save the file as **13Laser_xx**.
3. Switch to Grayscale view and move through the slides to see how the presentation looks in grayscale.
4. Display slide 6 and select the photo to activate the buttons in the Change Selected Object group.
5. Try each button in the group to see how the photo looks with each option.
6. Deselect the photo and change the view to Pure Black and White. Your slide should look like Illustration A.
7. Send the presentation to Microsoft Word, using the Notes next to slides and the Paste link options.
8. Save the Word document as **13Holmes_handouts_xx**.
9. Return to PowerPoint, restore the color view, and save the presentation.
10. Return to the Word document to see that the slide thumbnails are now in color because you linked this document to the presentation.

11. Print the Word document. Save and close the Word document and return to PowerPoint.

12. Preview the presentation and follow these steps:
    - Move through the slides using the Next and Previous buttons.
    - Display the presentation as an outline.
    - Display the presentation as handouts with 3 slides per page, and then as handouts with 6 slides per page (use the Print What list).
    - Close Print Preview.

13. Use the Print dialog box to print presentation materials as follows:
    - Print only the first slide as a Slide.
    - Print all slides as a handout with 6 slides per page in grayscale.
    - Print notes pages for the first three slides.
    - Print the presentation outline.

14. Save your changes, close the presentation, and exit PowerPoint.

Illustration A

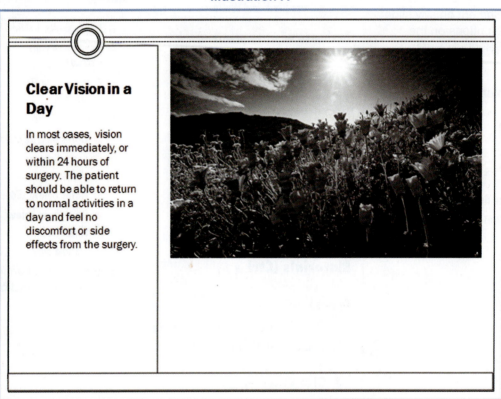

Clear Vision in a Day

In most cases, vision clears immediately, or within 24 hours of surgery. The patient should be able to return to normal activities in a day and feel no discomfort or side effects from the surgery.

ON YOUR OWN

1. Start PowerPoint and open the **OPP12_xx** presentation you created in the previous On Your Own Exercise, or open ⊙ **OPP13.doc**.

2. Save the file as **OPP13_xx**.

3. View the slides in grayscale and pure black and white, then return to color view.

4. Preview the presentation as an outline, then as handouts with four slides per page.

5. Send the presentation to Word with notes next to the slides. You do not need to link.

6. Save the Word document as **OPP13_handouts_xx**. If you are familiar with Word tables and formatting, you may want to apply text formats or adjust the size of the slide thumbnails to customize the handouts. Illustration A shows one way to set up the handouts.

7. Save your changes and close the Word document and print it.

8. Print four-slides-per page handouts in grayscale.

9. Print notes pages for the slides that have notes in color (if you have a color printer available).

10. Save your changes, close the presentation, and exit PowerPoint.

Illustration A

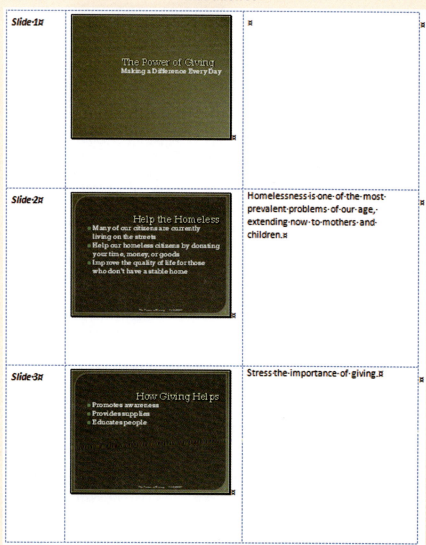

Critical Thinking

Application Skills   When presenting an advertising campaign to a client, you want to offer two or three different designs so that the client can compare layouts and then make a choice. In this exercise, you will create another sample presentation for your client Voyager Travel Adventures.

DIRECTIONS

1. Start PowerPoint and open the outline in **14Adventure.docx** to create a new presentation.

2. Save the presentation as **14Adventure_xx**.

3. Reset all slides, and then change the layout of slide 1 to Title and Content.

4. Add a new slide after slide 1 with the Title Slide layout. Type the title **Voyager Travel Adventures** and the subtitle **Everywhere You Want to Go**.

5. In Slide Sorter view, move this slide to become the first slide in the presentation.

6. Add a new slide after slide 1 with the Section Header layout. Type the title **WHAT WE OFFER**. In the text placeholder above the title, type the following text:

   Voyager Travel Adventures offers a variety of activities in some of the most beautiful locations in this country.

7. Copy slide 2 and paste it so it becomes the second-to-last slide in the presentation.

8. On the new slide 7, change the title to **TALK TO US** and the text to:

   Testimonials and customer satisfaction surveys agree: Voyager Travel Adventures is the best!

9. On slide 8, adjust the text as follows:
   - Position the insertion point just to the left of the number 450 in the Address bullet item, press ⏎Enter, and then press Tab⇥ to create a second-level bullet.
   - Repeat the process to create a second-level bullet for each of the contact entries.

10. Check spelling in the presentation. You can ignore heliskiing, which is spelled correctly.

11. Apply the Solstice theme and change the theme colors to Aspect.

12. Apply the Module theme fonts (Corbel and Corbel).

13. On slide 6, change the layout to Two Content. Look for and insert a clip art graphic or photograph that illustrates one of the destinations, such as a skiing, mountain, or beach image. Illustration A shows one option.

14. Resize the image and position it on the right side of the slide if necessary.

15. Add the following note to slide 6:

    Foreign adventures include skiing in Switzerland, bicycling in France, and hiking in England and Scotland.

16. Apply a date, slide numbers, and the following footer to all slides except the title slide: **Voyager Travel Adventures**. Apply a date, page numbers, the header **Everywhere You Want to Go** and the same footer for notes and handouts.

17. View the slides in Slide Show view.

18. Add the following properties:
    Author: **Your name**
    Title: **Voyager Travel Adventures**
    Subject: **Domestic and foreign travel**
    Keywords: **travel**
    Status: **Draft**
    Comments: **Version 2 of Voyager presentation**

19. View the presentation in grayscale.

20. Send the presentation to Microsoft Office Word with blank lines next to slides and the Paste link option active.

21. Save the handouts in Word as **14Travel_handouts_xx**. Print the document and then close it.

22. Restore the presentation colors and preview the presentation to see how handouts with 4 slides per page will look in pure black and white.

23. Print the handouts in grayscale.

24. Print slide 6 as a notes page in grayscale.

25. Save your changes, close the presentation, and exit PowerPoint.

Illustration A

Exercise | 15

Curriculum Integration

Application Skills   Your American Literature class will soon begin a study of Arthur Miller's play *The Crucible*. You have been asked to prepare a presentation that explains Miller's use of the Salem witch trials to comment on the actions of Joseph McCarthy, the senator whose investigations into alleged Communist infiltration of the U. S. Army and the entertainment industry were likened to a modern-day witch hunt. Before you begin the project, locate the following information:

- A summary of *The Crucible*

- Information on Joseph McCarthy and his actions in the early 1950s

- Biographical information on Arthur Miller

DIRECTIONS

Begin a new blank presentation and save it with an appropriate name, such as **15Crucible_xx**. Insert an appropriate title and subtitle on the first slide. Apply a theme, customizing theme colors and fonts if desired.

Add a slide with an appropriate layout and use it to supply brief biographical information on Arthur Miller, including where and when he was born and successful plays before *The Crucible*.

Add a slide with an appropriate layout and use it to provide a brief synopsis of the play. You may want to use two slides for this task. (You can use a site such as SparkNotes to find a synopsis of the play, if you are not already familiar with it.)

Add a slide and use it to provide a brief summary of Joseph McCarthy's activities in the early 1950s.

Add a slide with the Comparison layout and list some of the key parallels between the play and McCarthy's actions. Illustration A shows a sample comparison.

Add another slide that includes a quote from the play (you can find quotes on sites such as SparkNotes) and the rebuke given to McCarthy by Joseph Welch (you can find this information on a site such as Wikipedia). Change the slide background of this slide only to make it stand out. Add a clip art image that relates to courts or judgment on the slide and resize and position it as necessary.

Use Slide Sorter view to rearrange slides if necessary. Check spelling.

Add notes to the slides to indicate your sources. Insert properties if desired to identify the presentation by your name and class.

Add slide numbers and a date that updates automatically to all slides except the title slide. Add a header and footer for notes and handouts.

View the slides in Slide Show view, and then preview the handouts you will need to provide to the class. Print the slides as handouts with four slides per page.

Send the slides to Word using one of the options in the Send To Microsoft Office Word dialog box. If you choose to send the outline, adjust the styles in Word to improve the look of the document.

Save the Word document with an appropriate name, print it, and close it.

Save changes to the presentation and close it. Exit PowerPoint

Illustration A

The Parallels

The Crucible

- Abigail Williams accuses people of being witches
- People believe Salem is overrun with witches
- Arrested witches are encouraged to confess and name other witches
- Witches are condemned to death

McCarthyism

- Joseph McCarthy investigates Communists
- People believe the U.S. is overrun with "Reds"
- Alleged Communists are urged to confess and name their associates
- Alleged Communists lose their jobs

▶ 6   7/19/2007

Lesson | 2

Work with Text Elements

Skills Covered

- **Select Text and Placeholders**
- **Change the Appearance of Text**

Software Skills Although themes and theme fonts are designed to produce a pleasing appearance, you may sometimes wish to modify the appearance of text by changing font, font style, font size, or font color.

Application Skills Great Grains Bakery is a subsidiary of Whole Grains Bread that operates upscale bakery restaurants featuring fresh-baked breads and other wholesome foods. Great Grains Bakery wants you to help them create a presentation to display at a trade show. In this exercise, you explore ways to improve the appearance of text in the presentation.

TERMS

Case The use of uppercase or lowercase letters.

Font style Attribute such as bold or italic that changes the appearance of text.

NOTES

Select Text and Placeholders

- Manipulating text in a presentation requires you to know some basics about selecting text and placeholders to ensure you are working efficiently.

- As in a word processing document, you can select text by dragging the I-beam mouse pointer over it, highlighting the selected text. You can also double-click a single word to select it.

- As you are working with text in a placeholder, the placeholder displays a dashed line, sizing handles, and a rotation handle, as shown in the following illustration.

Selected text and a selected placeholder

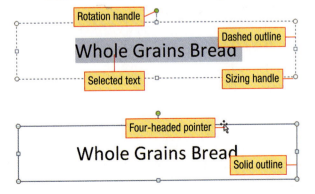

- You can also select the placeholder by clicking its outline with the four-headed pointer. The selected placeholder has a solid outline, as shown in the previous illustration.

- While a placeholder is selected, any change you make using text tools will apply to all text in the placeholder. When you want to make a change to all text in a placeholder, it is speedier to select the placeholder rather than drag over the text to select it.

Change the Appearance of Text

- PowerPoint's themes guarantee a presentation with a sophisticated design, and that includes the appearance of text. You can, however, easily customize text appearance to emphasize it or to make your presentation more readable, interesting, or unique.

- Text appearance attributes include font family, size, color, style, and special effects. You can also change the case of text to control use of uppercase and lowercase letters.

Apply a Different Font

- As you learned earlier, a *font* is a design of type. Fonts are generally divided into two main types:
  - Serif fonts have small cross strokes called *serifs* at the ends of vertical strokes. A common serif font is Times New Roman.
  - Sans serif fonts do not have serifs. A common sans serif font is Arial.
- You have several options for changing the font of any text in a presentation. You can use the Font list, the Font dialog box, and the Mini toolbar. You can also replace a single font throughout a presentation.
- The Font list can be found in the Font group on the Home tab in all Office 2007 applications. Clicking the list's down arrow displays a palette of the fonts available for use on your computer, as shown in the following illustration.

Font list on the Home tab

- The current theme fonts are shown at the top of the list. Scroll to see additional fonts.
- Fonts display on the list in their actual appearance so you can easily see what each font looks like.
- To change an existing font to a new font, select the text to change or select the placeholder that holds the text to change.

- If you want to make a number of text appearance changes, you can use the Font dialog box, shown in the following illustration.

Font dialog box

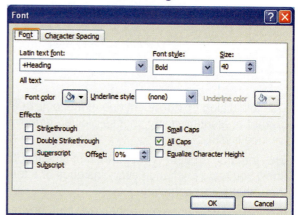

- By default, the font displayed in the Latin text font box is either +Body or +Heading, depending where the insertion point is currently located in a placeholder. These designations refer to the Body and Heading theme fonts.
- To choose a different font in the Font dialog box, click the Latin text font box's down arrow.
- You learned in the Basics section of this book that when you select text in most Office 2007 applications, the Mini toolbar displays, becoming opaque as you move the pointer toward it.
- You can select a new font on the Mini toolbar by clicking the Font down arrow as shown in the following illustration. Select a new font from the list that opens after you click.

Use the Mini toolbar to change a font

- Another way to change a font in a presentation is to use the Replace Fonts command, located on the Replace submenu in the Editing group on the Home tab.

- Selecting this command opens the Replace Font dialog box, shown in the following illustration.

Replace Font dialog box

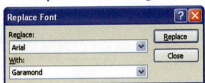

- Use this dialog box to select one of the fonts in the current presentation and choose a different font to replace it with.

- This feature can be a great savings of time if you know you want to change every instance of a font throughout a presentation.

- If you need to change more than one font, however, it is more efficient to adjust fonts using the slide master, where you can adjust the font in one location and have it apply to all current and new slides based on that master.

  ✓ *You will learn about slide masters in Exercise 38.*

- Keep in mind that PowerPoint's themes use no more than two fonts to display text (and several themes use only a single font). Using more than two fonts can result in a disorganized-looking presentation that sacrifices unity.

Change Font Size and Character Spacing

- Font sizes in a presentation are determined by the current theme. They are designed to present text clearly and attractively.

- You can change the font size of selected text to create a special effect or fit more text in a placeholder.

- Use the Font Size list in the Font group on the Home tab to select a size from the drop-down list. You can also, if desired, type a specific font size if the list does not have the size you want.

- You will find the same Font Size list on the Mini toolbar.

- In the Font dialog box, the Size increment box allows you to adjust the font size by tenths of a point if you want to be very accurate.

- If you don't need to be so accurate, you can use the Increase Font Size and Decrease Font Size buttons in the Font group on the Home tab. These buttons increase or decrease font size by the same set amounts that are displayed on the Font Size list. You can click these buttons until you have achieved a size that looks right to you.

- The Character Spacing button allows you to control the amount of space between characters of text. Clicking this button displays the palette shown in the following illustration.

Character Spacing palette

- Choose one of the options on the palette to control the space or click the More Spacing option to set character spacing to a specific amount using the Character Spacing tab in the Font dialog box.

Apply a Font Style or Effect

- A **font style** changes the appearance of text without changing its font. Common font styles include bold, italic, underline, and shadow.

- Apply a font style easily by clicking the desired button in the Font group on the Home tab.

  ✓ *You can click more than one font style button to apply multiple styles to selected text.*

- You can also apply font styles from the Font dialog box or the Mini toolbar, although the Mini toolbar offers only bold and italic.

- The Font dialog box lists a number of font effects you can use to format text, including Strikethrough and Double Strikethrough and special effects such as superscript and subscript.

  ✓ *In addition to offering Bold and Italic, the Font Style list in the Font dialog box offers Bold Italic.*

- Use font styles and effects sparingly and consistently to avoid a chaotic appearance.

Change Font Color

- Like other formatting options in any presentation, the current theme determines the color of text. You can change font color at any time, however, using the Font Color button in the Font group on the Home tab.

- Clicking the Font Color button displays the palette shown in the following illustration.

Font Color palette

- You'll notice that this is the same palette you see if you want to change theme colors. By default, PowerPoint displays the colors used for the current theme so that any changes you make to text, backgrounds, shapes, or other elements use the same basic colors.

- You can choose from the Standard Colors or click More Colors to choose a new font color from the Colors dialog box.

- After you change a font color, the new color displays on the Font Color button, making it easy to reapply the same color elsewhere in the presentation.

- As you select font colors, make sure they are readily visible on your slides and work well with existing colors in the theme.

Change Case

- **Case** determines whether text is in capital (uppercase) letters or small (lowercase) letters. The case of text in a presentation may be determined by the current theme. In some themes, for example, the title on a Title slide is automatically formatted in all capital letters.

- You can quickly change the case of text using the Change Case palette shown in the following illustration.

Change Case palette

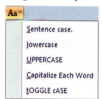

- Selecting one of these options immediately changes the case of all selected text to the chosen pattern.

Clear Text Formatting

- You may find after you have applied a number of formatting changes that you are not pleased with the result and wish to restore the default appearance of text.

- Use the Clear All Formatting button in the Font group of the Home tab to remove all formats you have applied. The text is restored to its original appearance.

PROCEDURES

Select Text

- Double-click to select a word.
- Click the I-beam at the beginning of text to select and drag the mouse pointer to the end of the text.

Select a Placeholder

- Click anywhere on a text placeholder to open the placeholder for text editing.
- Click the outside border of the placeholder to select the placeholder and everything within it.

Change Text Appearance

- Select specific text to modify or select placeholder to modify all text in the placeholder.

To change font:

Using the Home tab
1. Click **Home** tab .... Alt + H

   Font Group

2. Click **Font** down arrow .... F, F, ↓
3. Select a new font from the font list .... ↓ or ↑, ↵Enter

Using the Mini toolbar
1. Move the mouse pointer away from the selected text and toward the Mini toolbar until the toolbar is opaque.
2. Click **Font** down arrow.
3. Select a new font from the font list.

Using the Font dialog box
1. Click **Home** tab .... Alt + H

   Font Group

2. Click **Font** group dialog box launcher 🗗.

3. Click the **Latin text font** down arrow .... Alt + F , ↓

4. Select the desired font.

5. Click [OK] .... ↵Enter

Using the Replace Font dialog box

1. Click **Home** tab .... Alt + H

Editing Group

2. Click **Replace** button .... R

3. Click **Replace Fonts** .... O

4. Click **Replace** down arrow .... Alt + P , ↓

5. Select font from list.

6. Click **With** down arrow .. Alt + W

7. Select font from list.

8. Click [Replace] .... ↵Enter

To change font size:

Using the Home tab

1. Click **Home** tab .... Alt + H

Font Group

2. Click **Font Size** down arrow .... F , S , ↓

3. Select a new font size from the size list ...... ↓ or ↑, ↵Enter

Using the Mini toolbar

1. Move the mouse pointer away from the selected text and toward the Mini toolbar until the toolbar is opaque.

2. Click **Font Size** down arrow.

3. Select a new font size from the font list.

Using the Font dialog box

1. Click **Home** tab .... Alt + H

Font Group

2. Click **Font** group dialog box launcher ▣.

3. Click the **Size** up or down arrow .... Alt + S , ↑ or ↓

4. Click [OK] .... ↵Enter

Using the Increase or Decrease Font Size buttons

■ Click **Increase Font Size** button A⁺ .... F , G to immediately increase font size by a set amount.

■ Click **Decrease Font Size** button A⁻ .... F , K to immediately decrease font size by a set amount.

To change character spacing:

1. Click **Character Spacing** button AV↔ ▾ 6

2. Select the desired spacing option:

■ **Very Tight** I

■ **Tight** .... T

■ **Normal** .... N

■ **Loose** L

■ **Very Loose** V

To change font style:

Using the Home tab

1. Click **Home** tab .... Alt + H

Font Group

2. Click **Font Size** down arrow .... F , S , ↓

3. Select desired font style:

■ **Bold** B 1

■ *Italic* I 2

■ Underline U 3

■ Strikethrough abc 4

■ Shadow S 5

Using the Mini toolbar

1. Move the mouse pointer away from the selected text and toward the Mini toolbar until the toolbar is opaque.

2. Select desired font style:

■ **Bold** B .

■ *Italic* I .

Using the Font dialog box

1. Click **Home** tab .... Alt + H

Font Group

2. Click **Font** group dialog box launcher ▣.

3. Click the **Font style** down arrow .... Alt + Y , ↓

4. Select font style from list.

5. Click [OK] .... ↵Enter

To apply font effects:

1. Click **Home** tab .... Alt + H

Font Group

2. Click **Font** group dialog box launcher ▣.

3. Click any font effect in the Effects area to select it.

4. Click [OK] .... ↵Enter

To change font color:

1. Click **Font Color** button A ▾ down arrow .... F , C , ↓

2. Select a new color from the Theme Colors palette or Standard Colors palette.

OR

a. Click **More Colors** .... M

b. Mix a color on the **Custom** tab or click **Standard** tab and select a color.

c. Click [OK] .... ↵Enter

To change case:

1. Click **Change Case** button Aa▾ down arrow 7

2. Select the desired case:

■ **Sentence case** .... S

■ **lowercase** L

■ **UPPERCASE** .... U

■ **Capitalize Each Word** C

■ **tOGGLE cASE** .... T

To remove custom formatting:

■ Click **Clear All Formatting** button ▤ .... E

EXERCISE DIRECTIONS

1. Start PowerPoint and open 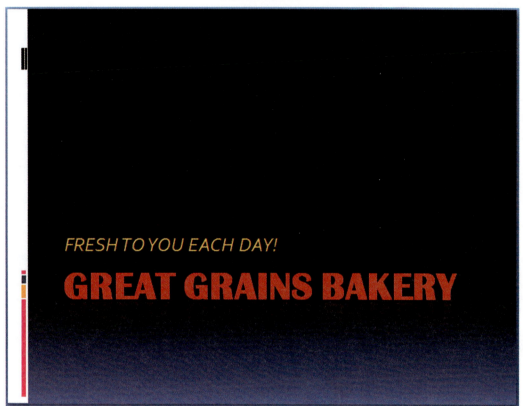**16Bakery**.

2. Save the presentation as **16Bakery_xx**.

3. On slide 1, select the title **GREAT GRAINS BAKERY** and enlarge its font size to 54 points. Change the font color to a dark orange red that you locate using More Colors.

4. Change the font of the title to Britannic Bold (or another sans serif face that fits the text on one line).

5. Select the subtitle text and change it to 28 points and italic. Change the color of the subtitle to one of the theme colors, Gold, Accent 3, Lighter 40%.

6. Change the case of the subtitle to Uppercase. Your slide should look similar to Illustration A.

7. Display slide 3. Format the text *7.00 a.m.* in bold and the gold accent Lighter 40% color.

8. Save your changes, close the presentation, and exit PowerPoint.

Illustration A

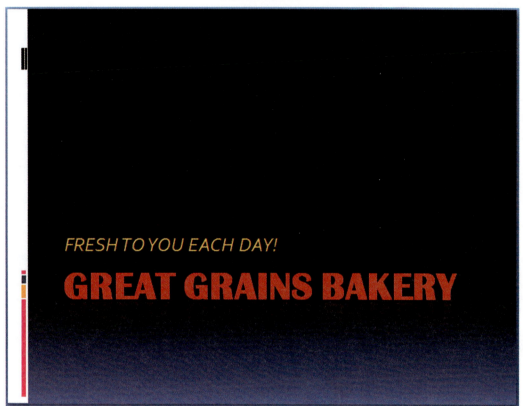

ON YOUR OWN

1. Start PowerPoint and open ⊙**OPP16**.
2. Save the presentation as **OPP16_xx**.
3. Use the Replace Font dialog box to replace the Arial Black font with another serif font such as Georgia.
4. Change the font color of the title to another color in the theme palette. Increase the size of the title font (click the Increase Font Size button until you like the size) and change its character spacing to Loose.
5. Change the font style of the subtitle by applying the Shadow style. Your slide might look similar to Illustration A.
6. Save your changes, close the presentation, and exit PowerPoint.

Illustration A

The Power of Giving
Making a Difference Every Day

Skills Covered

- **Use AutoFit Options**
- **Copy Text Formatting**
- **Create New Theme Fonts**

Software Skills When you have more text than will fit comfortably in a placeholder, you can choose how to fit the overflow text. Use the Format Painter to copy formatting from one slide to another. You can create new theme font combinations to easily apply in later presentations.

Application Skills You will continue to work with the Great Grains Bakery presentation to modify text and tweak formatting.

TERMS

AutoFit PowerPoint feature designed to reduce font size to fit text in the current placeholder.

Format Painter A tool that lets you copy text formatting from one text selection and apply it to any other text in the presentation.

NOTES

Use AutoFit Options

- If you enter more text than a placeholder can handle—such as a long slide title or a number of bullet entries—PowerPoint will by default use **AutoFit** to fit the text in the placeholder.

- You can control AutoFit options using the AutoFit Options button that displays near the bottom left corner of a placeholder. The following illustration shows the options available on the AutoFit Options drop-down menu.

AutoFit Options

- The default option is AutoFit Text to Placeholder. If you take no other action, PowerPoint reduces font size or line spacing (or both) to fit the text into the placeholder.

- If your text is very close to fitting in the placeholder, you may want to select Stop Fitting Text to This Placeholder to maintain the current font size and line spacing. If you take this action, make sure your text does not obscure other regions of the slide, such as the footer area.

- If you do not want to reduce font size and you have too much text to keep current sizes, you have three additional options:

  - Use Split Text Between Two Slides to move half of the text in the placeholder to a new slide. PowerPoint creates the new slide with the same title.

  - Use Continue on a New Slide as soon as you realize your placeholder is full. PowerPoint creates a new slide with the same title on which you can continue typing your content entries.

  - Use Change to Two Columns to create a new two-column layout on the slide to hold the text.

Copy Text Formatting

- Formatting text in a presentation to customize it to your needs can take time. If you know you want to use the same formats again on the same slide or another slide in the presentation, you can save time by applying the formats using the **Format Painter**.

- The Format Painter allows you to select existing formats and "paint" them over text to apply the same formats by clicking or dragging the mouse pointer.

- The following illustration shows how the formats of one bullet are being copied to unformatted text (top) and the final result of the format painting (bottom).

Using the Format Painter to copy formats

- *Formatted text*
- Nonformatted text `Format Painter pointer`

- *Formatted text*
- *Nonformatted text*

- To copy formatting one time, click the Format Painter button in the Clipboard group of the Home tab once. To apply formatting multiple times, double-click the button.

- It can be tricky to use the Format Painter when copying formats such as slide titles, which require you to click the pointer to open the placeholder and then drag over the title text. To copy formats successfully, click the Format Painter pointer just to the left of the first word of the text to which you are copying formats and immediately drag to the right.

Create New Theme Fonts

- PowerPoint makes it easy to change text appearance on one or more slides, but it would be inefficient to change the font on each slide in a presentation. You have already learned that you can use the Replace Fonts command to quickly change a single font throughout a presentation.

- If you want to change the font scheme for both headings and body text, you can create your own set of theme fonts and then apply them to change text on all slides at once.

- Create a new set of theme fonts in the Create New Theme Fonts dialog box, shown in the following illustration. As you choose a heading font and a body font, the Sample preview shows your choices.

Choose fonts to create your own set of theme fonts

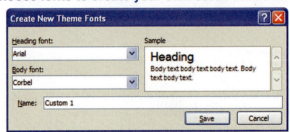

- After you name your set of theme fonts, the set appears at the top of the Theme Fonts gallery in the Custom section.

  ✓ *You can delete custom theme fonts by right-clicking the font set and selecting Delete.*

- Your custom fonts are available for use in any presentation.

- If you have applied fonts directly to text (using the Font list, for example) before applying new theme fonts, the new theme fonts will not override the direct formatting.

- If you wish to remove the direct formatting so that your new theme fonts will be used throughout the presentation, remove direct formatting using the Clear All Formatting button that you learned about in Exercise 16.

Curriculum Connection: Language Arts

Elements of Literature

In the study of literature, there are many terms used to discuss and evaluate particular elements or components of a literary work. The most basic include plot, characters, setting, and theme.

Present a Story

Pick your favorite literary work. It can be a novel, short story, play, etc., so long as it has the main elements of literature. Create a PowerPoint presentation in which you describe the major elements of your story. Describe the major characters, the plot, setting and the major theme(s). Use pictures to enhance your presentation, as well as different backgrounds and theme colors.

PROCEDURES

Use AutoFit Options

1. Click **AutoFit Options** button to display menu of options.

   ✓ *Button will appear at lower-left corner of a placeholder if the placeholder is full.*

2. Select an AutoFit option:
   - **AutoFit Text to Placeholder** Ⓐ
   - **Stop Fitting Text to This Placeholder** Ⓢ
   - **Split Text Between Two Slides** Ⓣ
   - **Continue on a New Slide** Ⓝ
   - **Change to Two Columns** Ⓒ

Copy Text Formatting

1. Select text containing format you want to copy.
2. Click **Home** tab .... Alt+Ⓗ

   Clipboard Group

3. Click **Format Painter** button 🖌 .... Ⓕ, Ⓟ
4. Select text that you want to change.

   ✓ *To change more than one instance, double-click the Format Painter button.*

Create New Theme Fonts

1. Click **Design** tab .... Alt+Ⓖ

   Themes Group

2. Click **Theme Fonts** button Ⓐ .... Ⓣ, Ⓕ
3. Click **Create New Theme Fonts** .... Ⓒ
4. Click the **Heading font** down arrow .... Alt+Ⓗ, ↓ and select a heading font.
5. Click the **Body font** down arrow .... Alt+Ⓑ, ↓ and select a body font.
6. Click [Save] .... ↵Enter

EXERCISE DIRECTIONS

1. Start PowerPoint and open **16Bakery_xx** or open ⊙**17Bakery**.
2. Save the presentation as **17Bakery_xx**.
3. Create new theme fonts using Arial as the heading font and Corbel as the body font. Save the fonts as **Bakery** and then apply them to the current presentation if they are not automatically applied.
4. Display slide 3. You forgot to format the *9:00 p.m* text when you formatted the *7:00 p.m.* text. Use the Format Painter to quickly apply the formats from *7:00 p.m.* to *9:00 p.m.*

5. Display slide 5. Type the following bullet items:

   Locally grown herbs

   Whole grain flours

   Fresh creamery butter

   Free range eggs

   Turbinado sugar

   Locally produced honey

   Fair trade coffee and chocolate

   Certified organic fruits and vegetables

6. Now enter one more item: **Gourmet sea salt**. PowerPoint AutoFits the text into the placeholder. Use an AutoFit option to make the text two column, and then add the final entry, **Local and imported cheeses**. Your slide should look like Illustration A.

7. Save your changes, close the presentation, and exit PowerPoint.

Fresh Is Best!

- Locally grown herbs
- Whole grain flours
- Fresh creamery butter
- Free range eggs
- Turbinado sugar
- Locally produced honey
- Fair trade coffee and chocolate
- Certified organic fruits and vegetables
- Gourmet sea salt
- Local and imported cheeses

ON YOUR OWN

1. Start PowerPoint and open **OPP16_xx** or open **OPP17**.

2. Save the presentation as **OPP17_xx**.

3. Create a new set of theme fonts for the presentation. Save them with an appropriate name and apply them.

   ✓ *You should use the font you chose to replace Arial Black in Exercise 16 as the heading font for your new theme fonts. If you did not do the On Your Own in Exercise 16, use Georgia as the heading font for the new theme font scheme.*

4. On slide 3, change formatting of the first word in the bullet list, *Promotes*. Copy the formatting to the first word of the next two bullet items. Illustration A shows an example of formats you could use.

5. Save your changes, close the presentation, and exit PowerPoint.

Illustration A

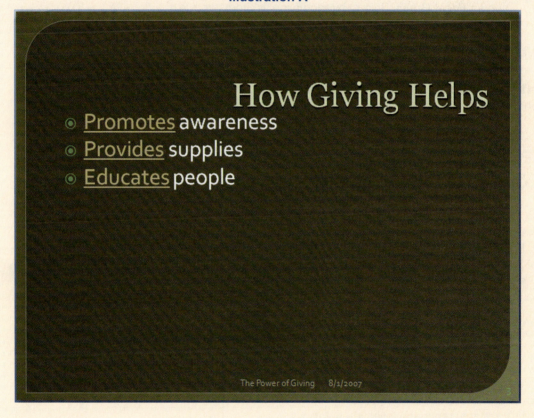

113

Skills Covered

- **Work with Bulleted and Numbered Lists**
- **Align Text**

Software Skills   Other ways to modify the appearance of text on a slide include adjusting bullet and number formats and changing text alignment.

Application Skills   In this exercise, you continue to work on the presentation for Great Grains Bakery by modifying list items and text.

TERMS

Alignment   The position of text relative to the placeholder borders.

NOTES

Work with Bulleted and Numbered Lists

- Slide text content consists mostly of bulleted items. First-level bullets are supplied on content placeholders. PowerPoint supplies formatting for nine levels of bullets. Each subordinate level is indented below the previous level and may have a different font size and bullet character.

- Create subordinate levels of bullets as you type by pressing Tab⇆ at the beginning of a line. You can also use the Increase List Level and Decrease List Level buttons in the Paragraph group on the Home tab to apply subordinate level formatting.

- To return to a previous bullet level, press ⇧Shift+Tab⇆ until you reach the level you want.

- Themes supply bullet characters for all levels of bullets in specific sizes and colors. If you change a theme, you will notice that the bullet characters change along with colors, fonts, backgrounds, and placeholder layout.

- You can change the bullets for a text placeholder using the Bullets and Numbering dialog box, shown in the following illustration.

Bullets and Numbering dialog box

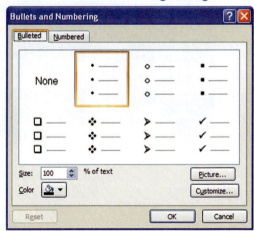

- Use the Bullets and Numbering dialog box to choose one of the other standard bullet characters, adjust the size of the bullet relative to text, or select a different color for the bullets.

- The Bullets and Numbering dialog box also allows you to select entirely new bullets from files of picture bullets or collections of symbols.

- To select a picture bullet, click the Picture button to display the Picture Bullet dialog box, shown in the following illustration.

Picture Bullet dialog box

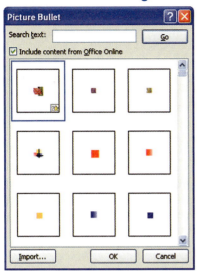

- If you have used earlier versions of Office or PowerPoint, you may recognize some of these bullets as those available for design templates and previous themes.

  ✓ *Some of these picture bullets may include a form of animation that changes the bullet display if the slide is viewed on the Web.*

- To select a new symbol to use as a bullet, click the Customize button in the Bullets and Numbering dialog box. The Symbol dialog box displays, as shown in the following illustration.

Symbol dialog box

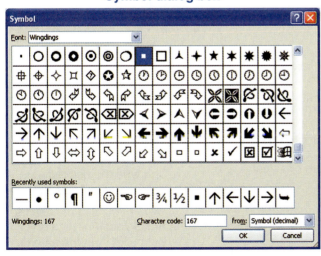

- The default font shown in the Symbol dialog box is one that includes many different types of graphic symbols that can be used for bullets. You can choose a symbol from this font or change the font to see other groups of appropriate symbols.

  ✓ *You can use this dialog box to insert many other kinds of symbols in slide text, as you will learn in Exercise 20.*

- As a general rule, you change bullet formatting on a single slide to emphasize the bullets. If you wish to replace all bullets in a presentation, you should do so on the slide master, discussed in Exercise 38.

- If the slide text has an obvious order, you can apply numbered list formatting, replacing bullets with consecutive numbers, roman numerals, or alphabetical letters. Use the Numbered tab in the Bullets and Numbering dialog box, shown in the following illustration, to format or customize numbers.

Numbered tab in Bullets and Numbering dialog box

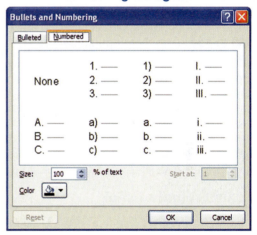

- You can turn off bullets or numbers to create a simple paragraph, but the text will retain the hanging indent used to create the bulleted or numbered list.

  ✓ *You can modify or remove the hanging indent as discussed in Exercise 22.*

Align Text

- Text **alignment** controls the position of text within a placeholder. PowerPoint allows you to specify both horizontal and vertical alignment.

- Themes control the default alignment of text in placeholders, but you can modify both horizontal and vertical alignment using buttons in the Paragraph group on the Home tab.

- The following illustration shows alignment options available in PowerPoint.

Horizontal and vertical alignment options

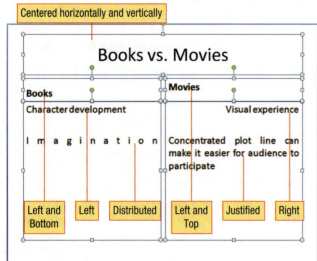

- Horizontal alignment options will be familiar to you from word processing applications. You can left-align, center, right-align, or justify text in any placeholder to add interest or enhance text appearance.

- Common horizontal alignments can be applied using buttons on the Home tab or the Mini toolbar. Distributed alignment is available only in the Paragraph dialog box's Alignment list.

- Vertical alignment options are available from the Align Text button's palette, shown in the following illustration.

Align Text options

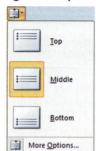

- Clicking the More Options command on this palette opens the Format Text Effects dialog box, where you can select from alignments as well as other special text effects.

  ✓ *You will learn more about this dialog box later in this lesson.*

- You can change horizontal alignment of any paragraph of text in a text placeholder without affecting other paragraphs of text. In a title placeholder, however, changing alignment of one paragraph realigns all paragraphs in that placeholder.

- If you change vertical alignment in any placeholder, all text within that placeholder changes to the selected alignment.

PROCEDURES

Create Subordinate Bullet Levels

- Press Tab⇄ at the beginning of a line to indent and display subordinate-level bullet and text formatting.
- Press ⬆Shift+Tab⇄ at the beginning of a line to return to the previous level.

  OR

1. Click in paragraph to promote or demote.
2. Click **Home** tab .... Alt+H

Paragraph Group

3. Click **Increase List Level** button .... A, I to increase indent.

  OR

  Click **Decrease List Level** button .... A, O to decrease indent.

Change Bullet Formatting

1. Click in bullet item or select placeholder.
2. Click **Home** tab .... Alt+H

Paragraph Group

3. Click **Bullets** button down arrow .... U
4. Select a different standard bullet character.

  OR

  a. Click **Bullets and Numbering** .... N
  b. Click a standard bullet character.
  c. Click **Size** .... Alt+S and type the desired percentage of text size.
  d. Click **Color** .... Alt+C and select a new color for the bullet from the palette.
  e. Click [OK] .... ↵Enter

To select a picture bullet:

1. Click **Home** tab .... Alt+H

   Paragraph Group

2. Click **Bullets** button ☰ ▾
   down arrow .... U
3. Click Picture... .
4. Select a bullet picture.
5. Click OK .... ↵Enter
6. Click OK again .... ↵Enter

To select a new bullet symbol:

1. Click **Home** tab .... Alt+H

   Paragraph Group

2. Click **Bullets** button ☰ ▾
   down arrow .... U
3. Click Customize... .
4. Select a symbol.

   ✓ *You may change the font in the Symbol dialog box to select from a different set of symbols.*

5. Click OK .... ↵Enter
6. Click OK again .... ↵Enter

Apply Numbered List Formatting

1. Click in bullet item or select placeholder.
2. Click **Home** tab .... Alt+H

   Paragraph Group

3. Click **Numbering**
   button ☰ ▾ .... N

   ✓ *Clicking the button starts a default list that begins with the number 1. To apply a different numbering format, click the button's down arrow.*

4. To format numbered list, use same steps as for formatting bullets using the Numbered tab in the Bullets and Numbering dialog box.

Change Text Alignment (Ctrl + L, Ctrl + E, Ctrl + R, Ctrl + J)

To change horizontal alignment:

1. Select text or placeholder, or click to place insertion point in any paragraph you want to align.
2. Click **Home** tab .... Alt+H

   Paragraph Group

3. Select desired alignment button:
   - **Align Text Left** ▤ .... A, L
   - **Center** ▤ .... A, C
   - **Align Text Right** ▤ .... A, R
   - **Justify** ▤ .... A, J

   OR

   - Use same alignment options on Mini toolbar.

     ✓ *Justify button is not shown on the Mini toolbar.*

   OR

1. Click **Home** tab .... Alt+H

   Paragraph Group

2. Click **Paragraph** dialog box launcher ▫ .
3. Click **Aligment** list
   arrow .... Alt+G
4. Select desired alignment.
5. Click OK .... ↵Enter

To change vertical alignment:

1. Click **Home** tab .... Alt+H

   Paragraph Group

2. Click **Align Text**
   button ▤ ▾ .... A, T
3. Select a vertical alignment:
   - **Top** .... T
   - **Middle** .... M
   - **Bottom** .... B

EXERCISE DIRECTIONS

1. Start PowerPoint and open 🔘 **18Bakery**.
2. Save the presentation as **18Bakery_xx**.
3. On slide 1, center the title and subtitle.
4. Change the vertical alignment of the subtitle text to Middle.
5. Display slide 2 and indent the four bullet items below *Breads* (*Croissants, Bagels, Muffins, Rolls*) to make them second-level bullet entries. Then indent the three items below *Sweet specialties*. Your slide should look like Illustration A.
6. Display slide 3 and change the bullet characters for both entries as follows:
   - Select the text placeholder.
   - Choose to customize bullets.
   - Select wingding 189, which looks like a clock set to 7 o'clock.
   - Change the bullet color to a darker blue.
7. Display slide 4 and change the bulleted list to a numbered list.
8. Display slide 6. Right-align the text in the placeholder to the left of the photo.
9. Save your changes, close the presentation, and exit PowerPoint.

A Variety of Baked Goods

- Breads
  - Croissants
  - Bagels
  - Muffins
  - Rolls
- Sweet specialties
  - Pastries
  - Cookies
  - Cakes

ON YOUR OWN

1. Start PowerPoint and open ⊙**OPP18**.
2. Save the presentation as **OPP18_xx**.
3. Apply left alignment to both the title and subtitle on slide 1.
4. Change the vertical alignment of the subtitle to improve the look of the slide.
5. Change the bullets on slide 4 to numbers, and change the number color and size.
6. Add subordinate bullet entries to some or all of the bullets on slide 5 to give further details about the suggestions of how to get involved. You may use events or programs you know about in your area to provide these details. Illustration A shows some sample subordinate items.
7. Center align the text in both placeholders on slide 6.
8. Save your changes, close the presentation, and exit PowerPoint.

Illustration A

How to Get Involved

⊙ Find a local chapter or organization
  • Try Web sites for lists of local chapters
⊙ Attend an event such as a walkathon or other benefit
  • MS Walk coming up in September
  • AIDS Awareness Week in November
⊙ Volunteer your services
  • Newspapers list volunteer opportunities on a weekly basis

The Power of Giving   8/1/2007

Skills Covered

- **Adjust Line Spacing**
- **Move and Copy Text**
- **Adjust and Format Placeholders**

Software Skills   Other ways to modify the appearance of text on a slide include adjusting line spacing. Move or copy text from slide to slide just as you would in a document. You can also move, resize, copy, or delete any placeholder on a slide or any object on a slide.

Application Skills   In this exercise, you continue to work on the presentation for Great Grains Bakery by modifying line spacing, moving and copying text, and adjusting placeholder formats.

TERMS

No new terms in this exercise.

NOTES

Adjust Line Spacing

- Adjust line spacing between bullets or other paragraphs to make text easier to read or to control space on a slide.

- To quickly adjust line spacing by set increments, use the Line Spacing button palette, shown in the following illustration.

- Line spacing affects all lines of a paragraph.

- With the insertion point in a single paragraph in a placeholder, the new line spacing option applies only to that paragraph. To adjust line spacing for all items in a placeholder, select them or select the placeholder.

- For greater control over line spacing, use the Paragraph dialog box, shown in the following illustration.

Line Spacing palette

The Paragraph dialog box

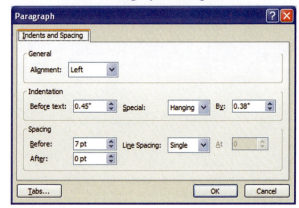

- The Line Spacing list offers a choice of Single, 1.5 lines, Double, Exactly, or Multiple.
  - Exactly allows you to set a line space that will not change. If you have set line spacing exactly and enter more text than can fit in a placeholder, PowerPoint maintains the desired line spacing and adjusts only the size of text when AutoFitting.
  - Multiple allows you to adjust line spacing as a percentage of single spacing. You enter a value that represents the percentage change in the At box.
- Besides setting line spacing options, you can use the Paragraph dialog box to specify an amount of space before or after a paragraph.
- When you use the Before or After setting, the spacing within the paragraph does not change; only the space above or below the paragraph changes.

Move and Copy Text

- As you review a slide or presentation, you may rearrange the text to make it easier to follow.
- You can move text in PowerPoint using drag-and-drop or cut-and-paste methods.
  - Use the drag-and-drop method to move text to a nearby location, such as within the same placeholder or on the same slide, or from the Outline pane to a slide. When you move text, a vertical line moves with the mouse to help you position the text.
  - Use the cut-and-paste method to move text between two locations that are some distance apart, such as from one slide to another or from one presentation to another.
- To copy text from one location to another, use either the drag-and-drop or copy-and-paste method. Hold down the Ctrl key while dragging to drag a copy of selected text.
- When pasting cut or copied text, you have the option of using the Paste Special command on the Paste button's drop-down list.

- The Paste Special dialog box, shown in the following illustration, allows you to paste Clipboard content in a variety of formats.

The Paste Special dialog box

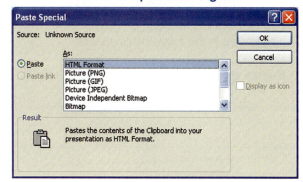

- The previous illustration shows the options available when the Clipboard contains text. A benefit to pasting text in any of the Picture formats is that you can then treat the pasted text as a picture and apply interesting formats to it.
- You can use this dialog box to paste, or embed, other objects such as Microsoft Excel charts or other Office objects. Depending on the object, you may also be able to paste link the object to create a link between the slide and the source of the object.

  ✓ *You will learn more about embedding and linking in Exercise 27.*

Adjust and Format Placeholders

- You can move or size any text or object placeholder to make room on the slide for other objects such as text boxes or images.
- You can also delete any placeholder to remove it from a slide, or copy a placeholder to use on another slide or in another presentation.
- To move, copy, size, or delete a placeholder and everything in it, select the placeholder so that its border becomes a solid line.
  - To move the placeholder, drag it by its border or use cut-and-paste to remove it from one slide and paste it on another.
  - To copy the placeholder, use copy-and-paste. A pasted placeholder appears in the same location on the new slide as on the original slide.

- Delete a placeholder by simply pressing Del while it is selected.

  ✓ *Be careful! If you have selected a placeholder that contains text and press Delete, the placeholder and all its text are deleted. Use Undo to restore the text.*

- To resize a placeholder, drag one of the handles as shown in the following illustration.

Resize a placeholder by dragging a handle

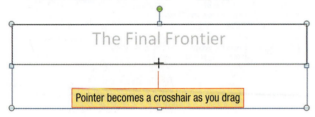

Pointer becomes a crosshair as you drag

- PowerPoint 2007 makes it easy to format a placeholder in interesting ways. Use a Quick Style, for example, to apply color and other effects to an entire placeholder, as shown in the following illustration.

Apply a Quick Style to a placeholder

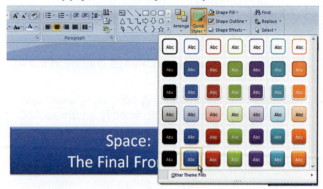

- You can also apply a fill, outline, or other shape effect to a placeholder, just as you would to a drawing shape.

  ✓ *You will learn more about applying fills, borders, and effects in later exercises.*

PROCEDURES

Adjust Line Spacing

1. Select paragraph(s) you want to adjust.
2. Click **Home** tab .... Alt+H

   Paragraph Group

3. Click **Line Spacing** button .... K
4. Select a spacing option from the drop-down list ....↓, ↵Enter

   OR

   a. Click **Line Spacing Options** L
   b. Click **Before** .... Alt+B and type a value for space before a paragraph.
   c. Click **After** .... Alt+E and type a value for space after a paragraph.
   d. Click **Line Spacing** .... Alt+N and select a line spacing option.
   e. Click OK .... ↵Enter

Move or Copy Text (Ctrl + X, Ctrl + C, Ctrl + V)

To move text using drag and drop:

1. Select text to move.
2. Hold down the mouse button and drag the selected text to a new location.

To move text using Cut and Paste:

1. Select text to be moved.
2. Click **Home** tab .... Alt+H

   Clipboard Group

3. Click **Cut** button .... X to move text.
4. Position the insertion point where you want to insert text.

5. Click **Paste** button V

   OR

   a. Click **Paste** button down arrow V
   b. Click **Paste Special** .... S
   c. Choose a format for the pasted content.
   d. Click OK .... ↵Enter

To copy text using drag and drop:

1. Select text to copy.
2. Hold down Ctrl and the mouse button and drag the selected text to a new location.

To copy text using Copy and Paste:

1. Select text to be copied.
2. Click **Home** tab .... Alt + H

   Clipboard Group

3. Click **Copy** button 🖺 C
4. Position the insertion point where you want to insert text.
5. Click **Paste** button 📋 V

   OR

   a. Click **Paste** button down arrow V
   b. Click **Paste Special** .... S
   c. Choose a format for the pasted content.
   d. Click [OK] .... ↵Enter

Adjust and Format Placeholders

To move a placeholder:

1. Select the placeholder to be moved.
2. Click on the placeholder border and drag the placeholder to the new position.

   OR

1. Select placeholder.
2. Click **Home** tab .... Alt + H

   Clipboard Group

3. Click **Cut** button ✂ X
4. Display the slide where you want to insert the placeholder.
5. Click **Paste** button 📋 .... Alt + H , V

To copy a placeholder:

1. Select the placeholder to be copied.
2. Hold down Ctrl, click on the placeholder border, and drag the placeholder to the new position.

OR

1. Select placeholder.
2. Click **Home** tab .... Alt + H

   Clipboard Group

3. Click **Copy** button 🖺 C
4. Display the slide where you want to insert the placeholder.
5. Click **Paste** button 📋 .... Alt + H , V

To delete a selected placeholder:

- Click Del .

To resize a selected placeholder:

- Drag any handle to enlarge or reduce placeholder.

To add Quick Style formatting to a selected placeholder:

1. Click **Home** tab .... Alt + H

   Drawing Group

2. Click **Quick Styles** button 🖌 .... S , S
3. Select the desired Quick Style from the gallery .... ← → ↑ ↓ , ↵Enter

EXERCISE DIRECTIONS

1. Start PowerPoint and open **18Bakery_xx** or open 💿 **19Bakery**.

2. Save the presentation as **19Bakery_xx**.

3. Display slide 3. Position the insertion point after the first bullet item, press ↵Enter, and type the text **Franchises available**. Move the last bullet item on the slide to be the first bullet item.

4. Display slide 4. Copy the first item and paste it at the end of the list. Add an exclamation point at the end of the word *Quality* in item 5. Then change the word *Four* in the slide title to *Five*.

5. Change the line spacing for all items in the text placeholder to 1.5.

6. Display slide 5. Delete the *Turbinado sugar* and *Gourmet sea salt* items and then drag the bottom of the placeholder upwards to redistribute the items so the *Fair trade* item does not break across the columns.

7. Display slide 6. Select the placeholder that is on top of the photo and delete it.

8. Copy the subtitle placeholder from slide 1 and paste it on slide 6. Move it below the photo and resize the placeholder to be the same width as the photo. You may also modify the placeholder's depth.

   ✓ *If the placeholder pastes in bulleted format, turn off the bullet.*

9. Apply a Quick Style to the placeholder. You may need to change the text color to make it stand out against the Quick Style formatting. Illustration A shows an example of one style.

10. Save your changes, close the presentation, and exit PowerPoint.

Great Grains Make Great Food!

Great food starts with great ingredients. At Great Grains Bakery, we strive to gather the finest, freshest ingredients to ensure quality products. You'll taste the difference when you buy Great Grains!

FRESH TO YOU EACH DAY

ON YOUR OWN

1. Start PowerPoint and open **OPP18_xx** or open **OPP19**.

2. Save the presentation as **OPP19_xx**.

3. The body text placeholders are very close to the title placeholders throughout this presentation. Adjust the height of each body text placeholder to allow more space between the body text and the titles.

4. Make the placeholders for the title and the subtitle on slide 1 the same width to further modify alignment on that slide.

5. On slide 3, add 6 points of space *after* each paragraph to make the text easier to read, but leave the line spacing the same.

6. On slide 5, move items to rearrange them on the slide.

7. On slide 6, adjust placeholder position and the position of the clip art as desired to make the slide more attractive. You may also change type size and color and add Quick Style formatting to the text placeholder if desired.

8. On slide 1, select and cut the subtitle text, and delete the empty subtitle placeholder box.

9. Use Paste Special to paste the text you cut in Picture (PNG) format. Format the pasted object as follows:

   ■ Select the pasted object, if necessary.

   ■ Click the Picture Tools Format tab, and then click the Picture Effects button in the Picture Styles group.

   ■ Click Preset and then select Preset 4 to apply a bevel, shadow effect to the object.

   ■ Adjust the position of the object as desired. Illustration A shows one example.

10. Save your changes, close the presentation, and exit PowerPoint.

Illustration A

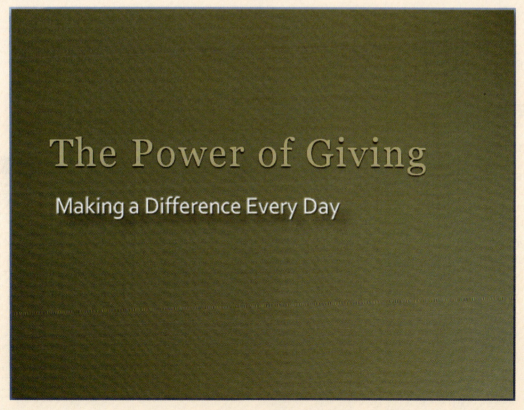

Skills Covered

- **Insert Symbols**
- **Insert and Remove Text Boxes**
- **Format Text Boxes**

- **Set Text Alignment and Orientation in a Text Box**
- **Create Column Text in a Text Box**
- **Change Margins in a Text Box**

Software Skills Insert symbols to handle special characters such as fractions or letters from other languages. Add a text box to a slide to position text in a location where there is no placeholder. PowerPoint 2007 allows you to control text in a text box by adjusting margins or setting text in columns.

Application Skills The Campus Recreation Center at your local university wants to bring in more members, particularly for the Aquatics Center, which is currently underused. The Aquatics Director has asked you to create a slide show that can be presented at a strategizing session. In this exercise, you continue to work with text by inserting symbols and creating and formatting text boxes.

TERMS

Symbols Characters that cannot be typed from the keyboard.

Text box A shape designed to hold text that can be positioned anywhere on a slide.

NOTES

Insert Symbols

- **Symbols** are characters that cannot be typed from the keyboard. Symbols can include decorative characters, foreign language characters, and mathematical or punctuation characters.

- Insert symbols from the Symbol dialog box, shown in the illustration at right.

The Symbol dialog box

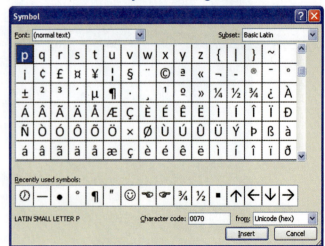

- To insert text characters rather than decorative symbols, make sure the Font box shows (normal text) as in the previous illustration. You can click the Font list arrow to display all fonts available on your system to find additional symbols.

- Use the Subset box to display subsets of symbols such as General Punctuation or Currency Symbols.

- The Recently used symbols section gives you quick access to symbols you use regularly.

- Each symbol has an identifying code displayed in the Character code box. This code can make it easy for you to use symbols consistently.

Insert and Remove Text Boxes

- A **text box** is a container for type that you can position anywhere on a slide. It is not a placeholder and not part of a slide layout.

- Like other slide objects, text boxes are inserted from the Insert tab. You have two options for inserting a text box:
  - You can click the text box pointer on the slide and begin typing to create a text box in which the text will not wrap. This option is suitable for short text insertions of a few words.
  - You can click the pointer on the slide and drag to create a box of a specific width in which text will wrap.

- Remove a text box the same way you would remove a placeholder: click the outside border of the text box to display the solid outline and then press Del.

Format Text Boxes

- You have a number of options for formatting a text box to make them visually appealing as well as easy to read on a slide.

- You can resize a text box as you would a placeholder, by dragging handles.

- Adjust the appearance of text in a text box using the text tools you have learned about in this lesson. You can change font, font size, font style, and font color, for example.

- Format the box itself using tools in the Drawing group on the Home tab or on the Drawing Tools Format contextual tab.
  - Use the Shape Fill palette, shown in the following illustration, to apply a fill (background) for the box. The fill can consist of a color, picture, gradient (gradations of color), or texture.

    ✓ *You will learn more about fill options in later exercises.*

Shape Fill palette

  - Use the Shape Outline palette, shown in the following illustration, to format a border for the box. You can choose an outline color, specify a weight (thickness), and select a dash style.

Shape Outline palette

- Click the Shape Effects button to see a palette of effects you can apply to the box, as shown in the following illustration. Click any of the palette categories to see a submenu of specific choices for that category.

Shape Effects palette

- If you do not want to take the time to choose a fill, outline, and effect, you can use the Quick Style gallery to apply preformatted styles to your text box the same way you apply styles to a placeholder.

Set Text Alignment and Orientation in a Text Box

- Text can be horizontally aligned in a text box as in any placeholder. Choose to align text left, center, right, or justified.
- You can also adjust the orientation or direction of text in a text box so that text reads from the bottom up or the top down. The following illustration shows options for changing text direction.

Text direction options

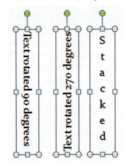

- You use the Text Direction button in the Paragraph group on the Home tab to change text direction.
- While you can actually change text direction in any placeholder, it is easier to control the size and position of text with a vertical orientation if you enclose it in a text box.

Create Column Text in a Text Box

- A new feature in PowerPoint 2007 is the ability to format text box type into columns. Use column text to break long lines into shorter ones that are easier to read.
- Use the Columns button in the Paragraph group on the Home tab to quickly divide text into two or three columns.
- For more control over the column text, use the Columns dialog box, accessed by clicking More Columns on the Columns palette, to select the number of columns and space between them, as shown in the following illustration.

Format text box text in columns

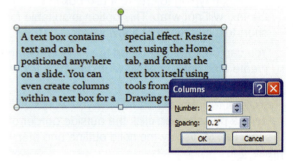

- You can create columns in any placeholder, not only text boxes. If you have fairly short bulleted entries, setting up two columns in a content placeholder can be a good way to display a fair quantity of text without crowding or AutoFitting.

Change Margins in a Text Box

- You may find that text in a text box crowds the edges of the box, which can result in a poor appearance if the text box has a color fill.

- To provide more space between text and the edges of the text box, you can adjust the text box's margins.

- Use the Text Box settings in the Format Shape dialog box, shown in the illustration at right, to adjust margins.

- Note that you can make other changes to text box formats in this dialog box, such as setting alignment and text direction options and choosing how text fits in the text box. You can also create columns from this dialog box by clicking the Columns button.

Format Shape dialog box's Text Box settings

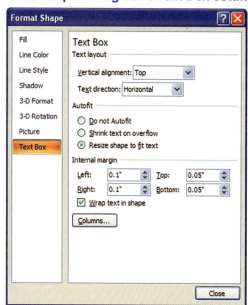

PROCEDURES

Insert Symbols

1. Position the insertion point where the symbol should appear.
2. Click **Insert** tab .... Alt + N

   Text Group

3. Click **Symbol** button Ω .... U
4. Select desired symbol.
5. Click [Insert] .... ↵Enter
6. Click [Close] .... ↵Enter

Insert a Text Box

1. Click **Insert** tab .... Alt + N

   Text Group

2. Click **Text Box** button A X
3. Click the text box pointer on the slide to create a nonwrapping text box.

   OR

   Click the text box pointer on the slide and drag to create a desired width in which text will wrap.

4. Begin typing to insert text.

Delete a Text Box

1. Click outside border of text box to select the text box.
2. Press Del.

Format a Text Box

1. Select the text box by clicking its outside border.
2. Click **Drawing Tools Format** tab .... Alt + J, D

   ✓ You can also use formatting tools on the Home tab in the Drawing group.

To add graphic formatting:

Shape Styles Group

- Click **More** ⊽ .... S, 3 to display Quick Style gallery and select a Quick Style.
- Click **Shape Fill** button 🖌 .... S, F to select a color or other fill option.

- Click **Shape Outline** button 🖉 .... S, O to select an outline color or style.
- Click **Shape Effects** button 🔲 .... S, E to select an effect.

Set Text Alignment

1. Select the text box by clicking its outside border.
2. Click **Home** tab .... Alt + H

   Paragraph Group

3. Click any alignment button to change horizontal alignment as directed in Exercise 18.

Set Text Orientation

1. Select the text box by clicking its outside border.
2. Click **Home** tab .... `Alt`+`H`

    Paragraph Group

3. Click **Text Direction** button `⫙ ▾` .... `A`, `X`
4. Select a text direction:
    - **Horizontal** .... `H`
    - **Rotate all text 90°** .... `R`
    - **Rotate all text 270°** .... `O`
    - **Stacked** .... `S`

Create Column Text in a Text Box

1. Select the text box by clicking its outside border.
2. Click **Home** tab .... `Alt`+`H`

    Paragraph Group

3. Click **Columns** button `▤ ▾` ...... `J`
4. Click a column option:
    - **One Column** .... `O`
    - **Two Columns** .... `T`
    - **Three Columns** .... `H`

    OR

    a. Click **More Columns** .... `M`
    b. Click **Number** .... `Alt`+`N` and type the number of columns.
    c. Click **Spacing** .... `Alt`+`S` and type a value for space between columns.
    d. Click `OK` .... `↵Enter`

Change Margins in a Text Box

1. Select the text box by clicking its outside border.
2. Click **Drawing Tools Format** tab .... `Alt`+`J`, `D`

    Shape Styles Group

3. Click **Shape Styles** group dialog box launcher `▣` .... `O`
4. Click **Text Box** in left column.
5. Make desired changes to Left, Right, Top, and Bottom margins by typing value or clicking increment arrows.
6. Click `Close` .... `↵Enter`

EXERCISE DIRECTIONS

1. Start PowerPoint and open 🔘**20Aquatics**.
2. Save the presentation as **20Aquatics_xx**.
3. Display slide 2 and draw a text box as shown in Illustration A. Type the following text, inserting the correct symbol é in the second word and the em dash symbol (—) in the second sentence.

    The Bédard Aquatics Center at CRC has an Olympic-sized pool that is primarily used in the winter by the swimming and diving team. The rest of the year, it is almost empty seven days a week—except for the occasional lonely lap swimmer or students taking required physical education courses. How can we market this facility to students, faculty and staff, alumni, and community members to keep it busier?

4. Change the text size to 16 point. Fill the text box with the Turquoise, Accent 3, Lighter 80% shape fill. Apply the first shape effect in the Shadow Outer group, Offset Diagonal Bottom Right.
5. Change the internal margins of the text box to 0.2 for the left and right margins. Then specify 2 columns with spacing of 0.2.
6. Adjust the width and height of the text box as necessary to balance the columns.
7. Insert another text box on the slide by clicking near the upper-left corner of the photo. Type the text **Aquatics Staff Report** in the text box.
8. Change the text direction in this text box to rotate it 270 degrees. Adjust the text box to be as tall as the photo and center the text in the text box.
9. Change the text color in the rotated text box to the Blue, Accent 1, Darker 25% theme color.
10. Apply an outline to the text box that uses the Blue, Accent 1 color and the Square Dot dash style.
11. Adjust the position of the rotated text box if necessary to leave a small amount of space between the text box and the photo. Your slide should look similar to Illustration B.
12. Display slide 1. You do not need the text box with the *Preliminary* text, so delete this text box.
13. Save your changes, close the presentation, and exit PowerPoint.

Illustration A

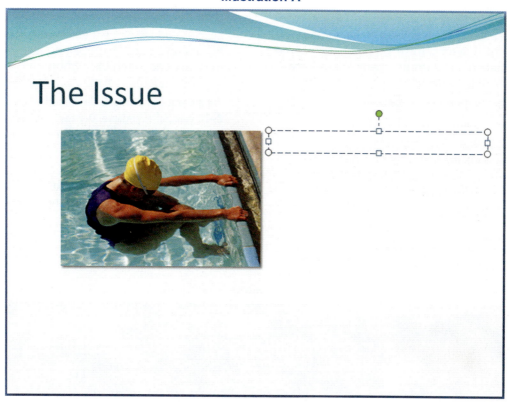

Illustration B

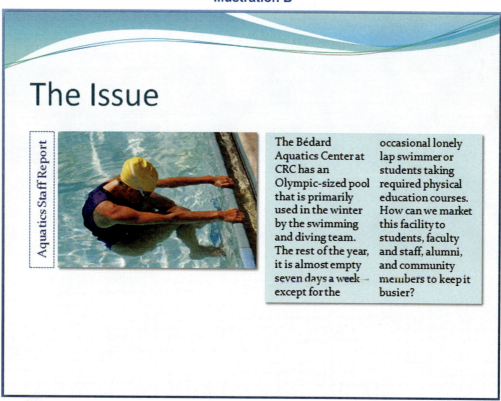

ON YOUR OWN

You have been asked by the owners of Restoration Architecture to help them complete a presentation that provides information about the company. You will create a first draft in this exercise.

1. Start PowerPoint and open 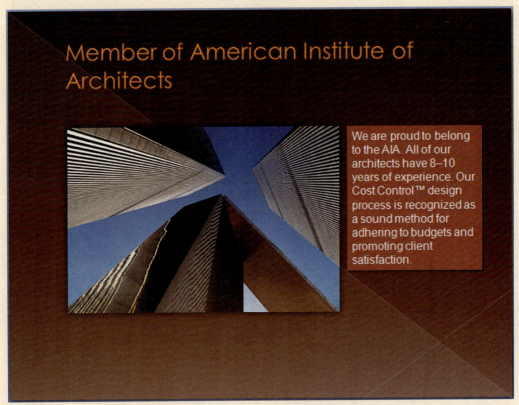OPP20.

2. Save the presentation as **OPP20_xx**.

3. On slide 1, create a text box in the upper-left corner that contains the text DRAFT. Choose the Stacked text alignment, and adjust text and text box formats as desired.

4. Display slide 3. Draw a text box to the right of the picture and insert the following text. You will need to locate and insert the symbols for an en dash and the trademark symbol.

   We are proud to belong to the AIA. All of our architects have 8–10 years of experience. Our Cost Control™ design process is recognized as a sound method for adhering to budgets and promoting client satisfaction.

5. Format the text box as desired, and change font size if necessary to fit the text neatly on the slide. Illustration A shows one arrangement you might use.

6. Save your changes, close the presentation, and exit PowerPoint.

Illustration A

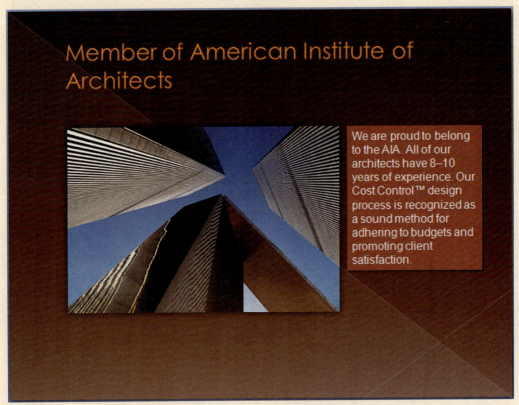

Exercise | 21

Skills Covered

- **Insert WordArt**
- **Apply WordArt Styles to Existing Text**
- **Modify and Format WordArt**
- **Copy Elements from Slide to Slide**

Software Skills Use WordArt to create a graphic from text. Once you have created the graphic, you can modify it by changing its shape or adjusting fill, outline, and effects. You can also apply WordArt styles to existing text for a special effect. If you have an element in one presentation that you want to use in another, you can use Copy and Paste to add the element to your current presentation.

Application Skills You will continue to work with the Campus Recreation Center presentation by adding a WordArt graphic and copying a logo symbol from another presentation to the aquatics presentation.

TERMS

Destination The location or application in which you place an element that was originally in another location or application.

Source The original location or application of an element you intend to place in another location or application.

WordArt Office feature that allows you to create a graphic from text.

NOTES

Insert WordArt

- **WordArt** is an Office feature that allows you to create a graphic from text. WordArt graphics can add a custom touch to text and provide visual interest to a slide.

- Begin the process of creating a WordArt graphic by clicking the WordArt button on the Insert tab and choosing a style from the WordArt gallery, shown in the illustration at right.

WordArt gallery

- Colors of the WordArt styles are controlled by the current theme. You can rest the mouse pointer on a style to see a description of the style.

- Styles are described according to fill, outline, and effect. The light blue style in the upper-left corner of the previous illustration, for example, is called Fill – Text 2, Outline – Background 2.

- After you choose a style, the WordArt graphic is created on the slide with placeholder text, as shown in the following illustration.

New WordArt graphic on the slide

- The placeholder text is selected, so all you need to do to finish your graphic is type your text.

- It is generally a good idea to limit text to a few words for the best effect. A whole sentence in a WordArt style such as the one in the previous illustration would be hard to read, not to mention bulky.

Modify and Format WordArt

- The default WordArt styles provide a variety of interesting graphics, but you have a number of options for customizing a WordArt graphic. Use tools on the Drawing Tools Format tab or the Format Text Effects dialog box to modify and format WordArt.

Modify Text and Shape

- You can change the text in a WordArt graphic at any time by selecting the existing text and typing new text to replace the selection.

- By default, WordArt graphics are created without any kind of transformation—all text sits on a horizontal baseline and the graphic itself has no shape.

- To apply a shape to the WordArt, use the Transform submenu on the Text Effects menu, part of which is shown in the following illustration.

WordArt Transform options

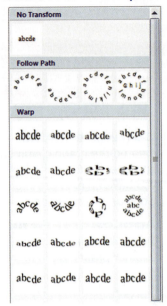

- Selecting any of the transformation options applies it immediately to your WordArt graphic, giving the graphic a more interesting appearance.

Format WordArt

- Use the options in the WordArt Styles group on the Drawing Tools Format tab to apply formats to a selected WordArt graphic.

- You can apply a different Quick Style from the WordArt Styles gallery. Some of these styles are designed to change all text in the shape, while others can be applied to portions of the WordArt text that you select.

- Use the Text Fill palette to choose a new fill color or apply a picture, gradient, or texture fill. In a WordArt graphic, the fill is the color or pattern applied to the characters in the graphic.

- Use the Text Outline palette to choose a new outline color, weight, or dash style. In a WordArt graphic, outline refers to the border around each character.

   ✓ *You do not have to have an outline around WordArt characters. To remove the outline, click the Text Outline button and select No Outline on the palette.*

- Use the Text Effects palette to choose an effect category such as Shadow, Reflection, Glow, or Bevel and then select an option from one of these category's submenu.

- If these fill, outline, and effect options look familiar to you, you should realize that they are the same options available when formatting shapes such as text boxes. Similar options are available for formatting drawing shapes, table and chart elements, pictures, SmartArt diagrams, and other graphic objects. This kind of consistency makes it easy for PowerPoint users to learn and employ PowerPoint 2007's enhanced graphic tools.

- Rather than select options on a number of different palettes, you can use the Format Text Effects dialog box to choose and apply formats.

- The Format Text Effects dialog box, shown in the following illustration, has a series of categories in the left pane that display options for that category in the main pane of the dialog box.

Format Text Effects dialog box

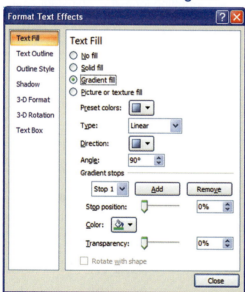

- Formats are applied to the WordArt graphic as soon as you choose them in this dialog box, so you never have to guess how a setting might affect your graphic.

  ✓ *Position the dialog box so that you can see your WordArt graphic as you select formats.*

- You can use this dialog box to select and customize fill, outline, and some effects.

- Note that the dialog box does not offer a Cancel button. If you decide against changes you make in this dialog box, you must use the Undo button to reverse them.

- The Format Text Effects dialog box offers many more options than can be covered in this text. You are encouraged to explore and experiment to become familiar with those you do not use in this exercise.

Apply WordArt Styles to Existing Text

- You have another option for using WordArt styles in a presentation: You can apply the styles to any text in the presentation for special visual effect.

- Use the WordArt Styles gallery on the Drawing Tools Format tab to apply a WordArt style to text. The text maintains its original size but takes on the WordArt style.

- The following illustration shows a presentation title and subtitle that have been formatted with WordArt styles.

Existing text formatted with WordArt styles

Campus Recreation Center
AQUATICS PROGRAM PLANNING

- WordArt styles can make a heading stand out on a slide, but use caution in applying WordArt styles to multiple lines of text.

Copy Elements from Slide to Slide

- You have already learned several ways to use information from other sources in your presentations, such as creating slides from Microsoft Word outlines or reusing slides from other presentations.

- You can copy any element from an existing presentation to paste in your current presentation. This makes it easy to reuse charts, graphics, pictures, diagrams, or other material, saving time and ensuring consistency.

- You can also copy elements from one slide to another within a presentation.

- The easiest way to transfer an element from one presentation or slide to another is to use the Copy and Paste commands that you have already used for copying text.

- When pasting or linking material from slide to slide, presentation to presentation, or application to application, it is helpful to use the terms **source** and **destination**.

- The *source* is the original location of material you are going to paste. The *destination* is the location where you paste that material.

- A source can be a slide in a presentation, another presentation, or another application.

- When you copy an object from one presentation or slide to another, it pastes in the same location on the destination slide that it occupied on the source slide.

- If an element that uses theme colors (such as a graphic created from shapes) is copied from one presentation to another, it will by default adjust to use colors of the destination presentation.

- If you wish to maintain the colors of the source presentation, click the Paste Options button that displays after the paste as shown in the following illustration and select Keep Source Formatting.

Paste Options choices

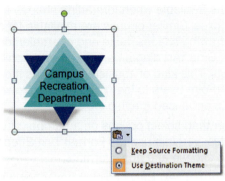

- The Paste Options button also displays if you copy other objects from one presentation to another, such as a text placeholder.

- You can choose whether to keep the original (source) formatting for text or adjust it to match the theme fonts of the destination presentation.

PROCEDURES

Insert WordArt

1. Click **Insert** tab .... Alt + N

2. Click **WordArt** button A .... W
3. Select a WordArt style from the gallery.
4. Type the desired text.

Change WordArt Text

1. Select existing text in WordArt graphic.
2. Type replacement text.

Modify WordArt Shape

1. Click WordArt graphic outline to select entire shape.
2. Click **Drawing Tools Format** tab .... Alt + J, D

   WordArt Styles Group

3. Click **Text Effects** button A down arrow .... T, X
4. Click **T**ransform .... T
5. Select desired shape on submenu.

Format WordArt

To apply a different style:

1. Select the WordArt graphic if necessary.
2. Click **Drawing Tools Format** tab .... Alt + J, D

   WordArt Styles Group

3. Click **More** button ⬇ .... K in WordArt gallery.
4. Select new style.

To select a different fill:

1. Select the WordArt graphic if necessary.
2. Click **Drawing Tools Format** tab .... Alt + J, D

   WordArt Styles Group

3. Click **Text Fill** button A ▾ down arrow .... T, I
4. Select a color, picture, gradient, or texture fill.

   OR

1. Click **WordArt Styles** group dialog box launcher 🗗 .... G
2. Click Text Fill category in left pane.
3. Select fill options in main pane.
4. Click Close .... Enter

To apply a different outline:

1. Select the WordArt graphic if necessary.
2. Click **Drawing Tools Format** tab .... `Alt`+`J`, `D`

> **WordArt Styles Group**

3. Click **Text Outline** button `✎▾` down arrow .... `T`, `O`
4. Select an outline color, weight, or dash style.

   ✓ *You must display the Text Outline palette repeatedly to make more than one change to the outline.*

   OR

1. Click **WordArt Styles** group dialog box launcher `▣` .... `G`
2. Click Text Outline or Outline Style category in left pane.
3. Select outline options in main pane.
4. Click `Close` .... `↵Enter`

To choose a different effect:

1. Select the WordArt graphic if necessary.
2. Click **Drawing Tools Format** tab .... `Alt`+`J`, `D`

> **WordArt Styles Group**

3. Click **Text Effects** button `Ⓐ` down arrow .... `T`, `X`
4. Select a category of effects.
5. Select an effect from the category's submenu.

OR

1. Click **WordArt Styles** group dialog box launcher `▣` .... `G`
2. Click Shadow, 3-D Format, or 3-D Rotation category in left pane.
3. Select effect options in main pane.
4. Click `Close` .... `↵Enter`

Apply WordArt Styles to Existing Text

1. Select existing text to which you want to apply WordArt styles.
2. Click **Drawing Tools Format** tab .... `Alt`+`J`, `D`

> **WordArt Styles Group**

3. Select any of the WordArt formatting tools to apply to selected text:

   ■ Click **More** button `▼` .... `K` to select a Quick Style from the WordArt gallery.
   ■ Click **Text Fill** button `A▾` down arrow .... `T`, `I` to apply a fill.
   ■ Click **Text Outline** button `✎▾` down arrow .... `T`, `O` to choose outline formats.
   ■ Click **Text Effects** button `Ⓐ` down arrow .... `T`, `X` to choose a category of effects.

Copy Elements from Slide to Slide

1. Display the slide that contains the element you want to copy.

   ✓ *The slide can be in the current presentation or in a different presentation.*

2. Click the element you want to copy to select it.
3. Click **Home** tab .... `Alt`+`H`

> **Clipboard Group**

4. Click **Copy** button `📋` .... `C`
5. Display the slide on which you want to paste the element.
6. Click **Paste** button `📋` .... `V`

To specify theme formatting of pasted element:

1. After paste action, click **Paste Options** button `📋`.
2. Select an option:

   ■ Click **Keep Source Formatting** .... `K` to maintain color, font, or other formatting from original.
   ■ Click **Use Destination Theme** .... `D` to allow formats to adjust to theme on destination slide.

EXERCISE DIRECTIONS

1. Start PowerPoint and open **20Aquatics_xx** or open ⊙ **21Aquatics**.
2. Save the presentation as **21Aquatics_xx**.
3. Your client wants a WordArt graphic included in the presentation that can also be used for the marketing campaign. Create the WordArt as follows:

   ■ Add a new slide at the end of the presentation with the Title Only layout and type the title **Proposed Logo**.
   ■ Insert WordArt using the Gradient Fill – Accent 4, Reflection style. Type the text **WORK THE WATER**.

   ■ On the Drawing Tools Format tab, display the Transform text effects, and apply the Wave 1 effect.
   ■ Display the Reflection effects and choose Half Reflection, touching.
   ■ With the WordArt placeholder selected, display the text fill options and apply the texture called Water droplets.

- Display the Format Text Effects dialog box (use the WordArt Styles dialog box launcher) and click Text Outline in the left column.
- Select the Solid line option, if necessary, and change the color to Blue, Accent 1, Lighter 40%.
- Position the WordArt in the center of the slide.

4. Display slide 1 and format the subtitle with a WordArt style of your choice.

5. You want to add to this slide a logo used on all Campus Recreation presentations.
- Open ⊙ **21Campus**.
- Copy the graphic object in the lower-left corner of the title slide.

- Paste the graphic on slide 1 of **21Aquatics_xx**. Note that the colors adjust to the current theme automatically. You want to maintain the original colors, so click the Paste Options button and select Keep Source Formatting. Your slide should look similar to Illustration A.

   ✓ *If the Paste Options button has already disappeared, delete the pasted graphic and re-paste it.*

6. Copy the logo graphic you just pasted and paste it on slide 3. Note that because you are pasting the element within the presentation, the Paste Options button does not appear.

7. Save your changes, close both presentations, and exit PowerPoint.

Illustration A

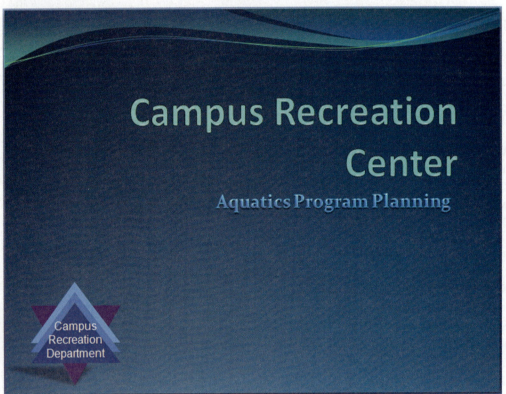

ON YOUR OWN

1. Start PowerPoint and open **OPP20_xx** or open OPP21.

2. Save the presentation as **OPP21_xx**.

3. Replace the title on slide 1 with a WordArt graphic that uses the same text as the title (*Restoration Architecture*). Format the WordArt as desired with a style, effect, color, and so on.

4. Position the WordArt above the subtitle.

5. Apply a WordArt style to the subtitle to make it stand out a bit more on the slide. Position both the title and subtitle to look attractive on the slide. Illustration A shows one combination of WordArt styles.

6. Save your changes, close the presentation, and exit PowerPoint.

Illustration A

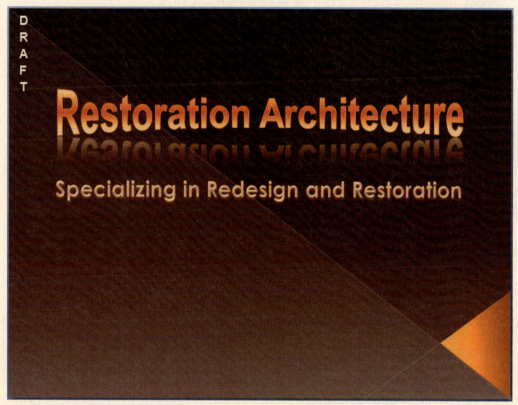

Skills Covered

Software Skills To fine-tune text on a slide, you can adjust the paragraph indent. Use tabs to align one or more lines of text on a slide.

Application Skills In this exercise, you begin work on a presentation for Yesterday's Playthings, a shop specializing in antique and collectible toys and games. You will adjust indents to improve the appearance of text on slides and use tabs to format a simple table of information.

TERMS

Hanging indent An indent in which the first line is not indented but all subsequent lines are indented.

Indent The amount of space a paragraph is set from the left edge of the placeholder.

Tab stops Incremental indents set for text so that each time you press the Tab key, the text indents to a set point.

NOTES

Adjust Paragraph Indent

■ An **indent** controls the amount of space between text and the left edge of the text's placeholder. You can adjust paragraph indents in PowerPoint just as you do in a word processing program such as Microsoft Word.

■ An indent may apply to an entire paragraph, to only the first line of the paragraph, or to all lines but the first line of the paragraph.

■ By default, bulleted text on a PowerPoint slide has a **hanging indent**. The first line is not indented, and subsequent lines indent and align under the first word of the paragraph.

■ If you turn off bullet formatting, the first line of the paragraph extends to the left margin of the place-holder and subsequent lines are indented, as shown in the following illustration.

Hanging indent applied to bulleted paragraphs

• A hanging indent has a first line that is not indented; subsequent lines are aligned on the first word of the paragraph

If the bullet formatting is turned off, the first line of the paragraph extends to the left margin of the placeholder

■ If you want to turn off bullet formatting to empha-size a paragraph of text (for example, to set a quo-tation by itself on a slide), you should adjust the indent to give your text a more professional appearance.

■ You have other indent options to choose from besides the default hanging indent.

 ● Apply a left indent to move an entire paragraph toward the right of the slide. You can use this indent in conjunction with a hanging indent to move a paragraph right and still maintain the hanging indent, as shown in the following illustration.

 ● Apply a first-line indent to indent only the first line of a paragraph, as shown in the following illustration. You generally apply this type of indent to a paragraph that does not have bullet formatting.

Left and first-line indents

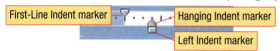

 • This paragraph has been indented 0.8 inches from the left margin and still has a hanging indent

 This paragraph has no bullet formatting and displays a first-line indent in which only the first line is indented

■ You have two options for adjusting indents: You can drag indent markers on the ruler, or you can specify the desired indent in the Paragraph dialog box.

■ The ruler displays indent markers for the currently selected paragraph, as shown in the following illustration.

Indent markers for a first-level bullet paragraph

First-Line Indent marker · · · · · · Hanging Indent marker
Left Indent marker

■ As you would expect, the First-Line Indent marker controls the indent of the first line of the paragraph. If it is to the left of the other indent markers, you have a hanging indent. If it is to the right of the other markers, you have a first-line indent.

■ The Hanging Indent marker (the upward-pointing marker) controls the indent of all lines of text following the first line.

■ The Left Indent marker (the rectangular marker below the Hanging Indent marker) controls both the First-Line Indent and the Hanging Indent markers. Dragging this marker will move the other two markers at the same time, maintaining their relative positions.

■ To adjust indents using the indent markers, simply drag them to the desired position on the ruler.

■ To adjust the indent of a single paragraph, click in the paragraph to position the insertion point and then make the adjustment. To adjust more than one paragraph, select the paragraphs and then adjust the indent.

■ The positions of the indent markers on the ruler are determined by the bullet level. If you click in a second-level bullet item, the markers look like the ones shown in the following illustration. Compare the position of the First-Line Indent marker with that for the first-level bullet markers in the previous illustration.

Indent markers for a second-level bullet paragraph

■ Using the ruler to set indents allows you to "eyeball" the indent positions. If you know the exact measurements you want to use for an indent, you can set them in the Paragraph dialog box.

■ Use the Indentation Before text and Special boxes in the Paragraph dialog box to set the amount of space before (to the left of) the first line and the indent type, such as First line or Hanging, as shown in the following illustration.

Specify an indent in the Paragraph dialog box

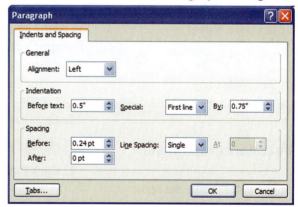

■ If you select a first-line or hanging indent, you must specify the amount of the indent in the By box. Choose (none) in the Special list if you want only a left indent.

Set Tab Stops

- You can set **tab stops** in a placeholder to control text position just as you would in a word processing document.

- Tab stops can be used to align text at the left, center, right, or on a decimal, as shown in the following illustration.

- By default, PowerPoint sets tab stops at 1 inch increments on the ruler. You can add tab stops where you need them by selecting a tab type from the tab selector and then clicking on the ruler.

- You can clear a tab by dragging the tab marker off of the ruler.

- Move a tab stop by dragging the marker to a new position.

- The previous illustration shows text aligned on a number of tab stops as a way of illustrating how tabs can be used. If you need to set up a number of columns and rows, however, you will find it easier to use a PowerPoint table.

  ✓ *Tables are discussed in Exercise 26 in the next lesson.*

Tab stops on the ruler control text on the slide

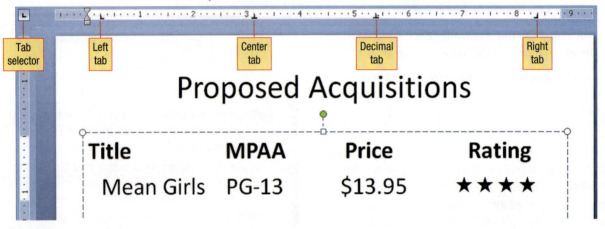

PROCEDURES

Display the Ruler

1. Click **View** tab .... Alt + W

   Show/Hide Group

2. Click **Ruler** .... R

Adjust Paragraph Indent

To adjust indent using the ruler:

1. Display the ruler and click in the paragraph to adjust or select multiple paragraphs.

2. Click and drag the appropriate indent marker on the ruler.

To adjust indent using the Paragraph dialog box:

1. Click in the paragraph to adjust or select multiple paragraphs.

2. Click **Home** tab .... Alt + H

   Paragraph Group

3. Click **Paragraph** dialog box launcher ▣ .... P , G

4. Click **Before text** .... Alt + R and type measurement or click increment arrow.

5. Click **Special** .... Alt + S

6. Select from Special list .... ↑ or ↓ , ↵Enter

7. Click **By** .... Alt + B if necessary and type measurement or click increment arrow.

8. Click OK .... ↵Enter

Set Tab Stops

1. Click in the paragraph for which you want to set tab stops, or select multiple paragraphs.

2. Display the ruler if necessary.

3. Click the **tab selector** ⌊ to the left of the ruler until the type of tab stop you want displays in the tab selector.

   - Left tab ⌊
   - Center tab ⊥
   - Right tab ⌐
   - Decimal tab ⊥

4. Click on ruler where tab stop should be positioned.

To delete a tab stop:
- Drag the tab stop marker off the ruler.

To adjust the position of the tab stop:
- Drag the tab stop marker on the ruler.

EXERCISE DIRECTIONS

1. Start PowerPoint and open 22Toys.
2. Save the presentation as **22Toys_xx**.
3. Display slide 4. Adjust indents as follows:
   - Turn off bullet formatting for all three bullet items in the content placeholder.
   - Remove the hanging indent for the first paragraph so that both lines align at the left margin.
   - Remove the hanging indent for the second paragraph and set a left indent of 0.5 inches.
   - Remove the hanging indent for the third paragraph and set a left indent of 1 inch.
4. Display slide 5. Remove the bullet formatting for all content items. Remove the hanging indent for the address information, but leave the hanging indent for the *On the Road* entries.
5. Display slide 6. In the content placeholder, turn off bullet formatting and remove the hanging indent. Insert the following tabular material.

Item	Originally	Sale Price
Keepsake marbles	$12.95	$8.95
Duncan yoyos	$15.50	$11.50
Vintage golf clubs	$35.00 – $75.00	$18.50 – $30.00

6. Set appropriate tabs to space the information attractively on the slide. Modify text formats of the table if desired (you may want to choose a different color for the column header items). Your table should look similar to Illustration A.
7. Save your changes, close the presentation, and exit PowerPoint.

Illustration A

Summer Show Specials . . .

Item	Originally	Sale Price
Keepsake marbles	$12.95	$8.95
Duncan yoyos	$15.50	$11.50
Vintage golf clubs	$35.00 - $75.00	$18.50 - $30.00

ON YOUR OWN

1. Start PowerPoint and open ⊙ **OPP22**.
2. Save the presentation as **OPP22_xx**.
3. Display slide 2. Remove bullet formatting from both paragraphs and adjust paragraph indents to improve the look of the slide.
4. Display slide 6. The second-level bullet items do not align neatly under the first-level bullet items. Adjust paragraph indents to solve this problem.
5. Display slide 7. Create a simple table that lists some sample goods you could contribute to a homeless or women's shelter. Illustration A shows a sample slide.
6. Save your changes, close the presentation, and exit PowerPoint.

Illustration A

Curriculum Connection: Science

Technology

In a school or office, many computer systems are networked together. This allows information to be shared among computers within the network. Yet as the ease of information sharing grows, there are increasing potentials for people to abuse network systems. For example, people can spy on others, pretend to be someone else, or steal personal information from others.

Identify Abuses

Create a PowerPoint presentation that identifies potential abuse and unethical uses of computers and networks. Explain how these abuses can affect a network in either a school or office setting.

Skills Covered

■ **Find and Replace Text**　　　　■ **Use the Reference Tools**

Software Skills　The Find and Replace features allow you to quickly locate and change text throughout a presentation. Use PowerPoint's reference tools to find synonyms, translate text, or locate online resources.

Application Skills　You continue working on the presentation for Yesterday's Playthings. In this exercise, you replace text and use the Thesaurus to finalize your presentation text.

TERMS

No new terms in this exercise.

NOTES

Find and Replace Text

■ In a slide show that consists of only a few slides, you may have no difficulty locating specific text. If your presentation has many slides, finding text can be time consuming.

■ And if you intend to replace the text you have found, you risk missing instances of the text if you simply scroll through the slides.

■ You can make the process of finding and replacing text more foolproof by using the Find and Replace options in the Editing group on the Home tab.

■ To simply find instances of a word or phrase, use the Find button to open the Find dialog box.

■ This feature functions the same way it does in a word processing program such as Microsoft Word: Type the text you want to find and then click the Find Next button.

■ PowerPoint searches the presentation and highlights the first instance that matches your text string, as shown in the following illustration.

Finding text using the Find dialog box

- You can save yourself some searching time by selecting options in the Find dialog box.

    - Select Match case to have PowerPoint search only for instances that match the exact capitalization of your search string.

    - Select Find whole words only to have PowerPoint find only complete words, not parts of words. You might select this option, for example, if you want PowerPoint to find only *the* and not *brother* or *therapeutic*.

- If you want to replace the text you have found, you can click the Replace... button in the Find dialog box to open the Replace dialog box, or click the Replace button on the Home tab if the Find dialog box is not already open.

- Specify the text to find, if necessary, and the replacement text, as shown in the following illustration, and then click the Find Next button to start the process.

Replace dialog box

- You have the same options in this dialog box for matching case and finding whole words. You can choose to replace an instance or replace all instances.

    ✓ *Replacing all instances can be risky unless you know your content well.*

- You can use Find and Replace in either the Slide pane or in the Outline tab of the Slides/Outline pane.

Use the Reference Tools

- The Proofing group on PowerPoint's Review tab contains a number of reference tools that can help you finalize a presentation.

- You have already used one of these tools, the spelling checker. Other tools you may find useful as you work on a presentation include the following.

    - The Research tool allows you to search for a word or phrase in a thesaurus, dictionary, or online reference site.

    - The Thesaurus lets you find synonyms and antonyms for a selected word.

- Translate allows you to translate a selected word or phrase into any of 14 languages.

- Use Language to specify the default language for the presentation. If a spelling dictionary is available for the chosen language, the presentation can be spell checked in that language.

- Of these tools, you may find the Thesaurus most useful. A thesaurus can help you replace overworked words with more interesting or specific ones.

- To use the Thesaurus, select a word in the presentation and then start the Thesaurus. It opens in a task pane as shown in the following illustration.

Thesaurus displays in the Research task pane

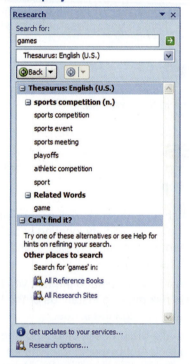

- To choose one of the suggested synonyms, point to one of the suggestions to display a down arrow at the right side of the pane and click Insert on the drop-down list.

- You can also choose to look up one of the suggestions by simply clicking it in the list. You then see synonyms for that word or phrase. Moving from word to word in this way, you can very often find a word or phrase that's exactly what you need.

PROCEDURES

Find and Replace Text

To find text:

1. Click **Home** tab .... Alt+H

   Editing Group

2. Click **Find** button 🔍 ...... F, D
3. Click in **Find what** box .... Alt+N
   and type search string.
   - Click **Match case** ...... Alt+C
     if desired to match capital-
     ization of search string
     exactly.
   - Click **Find whole words
     only** .... Alt+W
     if desired to find only whole
     words.
4. Click [Find Next] .... ↵Enter
   to find first instance.
5. Continue clicking [Find Next] to
   find additional instances.
6. Click [Close] to end process.

To replace text:

1. Click **Home** tab .... Alt+H

   Editing Group

2. Click **Replace** button 🔄 .... R
3. Click **Replace** .... R

   OR

   Click [Replace...] .... Alt+R
   in Find dialog box.
4. Click in **Find what** box ..... Alt+N
   and type search string.
5. Click in **Replace with**
   box .... Alt+P
   and type replacement string.
   - Click **Match case** ...... Alt+C
     if desired to match capital-
     ization of search string
     exactly.
   - Click **Find whole words
     only** .... Alt+W
     if desired to find only whole
     words.
6. Click [Find Next] .... ↵Enter
   to find first instance.
7. Click [Replace] .... Alt+R
   to replace instance.

   OR

   Click [Replace All] .... Alt+A
   to replace all instances.
8. Click [Close] to end process.

Use the Thesaurus

1. Select word for which you
   want to find a synonym.
2. Click **Review** tab .... Alt+R

   Proofing Group

3. Click **Thesaurus** button 📖 ...... E
4. Point to a word in the task
   pane you want to use as a
   synonym to display list arrow.
5. Click **Insert**.

To research a different word in the task pane:

- Click any word in the task
  pane results to see synonyms
  for that word.

EXERCISE DIRECTIONS

1. Start PowerPoint and open **22Toys_xx** or open
   ⊙ **23Toys**.
2. Save the presentation as **23Toys_xx**.
3. Find the first instance of the word *collector* in the
   presentation.
4. Choose to replace this word with the word
   collectible.
5. Replace each instance of *collector* with *collectible*,
   then close the Replace dialog box. Capitalize the
   word *collectible* that was replaced at the beginning
   of the third bullet on slide 2.

6. Display slide 3 and select the word *appreciated* in
   the second paragraph. Start the Thesaurus and
   replace the selected word with a more appropriate
   word.
7. Save your changes, close the presentation, and
   exit PowerPoint.

ON YOUR OWN

1. Start PowerPoint and open **OPP22_*xx*** or open ⊙ **OPP23**.
2. Save the presentation as **OPP23_*xx***.

3. Review the presentation to see if you can modify language in any way to make your meanings clearer.
   - You may want to replace some words throughout the presentation, such as *homeless* or *giving*. Illustration A shows a sample slide with the word *Homeless* replaced by a synonym.
   - Use the Thesaurus to find more meaningful words for some words in the presentation.
4. Save your changes, close the presentation, and exit PowerPoint.

Illustration A

Help the Dispossessed
- Many of our citizens are currently living on the streets
- Help our dispossessed citizens by donating your time, money, or goods
- Improve the quality of life for those who don't have a safe home

The Power of Giving   9/10/2007

Exercise | 24

Critical Thinking

Application Skills   Peterson Home Health Care has asked you to create a presentation that can be used at local health fairs to give viewers information about the company's home health care options. You will start work on that presentation in this exercise.

DIRECTIONS

1. Start PowerPoint and open ⊙**24Peterson**.
2. Save the presentation as **24Peterson_xx**.
3. Begin by creating new theme fonts for the presentation, using Corbel as the Heading font and Calibri as the Body font.
4. Make the following changes on slide 1:
   - Move the subtitle placeholder to the right to align at the right side with the title placeholder.
   - Change the alignment of both the title and subtitle to right alignment.
   - Adjust the height of the title placeholder so the top border of the placeholder is about the same distance above the first line of the title as the bottom border is below the last line of the title.
   - Apply a Quick Style format of your choice to the title placeholder.
5. On slides 2 and 3, the title has been mistakenly formatted with Top vertical alignment. Change the title alignment for these slides to Bottom.
6. On slide 2, remove the shadow formatting from the title and change the color to the Ice Blue, Accent 2, Darker 50% theme color.
7. Copy the title formats from slide 2 to the titles of slides 3–7.
8. Make the following changes to slide 2:
   - Remove bullet formatting from the three paragraphs in the content placeholder.
   - Remove the hanging indent on these three paragraphs.

- Center all three paragraphs.
- Change the font size to 32.
- Change the line spacing to 1.5.

9. On slide 3, change the bulleted paragraphs to numbered paragraphs. Choose a darker color for the numbers and increase their size to 90%.
10. Move the Long-term home care item to be second on the list. (You have not yet created the third item, so it is not included in this presentation.)
11. On slides 4, 5, and 7, change the bullet symbol to a different symbol, color, and size.

   ✓ *You may use one of the default symbols in the Bullets and Numbering dialog box or choose a new symbol by choosing to customize the bullets.*

12. On slide 4, insert a text box as follows:
   - Click to the left of the picture to insert the text box.
   - Change the text direction to rotate it 270 degrees.
   - Type the text **Gentle, professional home care**.
   - Adjust the position of the text box to leave room between it and the picture, and to be as tall as the picture. Apply a Quick Style of your choice and increase the font size so the text takes up more room in the text box. Your slide should look similar to Illustration A.
13. Copy the text box on slide 4 and paste it on slide 5. Delete the content placeholder behind the picture on the right side of slide 5. Change the text in the text box to read **Experienced nurses and helpers**.

14. On slide 6, turn off bullet and hanging indent formatting in the content placeholder and insert the following material, using tabs to space the columns of text:

	Hourly	Daily	Holidays
LPN	$18.50	$140.00	+$5.00/hour
RN	$25.00	$190.00	+$5.50/hour
Home helper	$9.50	$70.00	+$3.50/hour

15. Adjust the line spacing of the table so that there are 12 points of space after each line.

16. Reduce the height of the content placeholder to free up some space below the table. Create a text box that is about 6.5 inches wide below the table and type the following content:

   Fees listed above are sample rates that apply in many situations. Fees may vary according to personnel assigned, level of care required, amount of advance notice, and other circumstances. Please call to discuss your situation and we will provide you with a firm quote.

17. Format the text in the text box as follows:
   - Specify two columns with 0.2 inches of space between the columns.
   - Set margins to 0.2 inches on the left and right and 0.1 inch on the top and bottom.
   - Change the font to Calibri 20 point.
   - Italicize all text in the text box.
   - Apply a fill, outline, and effect of your choice to the text box.

18. On slide 7, indent the second, third, and fourth paragraph to make second-level bullet items.

19. Add a new slide with the Blank layout after slide 7 and insert a WordArt graphic using the text **Quality Home Care**.

20. Format the WordArt as desired by changing shape, fill, outline, and effect.

21. Find all instances of *prn* and replace them with **as needed**.

22. Use the Thesaurus to find a replacement for the word *Excellent* in the third paragraph on slide 2.

23. Print handouts with 4 slides per page.

24. Save your changes, close the presentation, and exit PowerPoint.

Illustration A

Curriculum Integration

Application Skills   For a global perspectives class, you have been asked to create a presentation giving information about a country in Europe. Your presentation should include statistics such as current population, largest cities, climate and terrain, currency, form of government, and so on. Before you begin this exercise, locate the following information:

■ A profile of a chosen country (the CIA World Factbook is a good place to start)

DIRECTIONS

Begin a new blank presentation and save it with an appropriate name, such as **25France_xx**. Create a title on the first slide using WordArt and format it as desired. Add a subtitle. Apply a theme, customizing theme colors and fonts if desired.

Add a slide with a Blank layout and insert a text box in which you give a brief history of your country. Use first-line indents to set off paragraphs of text. You may set the text in columns with appropriate margins and format the text box as desired. Add a vertical text box to the left of the history text box that includes the stacked text **HISTORY**. Adjust alignment, character spacing, and text box formats to make the stacked text look attractive. Illustration A shows an example.

Add a slide with an appropriate layout and use it to summarize the climate and terrain of your country. Use several levels of bullets as necessary, and use any symbols necessary to describe the country's features.

Add a slide to summarize information on your country's people. Insert the following information on the slide, using a tab to right align the number for each statistic at the right side of the placeholder.

■ Population
■ Median age
■ Population growth rate
■ Life expectancy (you may express this as total population or male and female, or all three)

Add a slide that lists in numeric order the five largest cities in your country, with their populations. Use number formatting for the list, and separate the city name from the population using tabs or an em dash (—) symbol. Indicate in a note on the slide if the population figure is for the city only or the city and suburbs. Adjust the size of the note text as desired. Adjust the line spacing of the list to 1.5.

Add a slide to summarize the country's government. Include the type of government, the branches of government, and any important information about each branch. Boldface each branch of the government.

Add a slide to summarize the country's economy. Include on this slide the currency, with its symbol, the chief exports and imports, and the gross domestic product (GDP) per capita.

Adjust formats for the slide titles of all slides except the first two slides and use the Format Painter to copy the formatting. Make any other changes to text formats that you wish to improve the look of the slides.

Save changes to the presentation and close it. Exit PowerPoint.

Illustration A

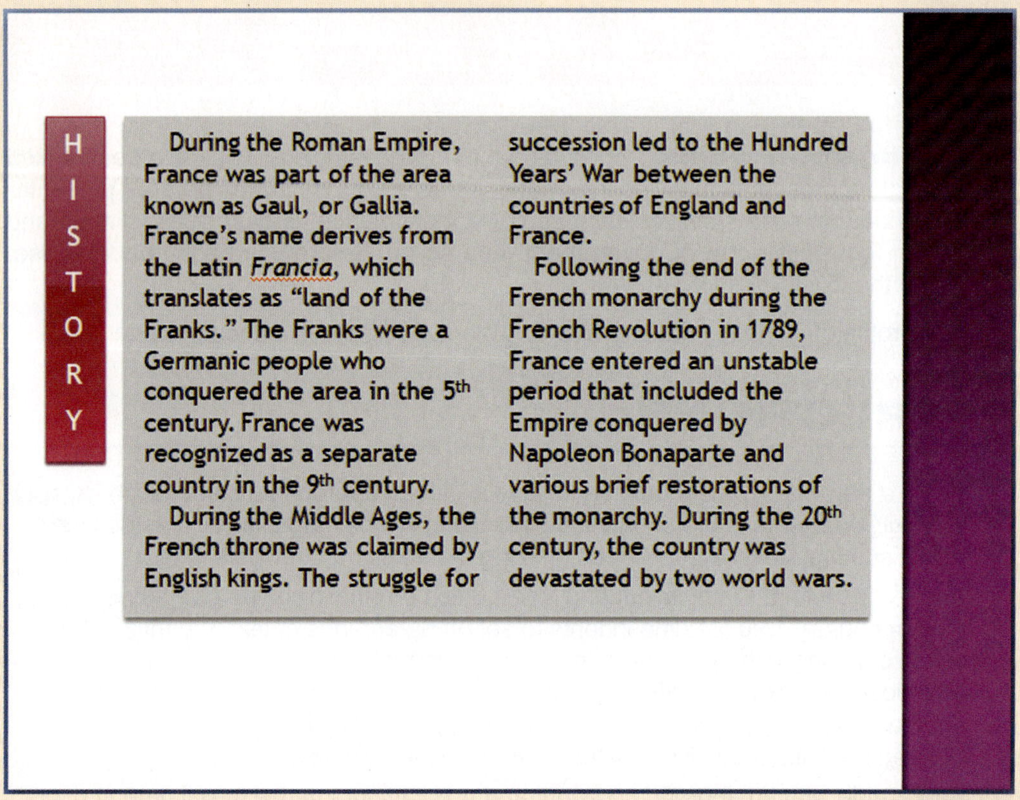

HISTORY

During the Roman Empire, France was part of the area known as Gaul, or Gallia. France's name derives from the Latin *Francia*, which translates as "land of the Franks." The Franks were a Germanic people who conquered the area in the 5th century. France was recognized as a separate country in the 9th century.

During the Middle Ages, the French throne was claimed by English kings. The struggle for succession led to the Hundred Years' War between the countries of England and France.

Following the end of the French monarchy during the French Revolution in 1789, France entered an unstable period that included the Empire conquered by Napoleon Bonaparte and various brief restorations of the monarchy. During the 20th century, the country was devastated by two world wars.

Lesson | 3

Work with Tables, Charts, and Diagrams

Skills Covered

- **Insert a Table**
- **Modify Table Layout**

- **Format a Table**
- **Add an Image to a Table**

Software Skills Use tables to organize data in a format that is easy to read and understand. You can restructure a table at any time by adding or deleting rows and columns. Table formats enhance visual interest and also contribute to readability. For additional interest, add an image to a table.

Application Skills In this exercise, you continue working on the presentation for the Campus Recreation Center. You insert and format two tables that list proposed programs and schedules and then modify and format the tables in a variety of ways.

TERMS

No new terms in this exercise.

NOTES

Insert a Table

- Use a table on a slide to organize information into rows and columns so it is easy for your audience to read and understand.

- You have several options for inserting a table on a slide:
  - Click the Insert Table icon in any content place-holder to display the Insert Table dialog box shown in the following illustration. After you select the number of columns and rows, the table structure appears on the slide in the content placeholder.

- Click the Table button on the Insert tab to display a grid that you can use to select rows and columns (see the following illustration). As you drag the pointer, the table columns and rows appear on the slide.

  ✓ *If you use this option on a slide that does not have a content layout, you may have to move the table to position it on the slide.*

Insert Table dialog box

Select columns and rows for a table

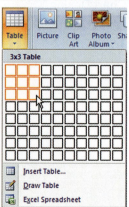

- Use the Draw Table command on the Table palette shown in the previous illustration to draw a table outline on a slide, as shown in the following illustration. You can then use the pointer to create the desired number of rows and columns by drawing them in the table outline.

Draw a table outline with the Draw Table pointer

- Note that the Table menu shown previously also allows you to access the Insert Table dialog box or insert an Excel worksheet to organize data. You'll learn more about using Excel worksheets in the next exercise.

- As soon as a table appears on a slide, the Table Tools contextual tabs become active on the Ribbon.

- You use the Table Tools Layout tab to restructure and control layout. Use the Table Tools Design tab to apply formats to a table.

- In the Table group, use the Select menu to quickly select the row or column of the currently active cell (the cell that contains the insertion point), or select the entire table. The View Gridlines button allows you to toggle gridlines off and on.

- The Rows & Columns group contains buttons that let you easily delete columns or rows, insert a row above or below the current row, or insert a column to the left or right of the current column.

- The Merge group contains buttons that let you merge cells (combine selected cells into one cell) or split cells (divide a selected cell into one or more rows or columns). The illustration below shows how merging works.

Merging cells

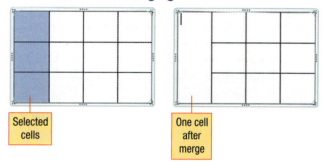

Selected cells

One cell after merge

Modify Table Layout

- The groups on the Table Tools Layout tab, shown in the following illustration, allow you to fine-tune table structure in a number of ways.

Table Tools Layout contextual tab

- Use the tools in the Cell Size group to specify exact height and width for a selected cell. The Distribute Rows and Distribute Columns buttons allow you to make all selected rows the same height or all selected columns the same width.

- The Alignment group provides a number of alignment options: You can align cell content both horizontally and vertically, change the text direction to rotate or stack it, and specify cell margins such as Narrow and Wide that adjust the amount of space around content in a cell.

- Use the Table Size group tools to specify an exact height and width for the table. If you select the Lock Aspect Ratio check box, any change you make to one dimension will resize the other dimensional proportionally.

- The Arrange group tools allow you to change the order of objects by moving them forward or backward. You will learn more about these tools in the next lesson.

- If you do not wish to enter specific measurements for cells and table size using the tools on the Table Tools Layout tab, you can adjust rows, columns, or the table itself by dragging borders. You can also drag the entire table to reposition it on the slide if necessary.

Format a Table

- The groups on the Table Tools Design tab, shown in the following illustration, give you a number of options for formatting a table.

- The check boxes in the Table Style Options group let you select parts of a table to receive special emphasis. Clicking the Header Row check box, for example, ensures that the first row of the table will have a fill and other formatting that make the row stand out. The Banded Rows and Banded Columns options will supply alternate fill colors for rows or columns to make it easy to differentiate content by row or column.

- The Table Styles group offers the Table Styles gallery of table formats that you can apply to an entire table with a single click. The Quick Styles in the gallery reflect the selections you have made in the Table Style Options group. As you select or deselect table style options, the Quick Styles change. The illustration below shows a portion of the Table Styles gallery.

Table Styles gallery

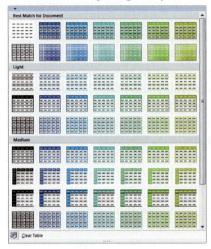

Table Tools Design contextual tab

- If you want to control styles yourself, you can use the Shading, Borders, and Effects buttons in the Table Styles group.

  - The Shading button allows you to select a color, picture, gradient, or texture fill for selected cells, or supply a background color or picture to fill the entire table.

  - The Borders button lets you select borders for any or all sides of a cell or table, including diagonal borders to split cells on the diagonal.

  - Use the Effects button to display categories of familiar effects such as Bevel, Shadow, and Reflection. Bevel effects can be applied to individual cells, but the Shadow and Reflection effects can be applied only to the entire table.

- Use the WordArt Styles group options to apply WordArt Quick Styles to text or modify WordArt text fill, outline, or effects. You can insert WordArt text in a table just as you would anywhere on a slide.

- The Draw Borders group contains tools you can use to draw a table (as you learned earlier) or borders in a table to create rows and columns.

  - Use the Pen Style, Pen Weight, and Pen Color tools to specify formats before you draw the table structure. You can also specify these formats after a table is created and use the Draw Table pointer to draw the formats on top of existing formats to change them.

  - Use the Eraser to remove any cell border in a table.

Add an Image to a Table

- You have several options for adding an image to a table: You can use the image as a background for a selected cell or cells, or you can use the image as the background for the entire table.

- To insert an image as the background for one or more selected cells, you can use the Picture command on the Shading palette to navigate to the image you want to insert. However, if you have selected more than one cell, the image is inserted into each cell, as shown in the following illustration.

Image inserted into selected cells

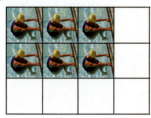

- This result is probably not what you have in mind, unless you wish to have multiple copies of an image in a table for a special effect.

- For better control over the process of adding an image to selected cells, use the Format Shape dialog box, shown in the following illustration.

Format Shape dialog box

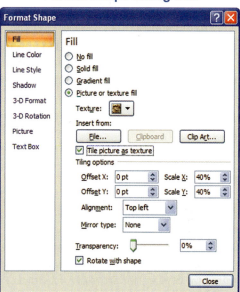

- When you select the Picture or texture fill option button in this dialog box, the controls below the option button become active, allowing you to select a texture from a palette of standard Office textures or insert a picture from a file or the Clip Organizer.

- You use the Tiling options to control how the image displays in selected cells. With the Tile picture as texture check box selected, you can specify how the image is positioned in the selection area and adjust the size of the image to better fit the area. The tiling options shown in the previous illustration result in the image shown in the following illustration.

Image stretched over selected cells

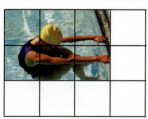

- If you want to use an image as a background for table cells, you can adjust transparency so that text can easily be read on top of the image background.

- You have the same general options when using an image as the background for an entire table. If you use the Table Background option on the Shading palette to insert a picture background, the image is spread out over all cells in the table, but you have no options for changing the position or transparency of the image.

- For best control of a table background image, select the cells in the table and use the Format Shape dialog box to insert and format the image.

- The following illustration shows a table background image that has a transparency of 58% to fade the image so it won't obscure text.

Background image with a transparency of 58%

- It can take some tweaking to get an image to fit the way you want in a table or table cells. You may need to adjust position and size and the table itself to keep from seeing multiple images tiled over the table. But the visual effect is worth the effort.

PROCEDURES

Insert a Table

Using any content placeholder:

1. Click **Insert Table** icon 🔲 in the content placeholder.
2. Type the number of columns.
3. Click **Number of rows** .... Alt+R and type number of rows.
4. Click ⬚ OK ⬚ .... ↵Enter

On any slide:

1. Click **Insert** tab .... Alt+N

   Tables Group

2. Click **Table** button 🔲 .... T

3. Drag the pointer over the grid or use arrow keys to select the desired number of columns and rows and then click or press ↵Enter to insert the table on the slide.

To draw table structure:

1. Click **Insert** tab .... Alt+N

   Tables Group

2. Click **Table** button 🔲 .... T
3. Click **Draw Table** .... D
4. Drag Draw Table pointer to create table outline.
5. Drag Draw Table pointer within outside border to create rows and columns.

Modify Table Layout

1. Click the table to select it.
2. Click **Table Tools Layout** tab .... Alt+J, L

To delete part of the table:

1. Select a portion of the table to delete.

   Rows & Columns Group

2. Click **Delete** button ❎ .... D
3. Select what to delete:
   - Click **Delete Columns** C
   - Click **Delete Rows** .... R

To insert a row or column:

1. Click in a table cell near where the new row or column should appear.

Rows & Columns Group

2. Click **Insert Above** button ⊞ .... Ⓥ to insert a row above the selected cell.

OR

■ Click **Insert Below** button ⊞ .... Ⓔ to insert a row below the selected cell.

OR

■ Click **Insert Left** button ⊞ .... Ⓛ to insert a column to the left of the selected cell.

OR

■ Click **Insert Right** button ⊞ .... Ⓘ to insert a column to the right of the selected cell.

To merge table cells:

1. Select the cells to merge.

Merge Group

2. Click **Merge Cells** button ⊞ ....Ⓜ

To distribute columns evenly:

1. Select a series of columns to distribute.

Cell Size Group

2. Click **Distribute Columns** button ⊞ .... Ⓤ, Ⓒ

To distribute rows evenly:

1. Select a series of rows to distribute.

Cell Size Group

2. Click **Distribute Rows** button ⊞ .... Ⓤ, Ⓡ

To change horizontal alignment:

1. Select text to align.

Alignment Group

2. Select desired alignment button:

■ **Align Text Left** ▤ .... Ⓐ, Ⓛ
■ **Center** ▤ .... Ⓐ, Ⓒ
■ **Align Text Right** ▤ .... Ⓐ, Ⓡ

To change vertical alignment:

1. Select text to align.

Alignment Group

2. Select desired alignment button:

■ **Align Top** ▤ .... Ⓞ
■ **Center Vertically** ▤ .... Ⓒ
■ **Align Bottom** ▤ .... Ⓑ

To change text direction:

1. Select table text to align.

Alignment Group

2. Click **Text Direction** button ▥ ▾ .... Ⓐ, Ⓧ

3. Select a text direction:

Horizontal .... Ⓗ
Rotate all text 90° .... Ⓡ
Rotate all text 270° .... Ⓞ
Stacked .... Ⓢ

To change cell margins:

1. Select table cell or cells.

Alignment Group

2. Click **Cell Margins** button ▥ .... Ⓝ

3. Select a margin option:

■ **Normal**.
■ **None**.
■ **Narrow**.
■ **Wide**.

To change table size:

1. Click anywhere in the table to size.

Table Size Group

2. Click **Table Height** button ▤ .... Ⓣ, Ⓗ and type new value or use spin arrow to set value.

OR

Click **Table Width** button ▤ .... Ⓣ, Ⓦ and type new value or use spin arrow to set value.

✓ *If Lock Aspect Ratio is selected, changing one dimension will automatically change the other a corresponding amount.*

Apply Table Formats

1. Click the table to select it.
2. Click **Table Tools Design** tab .... Ⓐⓛⓣ+Ⓙ, Ⓣ

To choose table style options:

1. Click in the table.

Table Style Options Group

2. Click check boxes to select portions of the table to receive special emphasis:

■ **Header Row** .... Ⓞ
■ **Total Row** .... Ⓙ
■ **Banded Rows** .... Ⓡ
■ **First Column** .... Ⓜ
■ **Last Column** .... Ⓝ
■ **Banded Columns** .... Ⓤ

To apply a Quick Style to an entire table:

1. Click in the table.

2. Click a thumbnail in the Table Styles gallery to apply it to the table.

   OR

1. Click **More** button ⊽ .... Ⓐ to view all available table styles.

2. Click a thumbnail to apply it to all slides. .... ←→↑↓, ↵Enter

To apply formats to selected cells:

- Click **Shading** button ▨▾ ...... Ⓗ and select a color, picture, gradient, or texture to fill table cells.

- Click **Borders** button ⊞▾ down arrow .... Ⓑ and select the desired border to apply to the current cell.

- Click **Effects** button ▨ .... Ⓕ and select from bevel, shadow, or reflection effects for the table.

Add an Image to a Table

To add an image to selected cells:

1. Select cells that will contain image.

2. Click **Table Tools Design** tab .... Alt+Ⓙ, Ⓣ

3. Click **Shading** button ▨▾ ...... Ⓗ

4. Click **P**icture .... Ⓟ

5. Navigate to location of picture and select picture.

6. Click ⟦ Insert ▾⟧ .... ↵Enter

OR

1. Select cells that will contain image.

2. Click **Home** tab .... Alt+Ⓗ

3. Click **Drawing** dialog box launcher ▣ .... Ⓞ

4. Click **P**icture or texture fill .... Alt+Ⓟ

5. Click ⟦ File... ⟧ .... Alt+Ⓕ

6. Navigate to location of picture and select picture.

7. Click ⟦ Insert ▾⟧ .... ↵Enter

8. Adjust the image position:

   - Click **Tile picture as texture** .... Alt+Ⓐ to spread the picture over all selected cells.

   - Adjust Offset measurements to move image horizontally or vertically from chosen alignment point.

   - Adjust Scale measurements to reduce image horizontally or vertically by a specified percentage from original size.

   - Choose an Alignment option to set the point at which the image aligns in the selected cells.

   - Drag the Transparency slider to make image increasingly transparent

9. Click ⟦ Close ⟧ .... ↵Enter

To add an image as a background for the entire table:

1. Select the table by clicking anywhere in it.

2. Click **Table Tools Design** tab .... Alt+Ⓙ, Ⓣ

3. Click **Shading** button ▨▾ ...... Ⓗ

4. Click **Table Background** .... Ⓑ

5. Click **P**icture .... Ⓟ

6. Navigate to location of picture and select picture.

7. Click ⟦ Insert ▾⟧ .... ↵Enter

   OR

1. Select all cells in the table.

2. Click **Home** tab .... Alt+Ⓗ

3. Click **Drawing** dialog box launcher ▣ .... Ⓞ

4. Click **P**icture or texture fill .... Alt+Ⓟ

5. Click ⟦ File... ⟧ .... Alt+Ⓕ

6. Navigate to location of picture and select picture.

7. Click ⟦ Insert ▾⟧ .... ↵Enter

8. Adjust the image position:

   - Click **Tile picture as texture** .... Alt+Ⓐ to spread the picture over all selected cells.

   - Adjust Offset measurements to move image horizontally or vertically from chosen alignment point.

   - Adjust Scale measurements to reduce image horizontally or vertically by a specified percentage from original size.

   - Choose an Alignment option to set the point at which the image aligns in the selected cells.

   - Drag the Transparency slider to make image increasingly transparent

9. Click ⟦ Close ⟧ .... ↵Enter

EXERCISE DIRECTIONS

1. Start PowerPoint and open 🔘 **26Aquatics**.

2. Save the presentation as **26Aquatics_xx**.

3. In PowerPoint, display slide 3 and then insert a Title and Content slide. Insert the title **Proposed Programs**.

4. Choose to create a table with four columns and seven rows. Then insert the table text shown in Illustration A.

5. Adjust the first column width to display all entries on single lines. Then distribute the remaining three columns evenly. Center all entries in all columns except the first.

6. Insert a row above the first row. In the second cell of the new row, type **Will Likely Appeal To . . .**

7. Merge the second, third, and fourth cell in the first row. Remove the shading in the first cell of the first row.

8. Turn on the First Row table style option and turn off all other styles except Header Row. Then apply a different Quick Style of your choice from the Table Styles gallery.

   ✓ *You may remove the fill from the first table cell in the first row if desired.*

9. Create another new slide using the Title Only layout. Insert the title **Proposed Pool Schedule**.

10. Use the Table button on the Insert tab to insert a table with four columns and eight rows. Then insert two more rows at the bottom of the table.

11. Resize the table and its columns as follows:
    - Size the first column to 0.7 inches.
    - Size the second column to 2.3 inches.
    - Size the third column to 2.2 inches.
    - Size the fourth column to 2 inches.

12. Insert the data shown in Illustration B in columns 2–4.

13. Select the row that contains the entry for Masters swimming and insert a 3 point black top border.

    ✓ *Hint: Select the 3 pt option in the Pen Weight palette before applying the border style.*

14. Select the four cells in the first column that are above the border and merge them. (Do not include the first table cell in the first row.) Then merge the five cells in the first column below the border.

15. In the merged cell above the border, rotate text direction 270 degrees and type **MORNING**. In the merged cell below the border, rotate text direction 270 degrees and type **AFTERNOON**.

16. Boldface the rotated text and apply center vertical and horizontal alignment.

17. Add an image as a background for some of the table cells as follows:
    - Select all cells except the first row and first column cells.
    - Open the Format Shape dialog box and choose to insert a picture fill.
    - Navigate to the data files and select 🔘 **26Swimmer**.
    - Choose to tile the picture. Make sure the Scale values are both 100%, and then change the Offset X value to 40 pt. The image should now fit neatly in the selected cell area.
    - Change transparency to 70%.

18. Adjust the colors of the first row and column if desired, and move the table so it sits below the slide title.

19. Save your changes, close the presentation, and exit PowerPoint.

Illustration A

	Students	Faculty/Staff	Community
Youth swim lessons		X	X
Adult swim lessons	X	X	X
Youth stroke clinic		X	X
Lifeguarding course	X		X
Masters swim team			X
Aquacize	X	X	X

Illustration B

Program	Weekdays	Weekends
Swim team	530 – 700	
Open swimming	700 – 900	600 - 1200
Classes	900 – 1100	
Aquacize	1100 – 1200 M W F	
Masters swimming	1200 – 230 T Th	1100 – 1230 S
Open swimming	230 – 330	1230 - 500
Adult lessons	300 - 430	
Youth lessons	400 - 530	230 – 400 S
Water Power	500 – 630 M W F	

ON YOUR OWN

1. Start PowerPoint and open ⊙**OPP26**.

2. Save the presentation as **OPP26_xx**.

3. Add a new slide at the end of the presentation with the Title Only slide layout. Insert the title **Planning Services Price List.**

4. Insert the table shown in Illustration A using the Table button on the Insert tab.

5. Adjust column widths to display all text on single lines. Change the table's width and height so text does not seem crowded.

6. You have decided to stop offering services for Zone 4. Delete the Zone 4 column.

7. Apply a different table style, and choose different table style options.

8. Center the entries in the last three columns, and position the table attractively on the slide.

9. Save your changes, close the presentation, and exit PowerPoint.

Illustration A

Service	Zone 1	Zone 2	Zone 3	Zone 4
Permits	$100	$250	$150	NA
Site Study	$1,500	$2,250	$3,000	$1,500
Planning	$60/hour	$70/hour	$85/hour	$60/hour
Design	$125/hour	$150/hour	$300/hour	$200/hour

Exercise | 27

Skills Covered

■ **Create an Excel Worksheet on a Slide**

■ **Insert an Existing Data File**

■ **Use Paste Special to Embed or Link Data**

Software Skills In the last exercise, you learned how to use tables to organize information on a slide. Another way to organize data is to create an Excel worksheet right on a slide or link worksheet data from Excel. Linked data updates on the slide when it is changed in the original worksheet. You can paste, embed, or link other materials from other Office applications to add content to slides.

Application Skills In this exercise, you continue working on the presentation for the Campus Recreation Center. You insert data from an Excel worksheet, and then link and update Excel data on another slide.

TERMS

Embed Insert data into a destination application from a source application so that you can edit it using the source application's tools.

Link Insert data into a destination application from a source application so that a link exists between the source and the destination data.

NOTES

Create an Excel Worksheet on a Slide

■ If you want to show data that may need to be calculated or otherwise manipulated, you can create an Excel worksheet object on a PowerPoint slide. You have two options for creating a worksheet on a slide: the Excel Spreadsheet command on the Table menu and the Insert Object dialog box.

■ Use the Excel Spreadsheet option on the Table menu to create a new worksheet object on a slide. This option displays a blank Excel worksheet as shown in the following illustration.

New Excel worksheet on a slide

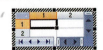

■ The worksheet object displays a diagonal-line or hatched border that indicates the object is **embedded** on the slide.

■ The Insert Object button on the Insert tab opens the Insert Object dialog box, shown in the following illustration. You can use this dialog box to select from a list of objects you might want to create on a slide, including an Excel Worksheet.

Insert Object dialog box

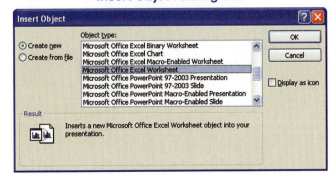

- The worksheet object inserted with the Excel Spreadsheet command is quite small, containing only four visible cells. If you use the Insert Object dialog box to insert a worksheet, you have many more rows and columns to work with.

- You can drag a sizing handle to display more worksheet cells or hide cells you don't need. The following illustration shows how to drag to reveal more cells in the worksheet.

Drag a handle to display more cells in the worksheet

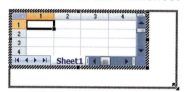

- When you enter text in an Excel worksheet you have inserted using either of these methods, you are actually working in Excel, so you can use all of Excel's features to calculate, manipulate, and format data.

- When you have finished working with the worksheet, click outside it on the slide to close the object. To modify data in the worksheet, double-click on the object to open it for editing in Excel.

- Clicking outside the worksheet displays a heavy light-blue selection border such as the one that surrounds any PowerPoint table. You can resize the embedded object by dragging a corner handle of this border.

Insert an Existing Data File

- If the data you want to display on the slide already exists as a file, you can insert the file on the slide using the Insert Object dialog box's Create from file option. This option displays the dialog box shown in the following illustration. You use the Browse button to navigate to the file you want to insert on the slide.

Browse for an existing file

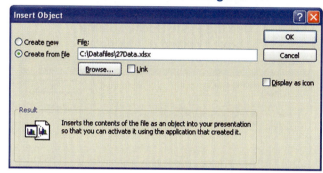

- Inserting data this way embeds the file on the slide so that you can work with the data using the tools from the file's original application. The embedded data is surrounded by a heavy blue selection border on the slide. To edit the object in its original application, double-click the object.

- Note that this feature inserts the entire file, or, in the case of Excel, an entire worksheet, on your slide. If you want only a portion of the data, you should use the Paste Special option discussed in the next section.

- You can also choose to **link** a file you insert using the Insert Object dialog box by clicking the Link check box in the dialog box.

- A linked file maintains a relationship between the inserted object and the original so that when the original file is modified, the object on the slide shows the same changes.

- If you double-click a linked object to edit it, the original file opens in its source application. You make all edits in the original file, rather than on the PowerPoint slide.

Use Paste Special to Embed or Link Data

- If you do not want to insert an entire file on a slide, you can use the Copy and Paste Special commands to embed or link only a selection of data from another application.

- After you copy the data in another application—for example, Word, Excel, or even Access in the Office 2007 suite—you use the Paste Special command on the Paste menu to open the dialog box shown in the following illustration.

Use the Paste Special dialog box to embed or link data

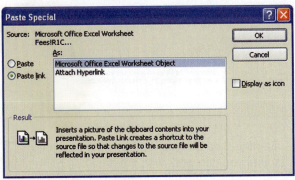

- If you choose the Paste option, the copied data is embedded on the slide and you can edit it using the tools of the original application.

- If you choose the Paste link option, the data is linked to the original file. Any change you make to the original data will also appear on the slide.

- The Paste Special dialog box offers different ways to paste data depending on the application in which the data was copied. Here are some of the options you have when pasting Office 2007 application data:

  - Data copied in Excel can be pasted in a variety of formats, including Microsoft Office Excel Worksheet Object, HTML Format, several picture formats, and Formatted Text (RTF) format. If you choose to paste link, you can select Microsoft Office Excel Worksheet Object or create a hyperlink from the data that will take the viewer directly to the Excel file during a presentation.

  - Data copied from Word, such as a Word table or a paragraph of text, can be pasted as a Microsoft Office Word Document Object, in HTML format, as a picture, and as formatted or unformatted text. The only option available for paste linking is Microsoft Office Word Document Object.

  - You can copy data from an Access table, or copy the entire table object and paste the data in HTML format or as formatted or unformatted data. You cannot paste link an Access table.

PROCEDURES

Insert an Excel Worksheet

To insert a blank worksheet:
1. Click **Insert** tab................. Alt + N

   Tables Group

2. Click **Table** button ▦ .... T
3. Click **Excel Spreadsheet** X

To insert an existing file:
1. Click **Insert** tab................. Alt + N

   Text Group

2. Click **Object** button 🗒 .... J
3. Click **Create from file** .... Alt + F
4. Click Browse... .... Alt + B
5. Navigate to the location of the file and select it.
6. Click OK .... ↵Enter
7. Click OK .... ↵Enter

Resize a Worksheet

To crop unnecessary blank cells:
1. Double-click worksheet object if necessary to display diagonal line border.
2. Click on handle in bottom center of border and drag upward to crop any blank cells below data.
3. Click on handle in center of right border and drag to the left to crop any blank cells to the right of data.
4. Click outside the worksheet.

To resize the worksheet object:

1. Click once on the worksheet object to display the thick light blue container border.
2. Click on the lower-right corner and drag to resize the entire container without distorting text in worksheet.

Insert or Edit Data in a Worksheet

1. Double-click the worksheet object to display the diagonal line border and the Excel Ribbon.
2. Type or edit text as you would in Excel.

Use Paste Special to Embed or Link Data

1. In the source application, select the data you want to paste or paste link.
2. Click **Home** tab .... Alt + H

Clipboard Group

3. Click **Copy** button 🗐 C
4. In PowerPoint, display the slide where the copied data will appear.
5. Click **Home** tab .... Alt + H

Clipboard Group

6. Click **Paste** button 🗐 down arrow V
7. Click **Paste Special** .... S
8. Click **Paste** .... Alt + P

   OR

   Click **Paste link** .... Alt + L
9. Select format for pasted data .... Alt + A, ↑, ↓
10. Click [OK] .... ↵Enter

EXERCISE DIRECTIONS

1. Start PowerPoint and open **26Aquatics_xx** or ⊙**27Aquatics**.
2. Save the presentation as **27Aquatics_xx**.
3. In Word, open ⊙**27Classes** and save the file as **27Classes_xx** in the same location that you saved the presentation file. In Excel, open ⊙**27Linkdata** and save it as **27Linkdata_xx** in the same location that you saved the presentation file. Close both files and their applications.
4. In PowerPoint, display slide 5 and then insert a Title Only slide. Insert the title **Program Details**.
5. Insert the existing Word file **27Classes_xx** on the slide. Open the document for editing and center values in all columns except the first.
6. Click outside the embedded document, then click on it and resize it to enlarge it somewhat on the slide. Position it attractively on the slide.

   ✓ *The text may look somewhat "fuzzy" on the slide, but it should look clear when viewed in Slide Show view.*

7. Add another new slide and insert the title **Fee Structure**.
8. Open **27Linkdata_xx** in Excel and copy the cells in the range A1:F6. Note that the parking fees have not yet been decided so these cells are empty.

9. Use Paste Special to paste link the copied data on the PowerPoint slide. Position the worksheet data attractively on the slide and adjust the size of the object container as desired.
10. You now have the parking fees. Switch to Excel and enter the following amounts in the Excel worksheet:

Parttime/Graduate Students	**10**
Faculty/Employees	**15**
Alumni	**18**
Community	**24**

11. On the Excel View tab, deselect the Gridlines options so gridlines do not show on the worksheet. Save and close the Excel worksheet. You should see the updated parking and total fees on the slide in PowerPoint, as shown in Illustration A. Note that the gridlines have disappeared to improve the look of the data on the slide.
12. Save your changes, close the presentation, and exit PowerPoint.

Fee Structure

	Membership		Parking/ Month	Monthly Total	Yearly Total
	Monthly	Yearly			
Parttime/Graduate Students	$20	$200	$10	$30	$320
Faculty/Employees	$40	$440	$15	$55	$620
Alumni	$50	$560	$18	$68	$776
Community	$60	$680	$24	$84	$968

ON YOUR OWN

1. Start PowerPoint and open **OPP26_xx** or  **OPP27**.
2. Save the presentation as **OPP27_xx**.
3. Add a new slide at the end of the presentation with the Title Only slide layout. Insert the title **Sample Costs by Style.**
4. Use the Excel Spreadsheet command on the Table button on the Insert tab to insert a new worksheet on the slide.
5. Enlarge the worksheet to show columns A through E and rows 1 through 6. Enter the data shown in Illustration A in the worksheet.
6. In the Total row, use Excel's Sum button to total the amounts for each style of house.

7. On Excel's Page Layout tab, click the Theme button and apply the Verve theme so the data in the worksheet matches the font of the presentation. Change the Theme Colors to those for Trek.
8. On Excel's Home tab, use the Cell Styles gallery to format the worksheet headings as desired. You may wish to fill cells with a background color using the Fill Color palette on Excel's Home tab so the black text shows up on the slide.
9. Change the font size of all text in the worksheet to 18 point and then adjust column widths to show all data. Adjust alignments as desired to display the data attractively. Illustration B shows one formatting option.
10. Save your changes, close the presentation, and exit PowerPoint.

Illustration A

	Victorian	Tudor	Arts & Crafts	Modernist
Permits	$100	$100	$100	$100
Site Study	$1,500	$1,500	$1,500	$1,500
Planning	$1,500	$1,500	$1,250	$1,300
Design	$5,000	$5,000	$4,500	$3,500
Total				

Illustration B

Sample Costs by Style

	Victorian	Tudor	Arts & Crafts	Modernist
Permits	$100	$100	$100	$100
Site Study	$1,500	$1,500	$1,500	$1,500
Planning	$1,500	$1,500	$1,250	$1,300
Design	$5,000	$5,000	$4,500	$3,500
Total	$8,100	$8,100	$7,350	$6,400

Exercise | 28

Skills Covered

- **Insert a Chart**
- **Modify Chart Design**
- **Modify Chart Layout**
- **Format a Chart**

Software Skills Add charts to a presentation to illustrate data in a graphical way that is easy to understand. Charts can be modified or formatted as needed to improve the display.

Application Skills In this exercise, you continue working on the presentation for the Campus Recreation Center. You insert a chart to show results of a usage survey.

TERMS

Data series The information in a worksheet column that is represented on a chart by a marker such as a column, bar, or line.

X axis The horizontal scale of a chart on which categories are plotted.

Y axis The vertical scale of a chart on which the value of each category is plotted.

NOTES

Insert a Chart

- You can add a chart to your presentation to illustrate data in an easy-to-understand format or to compare and contrast sets of data.

- In PowerPoint 2007, you create a chart using Excel 2007 if Excel is installed on your system. If you do not have Excel, charts are created using Microsoft Graph as in past versions of PowerPoint.

- Excel charts are *embedded* in PowerPoint. As you learned in the previous exercise, an embedded object becomes part of the destination file and can be edited using the source destination's tools. When you insert a chart in PowerPoint, you work with Excel's charting tools.

- You can insert a chart into a content slide layout or add it without a placeholder using the Chart button on the Insert tab.

- Your first task in creating a chart is to choose the chart type. The Insert Chart dialog box, shown in the following illustration, displays after you issue the command to insert a chart.

Insert Chart dialog box

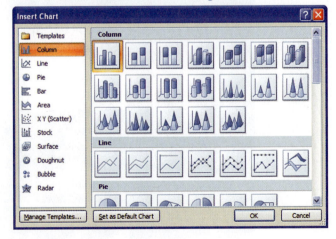

- The default chart type is a two-dimensional Clustered Column. You can, however, choose from several chart formats, including line, pie, bar, area, scatter, stock, surface, doughnut, bubble, and radar.

- Note that most chart types offer both two-dimensional and three-dimensional styles. Although choosing one over the other is largely a matter of personal preference, you should know that some formatting options are available only for two-dimensional styles.

- After you select a chart type and style, Excel opens in a split window with sample data. The chart associated with that sample data displays on the PowerPoint slide, as shown in the following illustration.

- You can type replacement data in the worksheet. As you change the data, the chart adjusts on the slide. You can save the Excel worksheet data for the chart and then close the worksheet to work further with the chart on the slide.

- Note the blue selection outline around the data in the Excel worksheet. This outline encloses the cells that are used to create the chart.

- If you do not need all the columns and rows provided in the sample data, you can delete them by selecting and pressing Del. But you must then drag the selection outline to enclose the remaining cells, or the empty columns and rows will be plotted on the chart.

Sample chart data displays in Excel window and on PowerPoint slide

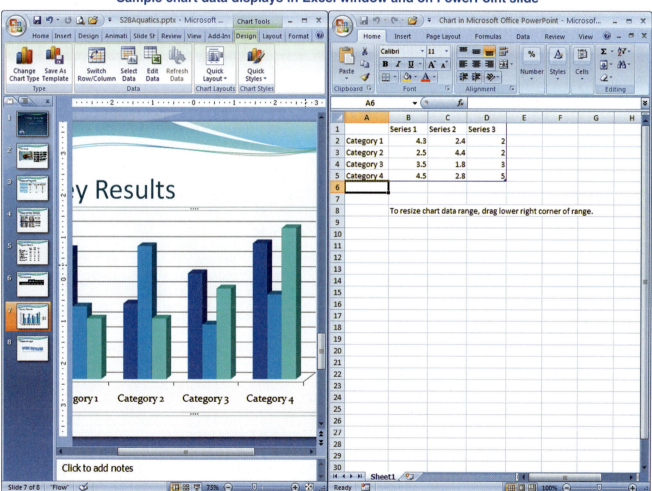

- Likewise, if you add more rows and columns of data in Excel than appear in the sample worksheet, you may need to drag the selection outline to enclose all cells with data to make sure they plot on the PowerPoint chart.

- PowerPoint sets up the chart feature for you to enter the data you want to use to plot the chart. You can use existing Excel data by copying the data and pasting it into the chart worksheet. You can also open an existing workbook and use the Select Data button (discussed in the next section) to choose the data range to chart.

- When you have finished working with a chart, click outside the chart object container to close it. You can reposition the chart by dragging the light blue outline to a new location on the slide. Delete a chart by pressing Del while the chart is selected.

- A chart created with default design, layout, and format may be perfectly adequate for your needs. To fine-tune a chart's appearance, use the three contextual tabs available for charts: Chart Tools Design, Chart Tools Layout, and Chart Tools Format. Options on these tabs are discussed in the following sections.

Modify Chart Design

- The groups on the Chart Tools Design tab, shown in the following illustration, allow you to make changes to the overall appearance of a chart.

- Use the Change Chart Type button in the Type group to open the Change Chart Type dialog box, which is virtually identical to the Insert Chart dialog box. Select a new chart type to immediately apply that type to the current chart.

  ✓ *Use caution when changing the chart type. Not all charts are interchangeable, and changing a column chart, for example, to a pie chart can result in an unusable chart.*

- The Save As Template button in the Type group allows you to save your current chart layout and formats as a template you can apply to other charts. You can apply these templates by opening the Templates folder in the Insert Chart or Change Chart Type dialog box.

- The Data group contains buttons for modifying the data used to create the chart.

  - Switch Row/Column allows you to change the direction the data is plotted, so that data that was plotted on the **X axis** (the horizontal axis) will instead be plotted on the **Y axis** (the vertical axis), and vice versa. This button is not active unless the Excel chart data worksheet is open.

  - Select Data allows you to specify the data range for the chart. This option is useful if you want to plot data from a worksheet other than the default chart worksheet.

Chart Tools Design tab

- Click the Edit Data button if you want to open the Excel data worksheet to make changes to the data. As you change the data in the chart worksheet, the PowerPoint chart on the slide changes to reflect the edit.
  - Click Refresh Data to update the chart after changes have been made to the data.
- The Chart Layouts gallery, shown in the following illustration, contains preformatted layouts with various combinations of layout elements and formats. Applying one of these layouts can minimize the time it might take to customize a default chart layout.

Chart Layouts gallery

- The Chart Styles gallery allows you to apply Quick Styles to the chart to modify colors of the **data series** markers and the chart background.

Modify Chart Layout

- Use tools on the Chart Tools Layout tab to customize a chart by choosing what chart elements to display.
- Before you can appreciate the tools on this tab, you should know the elements that make up a chart. The following illustration shows common chart elements.

Common chart elements

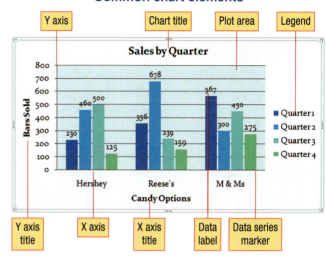

- The groups on the Chart Tools Layout tab, shown in the following illustration, make it easy to select these chart elements and apply very specific options for each element to speed the process of changing a chart's layout.

Chart Tools Layout tab

- Use the tools in the Current Selection group to select a specific chart element.
  - The Chart Elements drop-down list allows you to select a specific chart element, such as the plot area or the legend.
  - The Format Selection button opens a dialog box where you can find options for formatting the current selection.
  - The Reset to Match Style button lets you restore the theme styles if you have, for example, applied a color that is not part of the current theme.
- The Insert group buttons let you add a picture, shape, or text box to a chart.
- The Labels group provides buttons for chart elements that act as labels, such as the chart title or the axis titles. Clicking any of these buttons displays a menu of options for turning on or off the label and positioning it. The menu usually also includes a More Options command that opens a dialog box you can use to fine-tune the label format.
- The Axes group buttons let you choose view options for the horizontal and vertical axes and choose how to display the chart's gridlines.
- The Background group buttons control the appearance of the area behind the data series markers. These options vary according to whether the chart is 2-D or 3-D.
- The Analysis group contains buttons that control lines you add to charts to show trends and other lines and bars that help you to analyze plotted data. These options are not available in a 3-D chart.

- As you adjust the chart layout using the buttons on this tab, the chart immediately changes to reflect options you have turned on or off.

Format a Chart

- The groups on the Chart Tools Format tab, shown in the following illustration, contain tools that should be familiar to you from previous exercises.
- To make it easy to format a specific chart element, use the Chart Elements list in the Current Selection group to select a desired element.
- You can also simply click an element to select it. If you are selecting a data series marker, the first click selects all markers for that series, and a second click selects only that marker.
- You can then apply a Quick Style; apply fill, outline, or effect options; apply WordArt styles to selected text; change the arrangement of objects in the chart; and resize the chart precisely.
- The formatting options on this tab work the same way as when you apply them to text boxes or table elements.
- You can also use text formatting options on the Home tab to modify font, font size, font style, or font color and paragraph formatting options to adjust alignment.
- You can select text in a chart by clicking to display the text box. Clicking some items, such as data labels, will select all labels for that data series.

Chart Tools Format tab

PROCEDURES

Insert a Chart

1. Click **Insert Chart** icon 📊 in any content placeholder.

   OR

   a. Click **Insert** tab .... Alt + N
   b. Click **Insert Chart** button 📊 C

2. Select the desired chart type.
3. Click [OK] .... ↵Enter
4. Modify sample data in Excel by retyping or pasting existing data.
5. Close the Excel worksheet.

Modify Chart Design

To change chart type:

1. Click the chart to select it.
2. Click **Chart Tools Design** tab .... Alt + J , C

   Type Group

3. Click **Change Chart Type** button 📊 .... C to display a gallery of chart types.
4. Select a new chart type.
5. Click [OK] .... ↵Enter

To switch rows and columns:

1. Click the chart to select it, and open the Excel worksheet if it is not already open.
2. Click **Chart Tools Design** tab .... Alt + J , C

   Data Group

3. Click **Switch Row/Column** button 📊 .... W

To select data to chart:

1. Click the chart to select it.
2. Click **Chart Tools Design** tab .... Alt + J , C

   Data Group

3. Click **Select Data** button 📊 ..... E to open the Select Data Source dialog box.
4. Click on worksheet and select the desired data range.
5. Click [OK] .... ↵Enter

To edit the Excel data:

1. Click the chart to select it.
2. Click **Chart Tools Design** tab .... Alt + J , C

   Data Group

3. Click **Edit Data** button 📊 .... D to redisplay the Excel worksheet.
4. Modify data as desired and then close the worksheet.

To change chart layout:

1. Click the chart to select it.
2. Click **Chart Tools Design** tab .... Alt + J , C

   Chart Layouts Group

3. Click **More** button 🔽 .... L to view all available layout styles.

   OR

   Click **Quick Layout** button 📊 .... L if More button is not visible.

4. Click a layout to select and apply it.

To change chart style:

1. Click the chart to select it.
2. Click **Chart Tools Design** tab .... Alt + J , C

   Chart Styles Group

3. Click **More** button 🔽 .... S to view all available chart styles.

   OR

   Click **Quick Styles** button 📊 .... S if More button is not visible.

4. Click a chart style to select and apply it.

Modify Chart Layout

1. Click the chart to select it.
2. Click **Chart Tools Layout** tab .... Alt + J , A
3. Select the chart element to modify.
4. Click the button that offers options for modifying the selected element.
5. Click an option from the button's menu to select and apply it.

Modify Chart Format

1. Click the chart to select it.
2. Click **Chart Tools Format** tab .... Alt + J , O
3. Select the chart element to format.
4. Use the Shape Styles and WordArt Styles buttons as directed in previous exercises.

EXERCISE DIRECTIONS

1. Start PowerPoint and open **27Aquatics_xx** or **28Aquatics**. If you are prompted to update links, click Cancel.

2. Save the presentation as **28Aquatics_xx**.

3. Display slide 7 and then insert a Title and Content slide. Insert the title **Survey Results**.

4. Choose to create a chart using the 3-D Clustered Column chart type. Replace the sample data with the following data:

	Never	1 to 3	4 to 6	Every Day
Students	10	57	25	8
Faculty	18	60	15	7
Staff	25	48	13	14
Community	38	29	26	7

✓ Note that this data has more columns and rows than the sample data. The range should automatically adjust as you enter the data.

5. Switch rows and columns. If you find the *Every Day* data is missing from the chart, use the Select Data button to specify the correct rows and columns. Then close the Excel worksheet.

6. Change the layout to Layout 3 and the style to style 26.

7. Type the title **Visits per Week**.

8. Change the chart type to Clustered Cylinder.

9. Choose to edit the data and change the Students value for *1 to 3* to **47** and the value for *Every Day* to **18**. Close the worksheet.

10. On the Chart Tools Layout tab, select the Gridlines option, select primary vertical gridlines, and then choose to display major gridlines.

11. On the Chart Tools Format tab, use the Chart Elements list to select the Chart Area. Format this area as follows:

    ■ Choose to fill the shape with the lightest gray in the Shape Fill palette (White , Background 1, Darker 5%).

    ■ Apply an outline using a 1 1/2 pt weight and a dark gray color.

    ■ Apply a Shadow effect of your choice to the selected element. Your slide should look similar to Illustration A.

12. Save your changes, close the presentation, and exit PowerPoint.

Illustration A

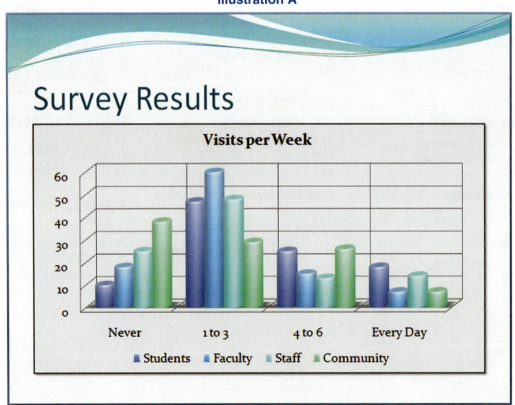

ON YOUR OWN

1. Start PowerPoint and open **OPP27_xx** or 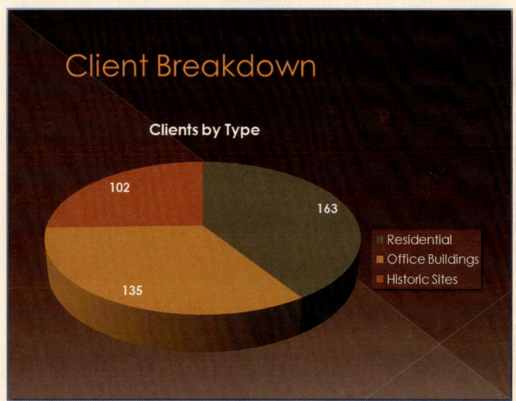**OPP28**.

2. Save the presentation as **OPP28_xx**.

3. Add a new slide at the end of the presentation with the Title and Content slide layout. Insert the title **Client Breakdown**.

4. Insert a pie chart using the following data:

   Clients by Type

Residential	163
Office Buildings	135
Historic Sites	102

5. Add data labels to the chart, choosing the Inside End format. Click any label to select all the data labels and apply bold style.

6. Select each slice of the pie and apply a different fill color from the Shape Fill palette, using theme colors.

7. Select the legend and choose a fill color and a shadow effect to make it stand out on the slide.

8. Drag the title text box to center it over the pie. Make any other changes you think will improve the look of the chart. Illustration A shows one example.

9. Save your changes, close the presentation, and exit PowerPoint.

Illustration A

Exercise | 29

Skills Covered

- **Insert a SmartArt Graphic**
- **Add Text to a SmartArt Graphic**
- **Create SmartArt from a Bulleted List**
- **Modify SmartArt Graphic Design**
- **Format a SmartArt Graphic**

Software Skills   SmartArt graphics are visual representations of different kinds of information. You choose a type of graphic and then add text to customize it. You can also create SmartArt from any bulleted list. Sophisticated tools allow you to modify and format the graphic.

Application Skills   In this exercise, you continue working on the presentation for the Campus Recreation Center. You will create two SmartArt graphics to make information on the slides visually exciting.

TERMS

SmartArt graphics   Professionally designed graphics that organize and display information in various graphic types such as lists, processes, or hierarchical displays.

NOTES

Insert a SmartArt Graphic

- **SmartArt graphics** are new in Office 2007. They replace diagrams and organization charts used in previous versions.

- You can insert a SmartArt graphic into a content slide layout or add it without a placeholder using the SmartArt button on the Insert tab.

- When you insert a new SmartArt graphic, the Choose a SmartArt Graphic dialog box opens, as shown in the following illustration.

Choose a SmartArt Graphic dialog box

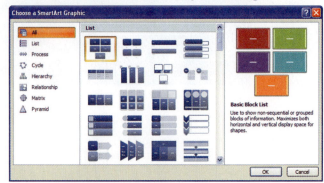

- Select a category of graphics and then a specific layout. The pane at the right side of the dialog box shows a detailed view of the selected graphic and explains what type of data the graphic is designed to display.

  - Use the List category layouts when your information can appear in any order.

  - Process layouts let you show information as a series of steps or points on a timeline.

  - Use Cycle layouts if you need to show a continual process.

  - Use Hierarchy layouts to create graphics such as organization charts that show levels of subordination.

  - Relationship layouts are used to show how items are interconnected.

  - Matrix layouts are used to show the relationship of parts to a whole.

  - Use Pyramid layouts when you want to show the importance of related items by size, from smallest to largest or vice versa.

- After you select a SmartArt graphic type, PowerPoint displays the graphic on the slide, as shown in the following illustration.

A new SmartArt graphic with Text pane displayed

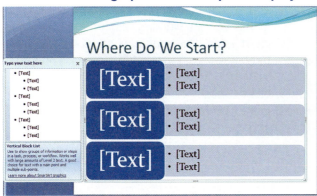

- The Text pane, which flies out to the left of the graphic as shown in the previous illustration, may or may not display with a new SmartArt graphic.

Add Text to a SmartArt Graphic

- As you can see in the previous illustration, a SmartArt graphic provides placeholders for text. Text may be insert in shapes (such as the darker blue, rounded-corner rectangles in the previous illustration) or as bulleted text in text boxes or other shapes.

- You can enter text in the Text pane by clicking a placeholder and typing the desired text. In the Text pane, the first-level bullet items represent the shapes in the graphic. The subordinate bullet items indented below the first-level bullets represent the bulleted text items in the graphic.

  ✓ *You can promote a bullet item so it becomes a shape or demote a shape so it becomes a bullet item. You will learn about promoting and demoting later in this exercise.*

- If you don't want to work in the Text pane, you can close the Text pane and type directly in the graphic as shown in the following illustration.

Type text in the SmartArt graphic

- As you enter text, font sizes adjust automatically to accommodate the longest line in a shape.

- Some SmartArt graphics have more room for text than others do. Consider as you create the graphic how much text you want to insert so you can choose an appropriate layout.

- Some graphics have placeholders not only for text but also for pictures. You can insert your own picture files into these placeholders for a unique graphic effect.

Create SmartArt from a Bulleted List

- If you have created a content slide with bullet items that you think would have more impact as a SmartArt graphic, you do not have to re-enter the text in a new graphic. You can instead simply convert the bulleted items to a graphic.

- Use the Convert to SmartArt Graphic button on the Home tab to display a gallery of graphic layouts you can choose among, as shown in the following illustration.

Convert a bulleted list to a graphic

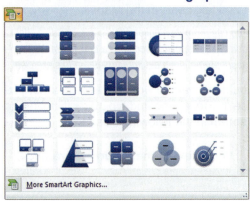

- As you rest your pointer on a layout in this gallery, the bulleted items in your placeholder display in that layout.

- If you do not find a layout you like, click the More SmartArt Graphics command at the bottom of the gallery to open the Choose a SmartArt Graphic dialog box where you have many more choices.

Modify SmartArt Graphic Design

- As for tables and charts, you can modify a graphic using Design and Format contextual tabs.

- Use the SmartArt Tools Design tab, shown in the following illustration, to change the layout and appearance of the graphic as a whole.

- The Create Graphic group supplies tools for changing the structure of the current graphic.

  - Use the Add Shape button to insert another shape in the graphic. Depending on the graphic layout, you have options to add a shape above, below, to the left, or to the right, or add an assistant if you are working with an organization chart.

  - The Add Bullet button lets you add a bullet item to an existing bullet list or to a shape that does not include a bullet item.

  - Use the Right to Left button to change the orientation of the graphic so that objects flip horizontally from one side of the graphic to the other.

  - The Layout button is active only for organization charts and allows you to specify how subordinate levels align under the top-level shape.

  - The Promote and Demote buttons let you change the display level of shapes and bullet items.

    - When you demote a shape, it becomes a bullet item.

    - When you demote a bullet item, it is indented to the next level.

    - When you promote a bullet item, it becomes a shape.

    - You usually cannot promote shape items, unless you are working with an organization chart. In an organization chart, you can promote any shape (except the top-level shape) to move it to the next higher organizational level.

  - Use the Text Pane button to show or hide the Text pane.

SmartArt Tools Design tab

■ The Layouts group contains a gallery of layouts for the current category type. You can usually change to a new layout in the same category without having to readjust text. If you want to select a layout from a different category, click the More Layouts command at the bottom of the gallery to open the Choose a SmartArt Graphic dialog box.

✓ *If you select a new category type to apply to the current graphic, you may need to adjust shape and bullet levels using the Text pane.*

■ The SmartArt Styles group includes the Change Colors and Quick Styles galleries. Use these galleries to apply a new color scheme using the current theme colors, as shown in the following illustration, or a Quick Style that applies to all objects in the graphic.

Change Colors gallery

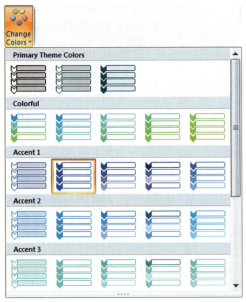

■ If you do not like the modifications you have made to a graphic, use the Reset Graphic button in the Reset group to restore the graphic to its original appearance.

Format a SmartArt Graphic

■ The tools on the SmartArt Tools Format tab, shown in the following illustration, allow you to modify individual shapes and text in the graphic.

■ The Shapes group gives you options to edit a shape in a two-dimensional view (available only if you have applied a three-dimensional style to a graphic), replace the currently selected shape with a different one from the Shapes gallery, or make the current shape larger or smaller.

■ The Shape Styles group offers the Shape Styles gallery of Quick Styles that can be applied to individual shapes. The familiar Shape Fill, Shape Outline, and Shape Effects buttons let you apply fill, outline, and effects to individual shapes.

■ Use the WordArt Styles group options to apply WordArt Quick Styles, fills, outlines, and effects to text in the graphic.

■ The Arrange group supplies options for rearranging the order of objects in the graphic.

■ The Size group lets you specify an exact width and height for the graphic.

■ You can also use text formatting tools from the Home tab to format graphic text and paragraph formatting tools to adjust alignment. Be careful when modifying text formats, however. If you make some text larger, PowerPoint may automatically downsize other text items to make room for it.

■ To select a shape so you can format it, click on the shape.

SmartArt Tools Format tab

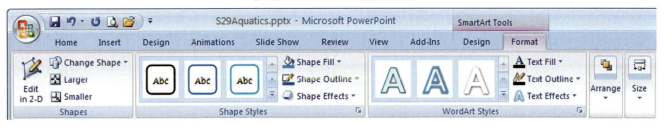

The Space Race

On July 21, 1969, Neil Armstrong became the first human to walk on the Moon. His feat capped what was essentially a decade-long race against the Soviet Union to be the first country to successfully put people on the Moon and bring them home safely. NASA's Mercury, Gemini, and Apollo missions set the stage for this final achievement.

Diagram the Missions

Create a presentation that lists the Mercury, Gemini, and Apollo missions in SmartArt graphics of your choice. Use different slides for each mission. You may elect to show all flights for each mission or only the high points. Add shapes and bullets to each graphic as necessary to show flight information such as the name(s) of the astronauts making the flight, the date of the flight, and the duration of the flight. You may use more than one slide for each mission if desired to avoid crowding too much information on a slide.

PROCEDURES

Insert a SmartArt Graphic

1. Click **Insert SmartArt Graphic** icon 🖼 in any content placeholder.

   OR

   a. Click **Insert** tab .... Alt + N
   b. Click **SmartArt** button 📊 .... M

2. Select the desired SmartArt category and layout.

3. Click [OK] .... ↵Enter

Add Text to a SmartArt Graphic

1. Click **[Text]** in the Text pane or in the graphic shape.

2. Type replacement text.

Create SmartArt from a Bulleted List

1. Select placeholder that contains bulleted items to be used for list.

2. Click **Home** tab .... Alt + H

   Paragraph Group

3. Click **Convert to SmartArt Graphic** button 📊▾ .... M

4. Select a layout from the gallery.

   OR

   a. Click **More SmartArt Graphics** .... M
   b. Select the desired SmartArt category and layout.
   c. Click [OK] .... ↵Enter

Modify SmartArt Graphic Design

To add a shape:

1. Select a shape near where you want to add the new shape.

2. Click **SmartArt Tools Design** tab .... Alt + J, S

   Create Graphic Group

3. Click **Add Shape** button 🔲 down arrow .... O

4. Click one of the choices for adding a shape after, before, above, below, or other option specific to the type of SmartArt graphic.

To delete a shape:

1. Click the shape to delete to select it.

2. Press Del.

To add a bullet to a shape:

1. Select a shape that should contain the bullet item.

2. Click **SmartArt Tools Design** tab .... Alt + J, S

   Create Graphic Group

3. Click **Add Bullet** button 📧 .... B

To promote or demote a shape or bullet item:

1. Select a shape or click in a bullet item.

2. Click **SmartArt Tools Design** tab .... Alt + J, S

   Create Graphic Group

3. Click **Promote** button ⬆ .... P

   OR

   Click **Demote** button ➡ .... D

To change the SmartArt layout:

1. Click the SmartArt graphic to select it.

2. Click **SmartArt Tools Design** tab .... Alt + J, S

   Layouts Group

3. Click **More** button ▼ .... L to view all SmartArt layouts for the current category.

4. Select a layout .... ←→↑↓, ↵Enter

To change graphic colors:

1. Click the SmartArt graphic to select it.
2. Click **SmartArt Tools Design** tab .... Alt +J, S

   SmartArt Styles

3. Click **Change Colors** button 🎨 C
   to display a gallery of color options.
4. Select a color combination ... ← → ↑ ↓, ↵Enter

To change graphic style:

1. Click the SmartArt graphic to select it.
2. Click **SmartArt Tools Design** tab .... Alt +J, S

   SmartArt Styles Group

3. Click **More** button ▼ .... S
   to display a gallery of style options.
4. Select a style option .... ← → ↑ ↓, ↵Enter

Format a SmartArt Graphic

To adjust shape size:

1. Click the shape to select it.
2. Click **SmartArt Tools Format** tab .... Alt +J, O

   Shapes Group

3. Click **Smaller** button 🔳 .... D
   to reduce size of shape.

   OR

   Click **Larger** button 🔳 .... N
   to increase size of shape.

To format individual shapes:

1. Select the shape by clicking it.
2. Click **SmartArt Tools Format** tab .... Alt +J, O

   Shape Styles Group

- Click **More** button ▼ .... S, S
  to display Shape Style gallery and select a Quick Style.
- Click **Shape Fill** button 🎨 .... S, F
  to select a color or other fill option.
- Click **Shape Outline** button 🖊 .... S, O
  to select an outline color or style.
- Click **Shape Effects** button 🔷 .... S, E
  to select an effect.

  ✓ *You can also use formatting tools on the Home tab in the Drawing group.*

EXERCISE DIRECTIONS

1. Start PowerPoint and open **28Aquatics_xx** or ⊚**29Aquatics**. If you are prompted to update links, click Cancel.
2. Save the presentation as **29Aquatics_xx**.
3. Display slide 8 and insert a new Title and Content slide. Insert the title **Where Do We Start?** .
4. Create a SmartArt graphic using the Horizontal Bullet List type and insert the text shown in Illustration A.

5. You forgot to include a plan of action for staff. Choose to add a shape after the *Faculty* shape and type **Staff**. Add bullets below the new shape with the following text:

   Information via interdepartmental mail

   Brochures in departmental offices

6. Change the layout to Vertical Block List.

Illustration A

Students	Faculty	Community
• Campus newsletter • Brochures in student union	• Information via interdepartmental mail	• Local newspaper • Mailing to families within 5 miles of campus

7. To adjust the size of the blue shapes, select each one and click the Smaller button on the SmartArt Tools Format tab three times so the shapes and the text blocks are more in proportion.

8. Change the color scheme to one you like better, and apply a different SmartArt style.

9. Display slide 3. This bulleted list could have more impact as a SmartArt graphic. Convert the list to a graphic, using the Vertical Process layout from the Process category in the Choose a SmartArt Graphic dialog box.

10. The Vertical Process layout does not show the relationships among users that you want to emphasize. Change the graphic type to the Stacked Venn layout in the Relationship category.

11. Change the orientation using the Right to Left button.

12. Format the graphic as follows:
    - Boldface the text in the shapes.
    - Choose fill colors for each shape from the Shape Fill palette.
    - Make any other changes you think necessary to improve the look of the graphic.

13. Save your changes, close the presentation, and exit PowerPoint.

ON YOUR OWN

1. Start PowerPoint and open **OPP28_xx** or **OPP29**.

2. Save the presentation as **OPP29_xx**.

3. Display slide 4 and convert the bulleted list to a Cycle category graphic. Choose a layout that you like.

4. Modify font size and style, layout, and other formats as desired to improve the graphic.

5. Add a new slide at the end of the presentation and type the title **Company Structure**.

6. Insert a SmartArt graphic that will allow you to create an organization chart. Create the chart shown in Illustration A.

7. Modify and format the SmartArt graphic as desired to improve its appearance on the slide.

8. Save your changes, close the presentation, and exit PowerPoint.

Illustration A

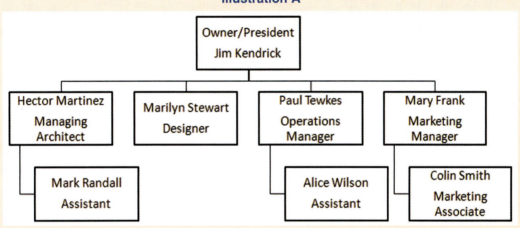

Critical Thinking

Application Skills The owner of Restoration Architecture wants you to create another presentation to show to owners of historic houses in your city. To start the presentation, he has supplied you with tabular information that he wants you to add to the slides to boost the visual appeal.

DIRECTIONS

1. Start PowerPoint to display a new, blank presentation.

2. Save the presentation as **30Architecture_xx**. Apply a theme of your choice.

   ✓ *You will create a new theme for this presentation in Exercise 41.*

3. On the title slide, type the title **RESTORATION ARCHITECTURE** and the subtitle **Design For Life—Design That Lasts**.

4. Add a new slide and type the title **Period Design Specialties**. Then insert the table shown below.

Period	Sample Project	Project Cost
Queen Anne	22 Hastings St	$132,333
Tudor Revival	4 Bellevue Ave	$101,993
Georgian	123 Elm St	$114,432

5. Format the table and its content as desired. At a minimum, you should apply a Quick Style and adjust table style options. You may also want to adjust the width of the table and distribute columns evenly.

6. Add a new slide and type the title **Sample Project Costs**.

7. Embed the Excel worksheet data contained in **30Costs**. You may copy the data and use Paste Special to paste it or use the Insert Object dialog box to insert the worksheet.

8. After embedding the worksheet data, open it for editing in Excel. Format the column and row headings as desired and apply a cell style for the totals. You may also turn off gridlines in Excel if desired.

9. Enlarge the font size so the data will show up more clearly on the slide.

10. Add a slide and insert the content shown in Illustration A.

11. Add a slide and type the title **You're Part of the Process**. Insert a SmartArt graphic that will show a process and enter the following text in the graphic:

    1 **You contact us**
    2 **We visit your site**
    3 **We prepare a design and budget**
    4 **You accept the design and budget**
    5 **We start work**

12. Format the SmartArt graphic as desired to display attractively on the slide. At a minimum, you should apply a Quick Style. You may also want to choose a different layout that better fits the information and change the colors used in the graphic.

13. Add another slide and type the title **Site Study Services**. Insert a bar chart using the following data:

Survey	Survey	Soils Testing	Drainage
Small property	$2,500	$2,000	$2,750
Medium property	$6,000	$2,000	$3,800
Large property	$10,000	$2,000	$5,000

14. Switch rows and columns and then modify the chart as desired to look attractive on the slide. At a minimum, you should relocate the legend, add a chart title, and apply a Quick Style.

15. Save your changes, close the presentation, and exit PowerPoint.

What Sets Us Apart

- ‣ Excellent customer service
- ‣ Advanced project management methods
- ‣ Environmentally friendly building materials
- ‣ Superior design work

Exercise | 31

Curriculum Integration

Application Skills   Your biology class is beginning a unit on taxonomy, the science of classification. You have been asked to prepare a presentation that presents some information about the Linnaean hierarchy, the basic system still used to classify living organisms. Before you begin this exercise, do some research to locate:

■ Charts or tables that show the basic Linnaean hierarchy and its components (for example, kingdom, phylum, class, and so on)

■ Classification lists that will help you compare the taxonomy of several species (i.e., lists that show the phylum, class, order, family, genus, and species of several common animals or plants)

DIRECTIONS

Begin a new presentation. You may use a blank presentation or use one of PowerPoint's online presentation templates. Save the presentation with an appropriate name, such as **31Taxonomy_xx**. Insert an appropriate title and subtitle on the first slide. Apply a theme if necessary, customizing theme colors and fonts if desired.

Add a slide on which you will show the basic Linnaean hierarchy, beginning with kingdom and ending with species. Type an appropriate title and then create a SmartArt graphic for the diagram. (Illustration A shows one way you could organize this information.) Format the diagram as desired to make it attractive.

Current classification discussions suggest that a three-domain model may be a more accurate way to begin classification than the five-kingdom model. Add a slide and create a table that shows the three domains under discussion and how kingdoms may be divided among them.

Add slide numbers and a date that updates automatically to all slides except the title slide. Add a header and footer for notes and handouts.

View the slides in Slide Show view, and then preview the handouts you will need to provide to the class. Print the slides as handouts with four slides per page.

Save changes to the presentation and close it. Exit PowerPoint.

Illustration A

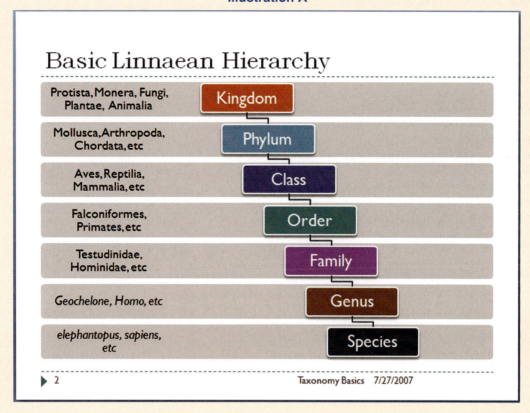

Lesson | 4

Work with Graphic Elements

Skills Covered

- **Customize Slide Backgrounds**
- **Create a Color or Gradient Background**

- **Create a Picture or Texture Background**

Software Skills Though themes provide you with interesting backgrounds, you can also customize your own backgrounds using color, a gradient, a texture, or a picture.

Application Skills You work for Thorn Hill Gardens, a park on the site of a former grand estate that is open for tours and conducts seasonal workshops in horticulture. You have been asked to prepare a presentation that can be shown to garden clubs and horticulture classes at nearby colleges. You will begin the presentation by customizing some backgrounds for the slides.

TERMS

Gradient Gradations of color usually from a light color to a darker color, although gradients can consist of more than two colors.

NOTES

Customize Slide Backgrounds

- You should by now be familiar with a number of PowerPoint's theme backgrounds. You may find yourself wishing as you apply a particular theme that you could change the background to create a different visual statement or to more closely meet your needs.

- You can use the Format Background dialog box, shown in the illustration at right, to create a number of background effects that will ensure your presentation is one of a kind.

Format Background dialog box

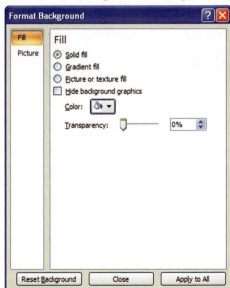

- Select from a solid, gradient, picture, or texture fill. The choices available in the lower portion of the dialog box change depending which fill option you choose.

- You will learn how to create these background fills in the following sections.

- You can use the Apply to All button to apply your new background to all slides in the presentation. If you don't click this button, the background applies only to the current slide.

- If you find that you don't like the changes you have made, you can click the Reset Background button to restore the default background.

- Note that the fill options available in the Format Background dialog box are also available for any object that can be filled, such as a text box or a shape. You can access the fill options in a dialog box such as Format Shape.

Create a Color or Gradient Background

- The easiest background fill to create is a solid color background. After you click the Solid fill option, the dialog box displays a Color button to open a theme color palette and a Transparency slider to adjust the opacity of the color.

- You can choose any color from the Color palette or one of the Standard colors at the bottom of the palette. Or, click More Colors to open the Colors dialog box so you can pick a color.

- As you drag the Transparency slider to the right, your chosen color is mixed with increasing amounts of white so that it lightens or fades.

   ✓ *Keep in mind that a background color should not overwhelm the type on a slide, so adjusting transparency is often a good way to keep the background under control.*

- A **gradient** is a color fill that shades from one color to another. Gradient fills give an object a more interesting look than a plain color fill because of the variation in color tone.

- Clicking the Gradient fill option in the Format Background dialog box displays the settings shown in the following illustration.

Gradient fill options in the Format Background dialog box

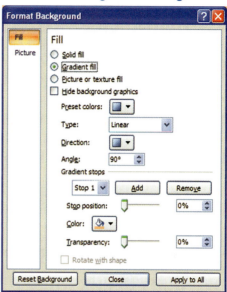

- Click the Preset colors box to see a gallery of gradients that have already been created for you.

- The Type list lets you choose how the gradient displays: Linear, for example, goes from one side of a slide to another, while Radial radiates out from the center of the slide.

- The following illustration shows two objects with gradient fills using two colors, the left with a linear gradient and the right with a radial gradient.

Linear gradient (left) and radial gradient (right)

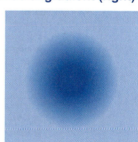

- After you choose a type, you can fine-tune the gradient appearance by selecting a direction that the gradient will flow. Directions for linear gradients, for instance, include Linear Diagonal, Linear Down, and Linear Left.

- Use the Angle setting to adjust the direction in which the gradient flows.

- Use the options in the Gradient stops area of the dialog box to choose the colors for the gradient. You can choose a color for each stop, and drag the Stop position slider to determine how much of the object will be filled with that color.

  ✓ *Or, set the position more precisely by typing a percentage.*

- Add a stop if you want to add another color to the gradient. Remove a stop to create a less complex gradient.

- Use the Transparency slider to soften the gradient by making the colors more transparent.

Create a Picture or Texture Background

- You learned in Exercise 26 how to use a picture as a background for a table or selected table cells. The process of applying a picture background to an entire slide is identical to applying a picture to a table.

- When you click the Picture or texture fill option, the Format Background dialog box displays options for selecting a picture or texture, as shown in the following illustration.

Picture or texture background options

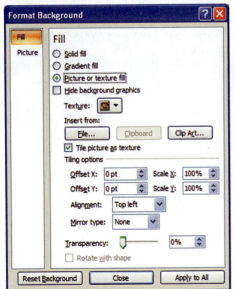

- Use the File or Clip Art button to locate a picture to use as a background. You will usually want to tile the picture as a texture so that it stretches over the entire slide background.

- You can adjust the position of the picture on the slide and scale it if necessary to fit on the slide.

- The Transparency option is very important for picture backgrounds. Washing out the picture can make it much easier to read type on the slide.

- Clicking the Texture button displays the gallery shown in the following illustration. These textures have been available in a number of previous PowerPoint versions, so they may look familiar to you.

PowerPoint's texture gallery

- Click any texture in the gallery to apply it immediately to the current slide.

- As for a picture, you may want to adjust transparency to avoid overwhelming the type on your slide with the sometimes strongly colored textures. You can also choose to change font color to contrast well with the darker textures.

PROCEDURES

Create a Color Background

1. Click **Design** tab .... `Alt`+`G`

   Background Group

2. Click **Background Styles** button 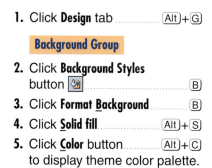 .... `B`
3. Click **Format Background** .... `B`
4. Click **Solid fill** .... `Alt`+`S`
5. Click **Color** button .... `Alt`+`C`
   to display theme color palette.
6. Select theme color or Standard color .... `←``→``↑``↓`, `↵Enter`

   OR

   a. Click **More Colors** .... `M`
   b. Select a color in the Colors dialog box.
   c. Click `OK` .... `↵Enter`
7. Drag **Transparency** slider .... `Alt`+`T`, `→`, `←`
   if desired to adjust opacity of color.
8. Click `Close` .... `↵Enter`
   to apply background to current slide only.

   OR

   Click
   `Apply to All` ...... `Alt`+`L`, `↵Enter`
   to apply to all slides in presentation.

Restore Default Slide Background

Restore background in Normal view:

1. Click **Design** tab ...... `Alt`+`G`

   Background Group

2. Click **Background Styles** button 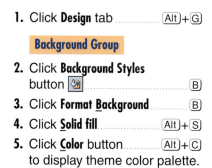 .... `B`
3. Click **Reset Slide Background** ...... `R`

Restore background while in Format Background dialog box:

- Click `Reset Background` ...... `Alt`+`B`

Create a Gradient Background

1. Click **Design** tab .... `Alt`+`G`

   Background Group

2. Click **Background Styles** button 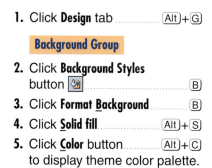 .... `B`
3. Click **Format Background** .... `B`
4. Click **Gradient fill** .... `Alt`+`G`

   ✓ *A gradient fill immediately fills background using shades of most recently created gradient.*

5. Click `Close` .... `↵Enter`
   to apply gradient background to current slide only.

   OR

   Click
   `Apply to All` ...... `Alt`+`L`, `↵Enter`
   to apply to all slides in presentation.

To choose a preset gradient:

1. Click **Preset colors** ...... `Alt`+`R`
2. Select a preset gradient .... `←``→``↑``↓`, `↵Enter`

To choose type of gradient:

1. Click **Type** .... `Alt`+`Y`
2. Select from list of gradient types. .... `↓`, `↑`, `↵Enter`

To change direction and angle of gradient:

1. Click **Direction** .... `Alt`+`D`
2. Select from gallery of preset directions ...... `←``→``↑``↓`, `↵Enter`
3. Click **Angle** .... `Alt`+`E`
4. Type desired angle.

   OR

   Click increment arrows to increase/reduce angle by 10 degree increments.

To adjust gradient colors and percentages:

1. With **Stop 1** displayed in Gradient stops area, click **Color** button .... `Alt`+`C`
   and select a color from the theme color palette or any other color palette.
2. Drag **Stop position** slider .... `Alt`+`O`, `←`, `→`
   if desired to specify percentage of background used by selected color.
3. Click **Stop 1** list arrow to display list of stops and select **Stop 2**.
4. Click **Color** button ...... `Alt`+`C`
   and select a color from the theme color palette or any other color palette.
5. Adjust Stop position if desired as directed in step 2.
6. Continue to select gradient stops and select colors until gradient is adjusted.

To add a stop to gradient:

1. Display stop in gradient stop list that will be before new stop.
2. Click `Add` .... `Alt`+`A`
3. Select a color and stop position for the new gradient stop.

To remove a stop from a gradient:

1. Display the gradient stop list.
2. Select gradient stop to remove.
3. Click `Remove` ...... `Alt`+`V`

Create a Picture Background

1. Click **Design** tab .... `Alt`+`G`

   Background Group

2. Click **Background Styles** button 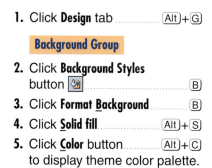 .... `B`
3. Click **Format Background** .... `B`

4. Click **Picture or texture fill** .... `Alt`+`P`

> ✓ *A texture may immediately fill the slide background.*

5. Click [File...] .... `Alt`+`F`

6. Navigate to location of picture and select picture.

7. Click [Insert ▾] .... `↵Enter`

8. Adjust the image position:
- Click **Tile picture as texture** .... `Alt`+`A` if necessary to spread the picture over the entire background.
- Adjust Offset measurements to stretch or contract image in any direction from point of alignment.
- Choose an Alignment option to set the point at which the image aligns on the background.

9. Drag **Transparency** slider .... `Alt`+`T`, `→`, `←` if desired to adjust opacity of image.

10. Click [Close] .... `↵Enter` to apply background to current slide only.

OR

Click
[Apply to All] .... `Alt`+`L`, `↵Enter`
to apply to all slides in presentation.

Create a Texture Background

1. Click **Design** tab .... `Alt`+`G`

> **Background Group**

2. Click **Background Styles** button 🔲 .... `B`

3. Click **Format Background** .... `B`

4. Click **Picture or texture fill** .... `Alt`+`P`

> ✓ *A texture may immediately fill the slide background.*

5. Click **Texture** .... `Alt`+`U`

6. Select texture from gallery .... `←``→``↑``↓`, `↵Enter`

7. Drag **Transparency** slider .... `Alt`+`T`, `→`, `←` if desired to adjust opacity of image.

8. Click [Close] .... `↵Enter` to apply background to current slide only.

OR

Click
[Apply to All] .... `Alt`+`L`, `↵Enter`
to apply to all slides in presentation.

EXERCISE DIRECTIONS

1. Start PowerPoint to open a new, blank presentation and apply the Trek theme.

2. Save the presentation as **32Thorn_xx**.

3. Type the title **THORN HILL GARDENS** and the subtitle **Four Seasons of Color**.

4. Begin by applying a picture background to the title slide to represent the spring season:
- Choose to insert a picture background and navigate to the 💿 **32Spring** picture in the data files.
- Insert the picture.
- Adjust transparency to 60% and close the Format Background dialog box.
- In Normal view, change the color of the subtitle and the title to Black to provide a slightly better contrast with the background. Your slide should look similar to Illustration A.

5. Add a new slide with the Title and Content layout. Create a solid color background for the summer season as follows:
- Choose to insert a solid fill background.
- The current theme colors do not have a good selection of greens that would be appropriate for summer. Click More Colors on the color palette to open the Colors dialog box.
- Choose a green color and then adjust transparency as desired to make a fresh green background. You may need to test several greens to find one you like.
- Insert the title text **SUMMER EVENTS**.

6. Add a new slide with the Title and Content layout. Create a gradient background for the fall season as follows:
- Choose to insert a gradient background.
- With the Linear type selected, choose the first option on the Direction palette, Linear Diagonal, and set the angle to 45 degrees, if necessary.
- With Stop 1 displayed in the Gradient stops area, choose the Light Yellow, Background 2, Darker 10% color from the theme colors palette. Move the Stop position slider to 20%.

- Select Step 2 and specify the Light Yellow, Background 2 color. Move the Stop position slider to 25%.

- Select Stop 3 and specify the Orange, Accent 1, Darker 25% color. Move the Stop position slider to 65%.

- If you do not have Stop 4 available, add this stop. Specify the Orange, Accent 1, Darker 50% color and move the slider to 90%.

- Remove any other gradient stops in the list and close the dialog box.

- Insert the title text **FALL FUN**.

7. Add a new slide with the Title and Content layout. Create a texture background for the winter season as follows:

   - Choose to insert a texture background.

   - Select the White marble texture and adjust transparency to 70%.

   - Insert the title text **WINTER WONDERLAND**.

8. Save your changes, close the presentation, and exit PowerPoint.

Illustration A

Four Seasons of Color

THORN HILL GARDENS

ON YOUR OWN

1. Open 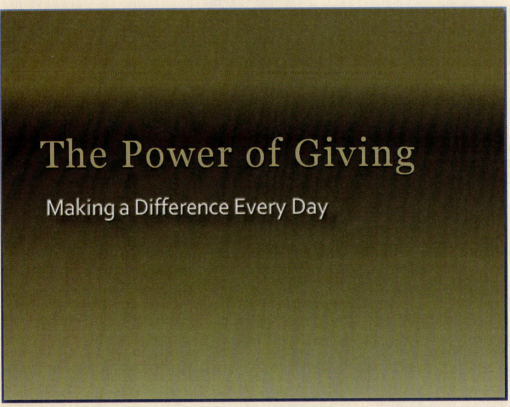OPP32.
2. Save the presentation as **OPP32_xx**.
3. On slide 1, adjust the colors and stop positions in the gradient to make the slide background a little more dramatic. Illustration A shows one option.

4. On slide 8, create a new background using color, a gradient, or a texture.
5. Save your changes, close the presentation, and exit PowerPoint.

Illustration A

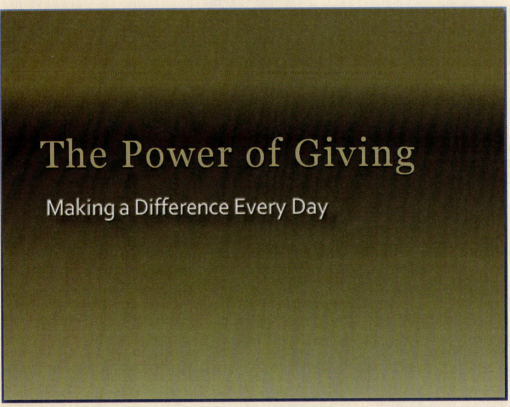

The Power of Giving

Making a Difference Every Day

Skills Covered

- **Display Rulers, Guides, and Gridlines**
- **Draw Shapes**
- **Modify and Format Shapes**
- **Add Text to Shapes**

Software Skills Use PowerPoint's many drawing tools to help enhance a presentation. You might use rulers and guides or the grid to line up text or drawing objects, for example. Use shape tools to draw logos, illustrations, or other objects to add to slides.

Application Skills Natural Light Ltd has asked you to create a presentation that can be used at trade shows to introduce the company's products and services. In this exercise, you will draw the shapes you need to create a simple illustration conveying the theme of natural light.

TERMS

Gridlines A regular grid of dotted lines displayed on a slide to help arrange objects.

Guides Nonprinting vertical and horizontal lines you can use to align objects on a slide.

Scale Specify a percentage of the original size to enlarge or reduce an object's size.

NOTES

Display Rulers, Guides, and Gridlines

- PowerPoint provides a vertical and a horizontal ruler that you can display or hide at any time.

- You have already learned that you can use the horizontal ruler to adjust indents or add tabs to text. You can also use both rulers to align objects on the slide.

- The ruler's origins (0 measurement on the ruler) change depending on whether you're working with text or an object. The origin appears on the edge of the ruler when you're working with text and in the center point of the ruler when you're working with an object.

- As you move the mouse pointer, an indicator moves on each ruler showing your horizontal and vertical locations. Watching these indicators as you position or draw an object can help you work more precisely.

- **Guides** are alignment tools that help you line up objects and text. In the following illustration, for example, the shape has been centered on the slide by moving it so its sizing handles have snapped to the vertical and horizontal guides.

Vertical and horizontal guides help to position graphics

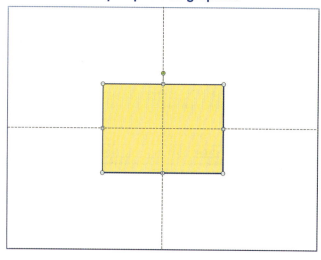

- By default, the guides display at the vertical and horizontal centers of the slide, as shown in the previous illustration, but you can move a guide to a new location by simply dragging it.

- You can also copy any guide to help you align objects at multiple locations on a slide.

- PowerPoint's **gridlines** display as a grid of dotted lines over the entire slide, as shown in the following illustration. Like guides, they can help you line up objects or position them attractively on the slide.

Gridlines displayed on a slide

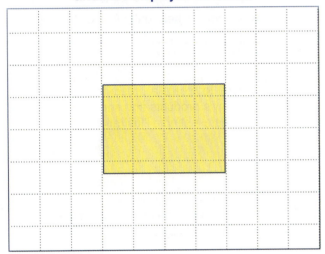

- By default, objects *snap* to the grid and guides as they are drawn or positioned on the slide, even if the gridlines are not currently displayed. Generally this is an advantage, but if you find you want to position an object more exactly, you can turn off the snapping feature or hold down Alt while dragging to temporarily disable the snapping feature.

- To turn off snapping or make other adjustments to the grid and guide settings, use the Grid and Guides dialog box, shown in the following illustration.

Grid and Guides dialog box

Draw Shapes

- The Shapes gallery on the Home tab, Insert tab, or Drawing Tools Format tab gives you access to many different types of shapes, from basic objects such as rectangles and lines to more complex graphic objects such as stars, banners, and block arrows.

   ✓ *If you have worked with previous versions of PowerPoint, you will recognize the objects in the Shapes gallery as AutoShapes.*

- The Shapes gallery is divided into several sections that organize shapes of various kinds (see the following illustration).

A portion of the Shapes gallery

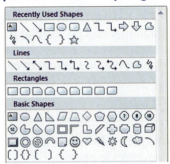

- Most shapes are drawn using the same basic steps: Select the shape, click on the slide to start the shape, and drag until the shape is the desired size.

- Use the Shift key while drawing to control shapes.
   - Hold down (⬆Shift) while drawing a rectangle or oval to create a perfect square or circle.
   - Hold down (⬆Shift) while drawing a line to create perfect horizontal, vertical, or 45-degree lines.

- Some shapes, such as connectors and callouts, require you to specify a starting and/or ending point.

- A connector, for example, starts at a handle on one shape and ends at a handle on another shape to show a flow or connection between the two shapes.

- You can copy a shape and paste the copy to create more than one version of the shape. The pasted copy displays almost on top of the original.

- To delete a shape, select it and then press (Del).

Modify and Format Shapes

■ You have many options for modifying shapes after you have drawn them. You can reposition the shape; change its size or appearance; or apply fill, outline, or effect options.

■ The Drawing Tools Format tab, shown in the following illustration, contains a number of tools you can use to modify and format shapes. You learn about some of these tools in following sections.

Drawing Tools Format tab

Reposition an Object on a Slide

■ To reposition a shape, you can simply drag it from one place to another.

■ To move an object in small increments, you can "nudge" the object using the arrow keys. Hold down Ctrl while pressing an arrow key to decrease the nudge increment for finer control.

■ If you need to be very precise about the position of a shape—or any other object such as a picture, placeholder, or text box—you can use the Size and Position dialog box shown in the following illustration.

Position tab of the Size and Position dialog box

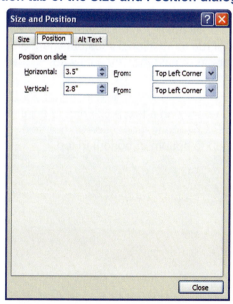

■ The Position tab in this dialog box allows you to specify exact horizontal and vertical measurements for the top left corner of an object or the center of an object. This level of control can be a great help when you need to position objects at the same coordinates on a number of slides.

Size or Scale an Object

■ Adjust a shape's dimensions by dragging a side or corner sizing handle, just as you learned to adjust a placeholder or text box in previous exercises.

✓ *Hold down* ⬆Shift *while dragging a corner handle to maintain the current ratio of height to width.*

■ You can specify an exact height or width for a shape using the measurement boxes in the Size group on the Drawing Tools Format tab.

■ You can also use the Size tab in the Size and Position dialog box, shown in the following illustration, to adjust the size of a shape or other object.

Size tab of the Size and Position dialog box

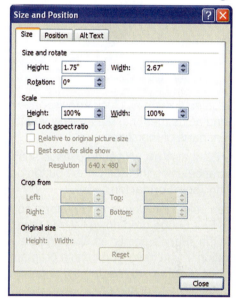

■ Specify an exact height and width for the shape, or **scale** the shape by specifying a percentage of the original size to enlarge or reduce the shape.

■ If you display this dialog box with a drawing shape selected, the Lock aspect ratio check box is not selected, which means you can adjust height and width independently.

■ If you have a picture selected when you display this dialog box, Lock aspect ratio is selected by default to help you maintain the original proportions of the image when resizing or scaling. The Crop settings also become active to allow you to trim the picture from any side.

✓ *You learn more about cropping in Exercise 35.*

Adjust Shape Appearance

- Some complex shapes allow you to adjust not only the overall size of the shape but also the appearance of the shape.

- If a shape has a yellow diamond adjustment handle, such as the one shown in the following illustration, you can drag the handle to change its appearance.

Adjusting a shape's appearance

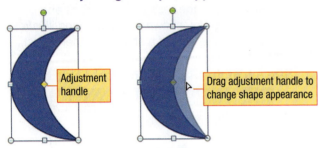

- Some objects, such as block arrows, have more than one adjustment handle to allow you to change different parts of the shape.

- PowerPoint also allows you to change shape appearance using the Edit Shape button on the Drawing Tools Format tab.

- You can select the Convert to Freeform command on the Edit Shape drop-down list and then choose to edit the shape's points, as shown in the following illustration. If you have worked in a program such as Adobe Illustrator, this is the same process you use to modify vector curves.

Edit a shape by adjusting its points

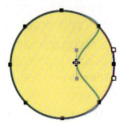

Apply Fill, Outline, and Effect Options to Shapes

- By default, shapes are formatted with the current theme colors. You can, however, use the tools on the Drawing Tools Format tab to modify fill, outline, and effects for any drawing object, or apply a Quick Style to format the shape.

- For easier access to advanced formatting options, use the Format Shape dialog box. Settings vary according to the currently selected shape. If you have selected a line, for example, there will be no fill setting options in the dialog box. Settings are applied as you choose them in the dialog box.

Add Text to Shapes

- You can add text to any filled shape. Simply click on the shape and start typing, as shown in the following illustration. PowerPoint handles line length and text wrap.

Add text to a shape

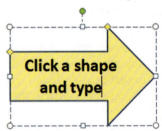

- If you enter more text than will fit in the shape, the shape does not automatically resize. Instead, the text will run to additional lines outside the shape borders. You must then manually adjust the shape to accommodate the text.

- You can edit and format text in a shape just as you would edit text in a text box. For a special effect, you can change text direction so that text reads from top to bottom or bottom to top.

Curriculum Connection: Mathematics

Triangles

A triangle is the simplest polygon because it is comprised of three sides and three angles. The sum of the three angles of a triangle is always equal to 180 degrees. Triangles can be classified either by the length of their sides or by their angles.

Identify Triangles

Create a PowerPoint presentation that identifies the different types of triangles in each classification. Explain how to determine the different types, and insert shapes to provide examples of what each triangle looks like.

PROCEDURES

Display Rulers, Guides, and Gridlines

To show/hide rulers:

1. Click **View** tab .... Alt + W

   Show/Hide Group

2. Click **Ruler** .... R

To display the guides:

1. Click **Home** tab .... Alt + H

   Drawing Group

2. Click **Arrange** button 🔲 .... G
3. Click **Align** .... A

   ✓ *You can also access the Align set-tings from the Drawing Tools Format tab.*

4. Click **Grid Settings** .... G
5. Click **Display drawing guides on screen** I
6. Click [OK] .... ↵Enter

   ✓ *To quickly turn guides on or off, press* Alt + F9.

To show/hide gridlines:

1. Click **View** tab .... Alt + W

   Show/Hide Group

2. Click **Gridlines** .... G

Draw Shapes

1. Click **Home** tab .... Alt + H

   Drawing Group

2. Click **More** button 🔽 .... S, H
   OR
   Click **Shapes** button 🔲 ..... S, H
   if More button is not visible.
3. Select a shape to draw.

4. Position crosshair on slide and drag to create object.

   ■ Hold down ⇧Shift to con-strain shapes to create squares, circles, and straight lines.

   ✓ *The drawing shapes gallery can also be accessed from the Insert tab or the Drawing Tools Format tab.*

Modify and Format Shapes

To reposition a shape:

1. Click a shape to select it.
2. Drag the selected shape to a new position.
   OR
1. Click a shape to select it.
2. Press any arrow key to "nudge" the shape in that direction.

   ✓ *Hold down* Ctrl *to reduce the nudge increment for finer control.*

   OR
1. Click a shape to select it.
2. Click **Drawing Tools Format** tab .... Alt + J, D

   Size Group

3. Click **Size** group dialog box launcher 🔲 .... S, Z
4. Click **Position** tab.
5. Specify position coordinates:

   ■ Click **Horizontal** ...... Alt + H
   and type a value or use spin arrows.

   ■ Click **From** .... Alt + F
   and select point from which to measure horizontal dis-tance.

   ■ Click **Vertical** .... Alt + V
   and type a value or use spin arrows.

   ■ Click **From** .... Alt + R
   and select point from which to measure vertical distance.

6. Click [Close] .... ↵Enter

To size a shape:

1. Click a shape to select it.
2. Drag a corner or side handle to enlarge or reduce shape size.
   OR
1. Click a shape to select it.
2. Click **Drawing Tools Format** tab .... Alt + J, D

   Size Group

3. Specify exact height and width:

   ■ Click **Shape Height** box ...... H
   and type value or use spin arrows to increase or decrease height.

   ■ Click **Shape Width** box ...... W
   and type value or use spin arrows to increase or decrease width.

   OR
1. Click a shape to select it.
2. Click **Drawing Tools Format** tab .... Alt + J, D

   Size Group

3. Click **Size** group dialog box launcher 🔲 .... S, Z
4. On **Size** tab, specify exact height and width:

   ■ Click **Height** .... Alt + E
   and type a value or use spin arrows.

   ■ Click **Width** .... Alt + D
   and type a value or use spin arrows.

5. Click [Close] .... ↵Enter

To scale a shape:

1. Click a shape to select it.
2. Click **Drawing Tools Format** tab .... Alt + J, D

   Size Group

3. Click **Size** group dialog box launcher 🔲 .... S, Z

4. On **Size** tab, specify percentage of original size:

- Click **H**eight .... `Alt`+`H` and type a value or use spin arrows.
- Click **W**idth .... `Alt`+`W` and type a value or use spin arrows.

  ✓ *If Lock aspect ratio box is cleared, you can specify height and width independently.*

5. Click `Close` .... `↵Enter`

To adjust shape appearance:

- Click the yellow diamond adjustment handle and drag it to modify the shape appearance.

  OR

1. Click a shape to select it.

2. Click **Drawing Tools Format** tab .... `Alt`+`J`, `D`

Insert Shapes Group

3. Click **Edit Shapes** button `⚎` .... `E`

4. Click **Con**v**ert to Freeform** .... `V`

5. Click **Edit Shapes** button `⚎` again .... `E`

6. Click **E**dit **Points** .... `E`

7. Drag any point to reshape the object.

To apply fill, outline, and effect options:

1. Click the shape to select it.

2. Click **Drawing Tools Format** tab .... `Alt`+`J`, `D`

Shape Styles Group

3. Select one of these options:

- Click **Shape Fill** button `🎨` .... `S`, `F` to remove the fill or select a new color, picture, gradient, or texture to fill the shape.

- Click **Shape Outline** button `✏` .... `S`, `O` to remove the outline or select a new outline color, weight, or dash style.

- Click **Shape Effects** button `▢` .... `S`, `E` to select effects such as shadow, glow, reflection, bevel.

OR

- Click **More** button `▼` .... `S`, `S` and select a Quick Style from the gallery.

To display the Format Shape dialog box:

1. Click the shape to select it.

2. Click **Drawing Tools Format** tab .... `Alt`+`J`, `D`

Shape Styles Group

3. Click **Shape Styles** group dialog box launcher `⌟` .... `O`

4. Click categories in the left side of the dialog box to display panes of settings in the right side of the dialog box.

5. Select desired settings to format object.

6. Click `Close` .... `↵Enter`

Add Text to Shapes

1. Click the shape to select it.

2. Begin typing text.

EXERCISE DIRECTIONS

1. Start PowerPoint to open a new, blank presentation. Change the first slide to a Blank slide layout.

2. Save the presentation as **33Light_xx**.

3. Display the rulers.

   ✓ *You will create three forms of natural light in the drawing: a sun, a moon, and a star. Then you will create additional shapes you need for the slide and complete the drawing in the next exercise.*

4. Create the sun drawing as follows:

- Choose the Sun shape in the Basic Shapes category and draw a sun shape anywhere on the slide that is about 2.5 by 2.5 inches. (Use the rulers to help you size the shape.)

- Remove the outline from the shape.

5. Now apply a gradient fill for the object as follows:

- Select the sun shape, if necessary, and open the Format Shape dialog box.

- Choose the Gradient fill option.

- Choose the Fire Preset color, change the Type to Radial, and change the Direction to From Center.

- Close the dialog box to apply the changes, and then move the sun toward the lower-left corner of the slide.

6. Create a moon graphic as follows:

- Use the Oval Basic Shape to draw a 2.25 by 2.25 inch circle. (Hold down Shift while drawing to create a perfect circle.) This is the full moon shape.

- Remove the outline from the shape and fill it with the Newsprint texture. Move the full moon shape to the lower-right corner of the slide.

- Use the Moon Basic Shape to draw a shape 2.25 inches high by 1.25 inches wide. Drag the yellow diamond adjustment handle to the left to make the moon into a narrower crescent shape.

- Position the crescent moon shape to the left of the full moon. Fill it with the Recycled paper texture, and remove the outline.

7. Create the star graphic as follows:

- Use the 4-Point Star from Stars and Banners shapes to draw a star about 1 inch by 0.75 inches in the upper-right corner of the slide.

- Remove the outline and fill the star with white. Don't worry if it disappears from view.

8. You need a background object on which to position the other objects, because they do not show up very well on the white background. Create a background shape as follows:

- Draw a rectangle that is about 6 inches wide and 4 inches high.

- Remove the outline.

9. Display the drawing guides or gridlines and use them to help you center the blue shape on the slide. Don't worry if the blue shape covers other objects. You will adjust this in the next exercise.

10. Choose a shape such as Explosion 2 and draw the shape in the upper-left corner of the slide. Apply a Quick Style of your choice and a shadow shape effect.

11. Add the following text to the shape: **NATURAL LIGHT, LTD**.

12. Format the text as desired, adjusting the size of the shape as necessary to display text attractively. Your slide might look similar to Illustration A.

   ✓ *The star shape does not show in this illustration because it is white on a white background.*

13. Save your changes, close the presentation, and exit PowerPoint.

Illustration A

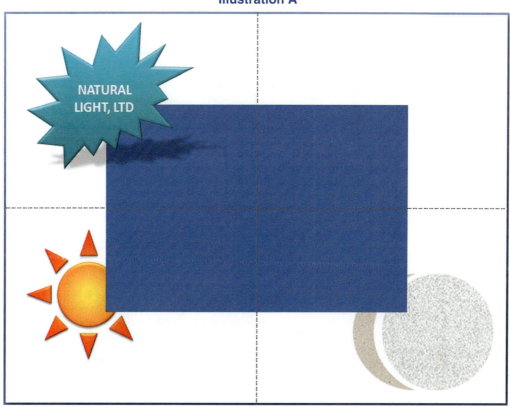

ON YOUR OWN

1. Open ⊙ **OPP33**.
2. Save the presentation as **OPP33_xx**.
3. Display the rulers and drawing guides, if necessary.
4. Drag the horizontal guide down to the 2.00 mark on slide 1.
5. Insert a shape on the title slide that sits on the horizontal guide. For example, insert an arrow, star, or any other object. Add a horizontal line above or below the shape, and then format both shapes. Add text to the shape if desired. Illustration A shows one option.
6. Use the drawing tools to draw a simple picture on a different slide, such as an arrangement of shapes that illustrates the text on slide 4. Try to use a block arrow and a polygon in your drawing. Add text to at least one of the shapes on this slide.
7. Reposition the shapes as desired and format them attractively with outline, fill, and effect options. Illustration B shows one arrangement.
8. Save your changes, close the presentation, and exit PowerPoint.

Illustration A

Illustration B

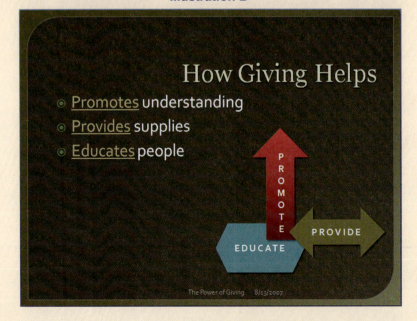

Skills Covered

- **Arranging Objects**
- **Order Objects**
- **Group and Ungroup Objects**
- **Align and Distribute Objects**
- **Rotate and Flip Objects**

Software Skills   PowerPoint provides a number of commands for arranging objects on a slide. You can change the order in which objects are stacked, group objects so they are easy to work with as a unit, align and distribute objects to position them relative to each other or the slide, and rotate or flip objects to change their orientation.

Application Skills   You continue to work with the Natural Light presentation in this exercise. You will arrange the objects you created in the last exercise to complete the drawing.

TERMS

Rotate Turn an object on a central axis to a new orientation.

NOTES

Arranging Objects

- PowerPoint offers a number of tools to help you arrange shapes and other objects on a slide.
- You can find tools for arranging objects by clicking Arrange on the Home tab or in the Arrange group on the Drawing Tools Format tab.
- The arrangement tools fall into three general categories: tools for ordering objects, tools for grouping objects, and tools for positioning objects relative to each other or the slide. PowerPoint also supplies tools for changing the orientation of an object by rotating or flipping it.

- To make it easy to select objects for arranging or other manipulation, use the Selection and Visibility pane, new in PowerPoint 2007 (see the following illustration).

Select any object easily in this pane

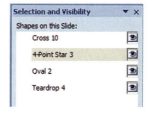

- The Selection and Visibility pane shows all objects currently displayed on the slide. To select any object, click it in the Selection and Visibility pane. This can be very helpful when objects are stacked. You can also click on the visibility symbol (the open eye) to hide an object.

- Objects in the Selection and Visibility pane are given default names (with accompanying numbers) that describe their shape or function. If you have four rectangles on a slide, however, it can be tedious to try to remember which is which.

- You can remedy this situation by renaming shapes in the pane. Click on an object name to open the default name for editing and then type your own names for objects.

  ✓ *Meaningful names for objects can also help you when you are creating animations for slide objects.*

Order Objects

- As you create objects on a slide, they stack up from the "back" (the first object created) to the "front" (the last object created), as shown in the following illustration.

Shapes stack up in the order in which they are created

- You can think of this process as creating a series of layers stacked on top of each other with an object on each layer.

- You may want to adjust the layers so that an object at the back of the stack comes to the front of the stack, or vice versa.

- To adjust how objects stack up on a slide, you use the order tools: Bring to Front, Send to Back, Bring Forward, and Send Backward.

  - The Bring to Front tool moves a selected object to the front or top of the stack so it is on top of all other objects.

  - The Send to Back tool moves the selected object to the back or bottom of the stack so it is below all other objects.

  - Use the Bring Forward tool to move an object one layer toward the front of the stack.

  - Use the Send Backward tool to move an object one layer toward the back of the stack.

Group and Ungroup Objects

- You can group the objects within a drawing to make them into one composition that can be treated as a single object. Grouping objects makes them easier to copy, move, or resize.

- A grouped object has only a single outline that surrounds the entire object, as shown in the following illustration. You only need to click once on a grouped object to select it.

Three rectangles grouped into a single shape

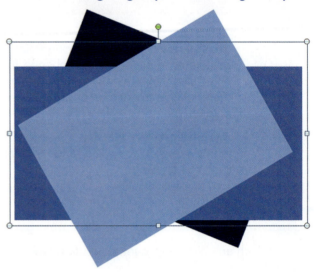

- To group objects, you select them and then use the Group option to combine the objects.

- Use Ungroup to separate a grouped object into its component parts so you can work with them individually.

- After you ungroup objects, they remain selected. Before you make any adjustment to the items, deselect them so you can work with them individually.

- You do not have to ungroup an object, however, if you want to make a change to a single object in the group. You can simply click on the object in the group to select it. The object is selected within the group outline, as shown in the following illustration.

Selecting a single item within a group

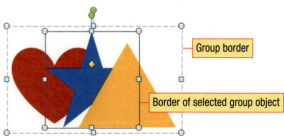

Group border

Border of selected group object

- Any changes you make will apply only to the selected object, not to the other objects in the group.
- If you ungroup objects to make changes, you can easily regroup the objects by clicking on one of the original group objects and then clicking Regroup.

Align and Distribute Objects

- When you have a number of objects on a slide, particularly similar shapes, you need to ensure that they display on the slide in a logical arrangement. It can be glaringly obvious to viewers when shapes do not line up with each other or are not evenly distributed on a slide.
- PowerPoint's alignment and distribution options make it easy to create an orderly arrangement of objects on a slide.
- You can align objects so they line up to the left, center, or right, or you can align them according to top, middle, or bottom, as shown in the following illustrations.

Shapes aligned at left, center, and right

Shapes aligned at top, middle, and bottom

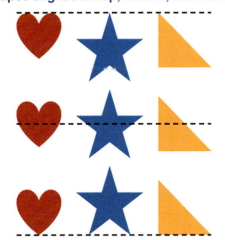

- Use the distribution options to make sure objects are evenly spaced on the slide. You can distribute objects vertically or horizontally.
- The following illustration shows a series of shapes that are not evenly spaced (top) and the result of distributing the shapes horizontally (bottom).

Unevenly spaced shapes (top) and distributed shapes (bottom)

- When aligning or distributing, you can choose whether to align or distribute objects relative to each other or relative to the slide. You may have to choose one of these options before you align or distribute objects to achieve the results you want.

Rotate and Flip Objects

- To provide more visual interest on a slide, you can rotate any object: shapes, pictures, text boxes, even PowerPoint's default placeholders. When you **rotate** an object, you turn it on a central axis to a new orientation.
- Drag a selected object's green rotation handle to rotate the object to a new orientation. As you drag the handle, the pointer changes shape and the object rotates as shown in the following illustration.

Rotate an object using the rotation handle

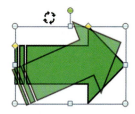

- You can also select a preset rotation such as Rotate Right 90° or Rotate Left 90° from the Rotate menu in the Arrange group or specify an exact degree of rotation on the Size tab of the Size and Position dialog box.

  ✓ *You can see this option in the Size and Position dialog box shown in Exercise 33.*

- If a shape or other object is not facing the way you want it to, you can use the flip options on the Rotate menu. Flip Vertical switches the object from top to bottom, and Flip Horizontal switches the object from left to right.

PROCEDURES

Display the Selection and Visibility Pane

1. Click **Home** tab .... Alt + H

   Drawing Group

2. Click **Arrange** button 🔲 .... G
3. Click **Selection Pane** .... P

   ✓ You can also open this pane by clicking the Select button on the Home tab or by clicking the Selection Pane button on the Drawing Tools Format tab.

Order Objects

1. Click the object to select it.
2. Click **Home** tab .... Alt + H

   Drawing Group

3. Click **Arrange** button 🔲 .... G
4. Click an option to change order:
   - **Bring to Front** .... R
   - **Send to Back** .... K
   - **Bring Forward** .... F
   - **Send Backward** .... B

   ✓ The order options can also be accessed from the Drawing Tools Format tab.

Group and Ungroup Objects

To group objects:

1. Click the first object.
2. Hold down ⬆Shift while clicking other objects to be grouped.
3. Click **Home** tab .... Alt + H

   Drawing Group

4. Click **Arrange** button 🔲 .... G
5. Click **Group** .... G

   ✓ The Group option can also be accessed from the Drawing Tools Format tab.

To ungroup shapes:

1. Click the grouped object.
2. Click **Home** tab .... Alt + H

   Drawing Group

3. Click **Arrange** button 🔲 .... G
4. Click **Ungroup** .... U
5. Click outside the objects to deselect all objects.

To regroup shapes:

1. Click an object that was previously grouped.
2. Click **Home** tab .... Alt + H

   Drawing Group

3. Click **Arrange** button 🔲 .... G
4. Click **Regroup** .... E

Align and Distribute Objects

To align objects:

1. Click the first object, hold down ⬆Shift, and click the other objects to align.
2. Click **Home** tab .... Alt + H

   Drawing Group

3. Click **Arrange** button 🔲 .... G
4. Click **Align** .... A
5. Click **Align to Slide** .... A
   if you want to align the shapes relative to the slide.

   OR

   Click **Align Selected Objects** .... O
   if you want to align the shapes relative to each other.

   ✓ If you made a change in how objects are aligned, you must click the Arrange button again and then click Align before you can select an alignment option.

6. Choose an alignment option:
   - **Align Left** L
   - **Align Center** C
   - **Align Right** .... R
   - **Align Top** .... T
   - **Align Middle** .... M
   - **Align Bottom** .... B

   ✓ Alignment options can also be accessed from the Drawing Tools Format tab.

To distribute objects:

1. Select the objects to be distributed.
2. Click **Home** tab .... Alt + H

   Drawing Group

3. Click **Arrange** button 🔲 .... G
4. Click **Align** .... A
5. Click **Align to Slide** .... A
   if you want to distribute the shapes relative to the slide.

   OR

   Click **Align Selected Objects** .... O
   if you want to distribute the shapes relative to each other.

   ✓ If you made a change in how objects are distributed, you must click the Arrange button again and then click Align before you can select a distribution option.

6. Choose a distribution option:
   - **Distribute Horizontally** .... H
   - **Distribute Vertically** V

   ✓ Distribution options can also be accessed from the Drawing Tools Format tab.

Rotate and Flip Objects

To rotate objects:

1. Click the object to rotate.
2. Click the green circular rotate handle at the top of the shape and drag to rotate the shape in the desired direction.

   OR

1. Click the object to rotate.
2. Click **Home** tab .... Alt + H

3. Click **Arrange** button .... G
4. Click **Rotate** .... O
5. Choose a rotation option:
   - **Rotate Right 90°** .... R
   - **Rotate Left 90°** L

   ✓ *Rotation options can also be accessed from the Drawing Tools Format tab.*

To flip objects:

1. Click the object to flip.
2. Click **Home** tab .... Alt + H

Drawing Group

3. Click **Arrange** button .... G
4. Click **Rotate** .... O
5. Choose a flip option:
   - **Flip Vertical** V
   - **Flip Horizontal** .... H

   ✓ *Flipping options can also be accessed from the Drawing Tools Format tab.*

EXERCISE DIRECTIONS

1. Start PowerPoint and open **33Light_xx** or open **34Light**. You are ready to use arrangement options to complete the drawing.
2. Save the presentation as **34Light_xx**.
3. First finalize the background shape:
   - Copy the blue rectangle in the center of the slide and paste it twice.
   - Rotate two of the shapes to create an interesting combination. (See Illustration A.) Adjust shape sizes if necessary. You may want to use the Selection and Visibility pane to quickly select rectangles as you arrange them.
   - Group the three rectangles and send them to the back.
4. Complete the sun drawing as follows:
   - Copy the sun shape and then paste it. Select both shapes and use the Align Center and Align Middle options to position the objects one on top of the other. Click outside the objects to deselect them.

   ✓ *Make sure the two shapes are exactly aligned before you go on to the next step.*

   - Rotate the top object to the left or right so the sun's "rays" are between those of the bottom object, giving the appearance of twice as many rays. (See Illustration A.)
   - Group the two objects, and then move the sun to a position at the lower-left of the background shape.
   - Scale the grouped object to 95% of its original size.

5. Finish the moon graphic as follows:
   - Copy the crescent moon currently to the left of the full moon shape.
   - Paste the copy, flip the copy horizontally, and position the second crescent to the right of the full moon. You may move all shapes as necessary to make room for the second crescent.
   - Align the moon shapes—the circle and the two crescents—by middle and distribute them horizontally relative to each other.
   - Group the moon shapes.
   - Center the moon object on the slide using the drawing guides or gridlines.
6. Use the Selection and Visibility pane to locate the white star if you can't see the shape, and then move it onto the blue shape if necessary.
7. Apply effects to the objects as follows:
   - Select the sun object and apply the Accent color 6, 5 pt glow effect.
   - Select the moon object and apply the same shadow effect you used for the shape with the text in it.
   - Select the star and choose the Glow effect. From the effect gallery, select More Glow Colors and choose white on the color palette.
8. Save your changes, close the presentation, and exit PowerPoint.

NATURAL
LIGHT, LTD

ON YOUR OWN

1. Open **OPP33_xx** or **OPP34**.

2. Save the presentation as **OPP34_xx**.

3. Use an alignment or distribution option to make sure the line and the shape on slide 1 align in a visually pleasing manner. Illustration A shows one option.

4. Group the line and the shape on slide 1 and rotate the shape as desired.

5. Use order tools to adjust layer order of the shapes in your drawing on slide 4. Use alignment or distribution options to fine-tune the arrangement of shapes. Illustration B shows a sample arrangement.

6. Save your changes, close the presentation, and exit PowerPoint.

Illustration A

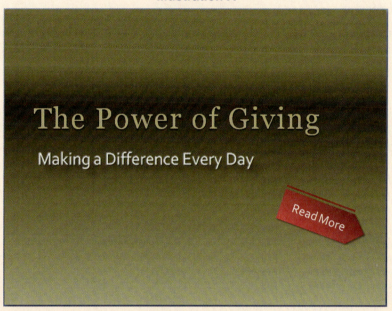

Illustration B

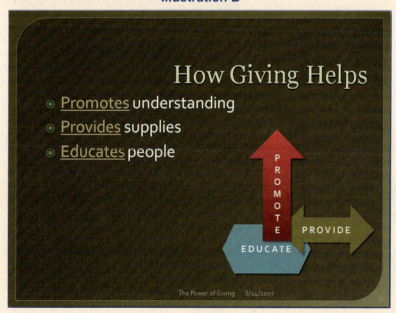

Skills Covered

- Insert a Picture from a File
- Modify and Format Pictures

Software Skills   You can insert your own pictures in a presentation and then use the enhanced picture tools to adjust the picture's appearance and apply special effects.

Application Skills   A local environmental group, Planet Earth, has asked you to prepare a presentation they can show on Earth Day. In this exercise, you begin the presentation by inserting and formatting pictures.

TERMS

Crop   Remove a portion of a picture that you don't want.

NOTES

Insert a Picture from a File

- You may be able to illustrate your presentations adequately using graphics and photos from PowerPoint's clip art files. But in some instances, you may want to include your own pictures of specific locations, events, or people.

- Use the Insert Picture from File icon in any content placeholder or the Picture button on the Insert tab to place your own picture file on a slide.

- This command opens the Insert Picture dialog box, shown in the following illustration, so you can navigate to and select the picture you want to insert.

Insert Picture dialog box

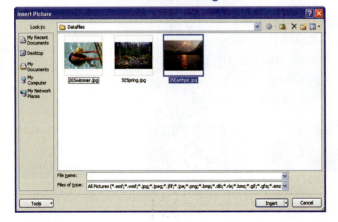

- A newly inserted picture is selected on the slide so that you can easily modify and format it if desired.

Modify and Format Pictures

- You can use some of the skills you have already learned to modify a picture. For example, you can resize a picture by dragging a corner handle, or reposition it by dragging it to a new location.

- For more control over the formatting process, use the tools on the Picture Tools Format tab, shown in the illustration at the top of the next page, to modify and enhance a picture.

- Options on this tab allow you to create interesting and unusual picture effects as well as specify a precise size.

Picture Tools Format tab

Adjustment Options

- Use the tools in the Adjust group to modify the appearance of the image. Some of these tools provide menus of preset adjustments so you can quickly apply an adjustment or give you the option of opening a dialog box for more control over the adjustment.

- Use the Brightness menu to adjust the lightness of the image. You can choose a brightness from the menu or use the Picture Corrections Options command to open the Format Picture dialog box, discussed later in this section.

- Use the Contrast menu to adjust the difference between light and dark areas of an image. Select from preset options or open the Format Picture dialog box for more control over contrast.

- The Recolor tool allows you to apply current theme colors to the selected image to create a special effect, as shown in the following illustration.

Original picture (left) and recolored picture (right)

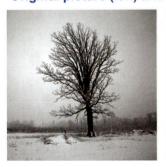 

- The Recolor gallery allows you to select any other color to use in the recoloring process and also gives you the option of making one or more colors in an image transparent using the Set Transparent Color command.

- When you click this command, a paintbrush icon attaches to the pointer. Click on the color you want to make transparent, as shown at left in the following illustration. All pixels of that color are removed to allow the background to show through, as shown at the right.

Click a color to make transparent (left) and the background shows through (right)

- Use the Compress Pictures option to reduce the file size of pictures embedded in a presentation. You will learn more about this option in Exercise 37.

- The Change Picture option reopens the Insert Picture dialog box so you can replace the currently selected picture with a different one.

- Use the Reset Picture option to restore a picture's original settings. Clicking this button reverses any changes you have made to size, brightness, contrast, or color.

- The Picture Correction Options command on the Brightness and Contrast menus opens the Format Picture dialog box, shown in the following illustration.

Format Picture dialog box

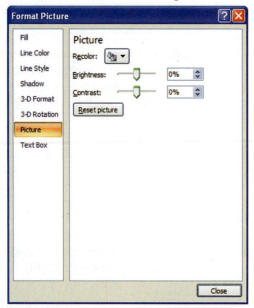

- You can use this dialog box to make a number of adjustments at one time to brightness, contrast, and color, or you can reset the picture to its original appearance.

- Note that this dialog box gives you a number of other options as well for modifying fill, border, and effects such as shadow and three-dimensional rotation.

Picture Styles Options

- The Picture Styles group lets you apply a number of interesting visual styles to your pictures.

- Use the Picture Styles gallery, shown in the following illustration, to apply a Quick Style to a picture. Quick Styles can include shapes, borders, and effects.

Picture Styles gallery

- Use the Picture Shape, Picture Border, and Picture Effect options if you want more control over the formats you apply to a picture. Clicking the Picture Shape button displays the Shapes gallery in which you can select any shape to apply to a picture.

Arranging and Sizing Options

- The Arrange group contains the arrangement tools you learned about in the previous exercise. If you have more than one image on a slide, you can use these tools to adjust order, alignment, distribution, rotation, and so on, or use the Group options to combine pictures into a single group that will be easy to manipulate.

- The Size group supplies width and height settings that allow you to precisely size a picture.

- The Crop option in the Size group allows you to **crop** a picture to remove portions of the picture you don't need, as shown in the following illustration. You can restore the hidden portion of the picture by using the Crop tool again.

Drag one of the crop handles to remove a portion of the picture

- If you prefer to scale a picture, you can click the Size group's dialog box launcher to open the Size and Position dialog box, where you can specify a percentage enlargement or reduction for the picture.

- You can also specify rotation and crop settings in the Size and Position dialog box or reset the picture to its original size.

PROCEDURES

Insert a Picture from a File

1. Click **Insert Picture from File** icon 🖼 in any content placeholder.

   OR

   a. Click **Insert** tab .... Alt+N

   ### Illustrations Group

   b. Click **Picture** button 🖼 ..... P

2. Navigate to the location where the file is stored and select the file.

3. Click [Insert] .... ↵Enter

Modify and Format Pictures

To adjust brightness and contrast:

1. Click the picture to select it.

2. Click **Picture Tools Format** tab .... Alt+J, P

   ### Adjust Group

3. Click **Brightness** button ☀ ...... B

   OR

   Click **Contrast** button ◐ .... N

4. Select a preset brightness or contrast option .... ↓, ↵Enter

   OR

   a. Click **Picture Corrections Options** C

   b. Drag the Brightness or Contrast slider, or use spin arrows to adjust the percentage of change.

   c. Click [Close] ↵Enter

To recolor a picture:

1. Click the picture to select it.

2. Click **Picture Tools Format** tab .... Alt+J, P

   ### Adjust Group

3. Click **Recolor** button 🖼 .... E

4. Select a theme color to apply .... ←→↑↓

5. Press ↵Enter.

To set transparent color:

1. Click the picture to select it.

2. Click **Picture Tools Format** tab .... Alt+J, P

   ### Adjust Group

3. Click **Recolor** button 🖼 .... E

4. Click **Set Transparent Color** ... S

5. Click on the color on the image to make transparent.

To apply picture style options:

1. Click the picture to select it.

2. Click **Picture Tools Format** tab .... Alt+J, P

   ### Picture Styles Group

3. Click **More** button ▼ .... K to display the Picture Styles gallery.

4. Select a style to apply .... ←→↑↓, ↵Enter

   OR

1. Click the picture to select it.

2. Click **Picture Tools Format** tab .... Alt+J, P

   ### Picture Styles Group

3. Select a formatting option:

   ■ Click **Picture Shape** button 🖼 .... I to select a shape for the picture.

   ■ Click **Picture Border** button 🖼 .... S, O to select a border color, weight, or style.

   ■ Click **Picture Effects** button 🖼 .... F to select an effect.

To crop a picture:

1. Click the picture to select it.

2. Click **Picture Tools Format** tab .... Alt+J, P

   ### Size Group

3. Click **Crop** button 🖼 C

4. Position the crop pointer on one of the cropping handles that display on the picture.

5. Drag to crop the picture as desired.

6. Click **Crop** button 🖼 .... Alt+J, P, C to complete the crop action.

To size a picture or other object:

1. Click the picture to select it.

2. Click **Picture Tools Format** tab .... Alt+J, P

   ### Size Group

3. Click in **Height** or **Width** box .... H or W

4. Type a precise height or width.

5. Press ↵Enter.

To scale a picture:

1. Click a picture to select it.

2. Click **Picture Tools Format** tab .... Alt+J, P

   ### Size Group

3. Click **Size** group dialog box launcher 🖼 .... S, Z

4. On **Size** tab, specify percentage of original size:

   ■ Click **Height** .... Alt+H and type a value or use spin arrows.

   ■ Click **Width** .... Alt+W and type a value or use spin arrows.

   ■ If Lock aspect ratio box is cleared, you can specify height and width independently.

5. Click [Close] ↵Enter

To reset a picture to its original appearance:

1. Click the picture to select it.

2. Click **Picture Tools Format** tab .... Alt+J, P

   ### Adjust Group

3. Click **Reset Picture** button 🖼 .... Q

EXERCISE DIRECTIONS

1. Start PowerPoint and open 35Earth.

2. Save the presentation as 35Earth_xx.

3. On slide 1, note that the gray area surrounding the earth logo is distracting. Make this gray color transparent.

   ✓ *You must click directly on some part of the earth to select this picture for editing.*

4. With the earth picture still selected, apply the 2.5 pt Soft Edges effect to the earth. Change the effect to the 5 pt Soft Edges effect.

5. This effect doesn't contribute to the picture, so remove it by selecting the No Soft Edges option on the Soft Edges palette.

6. Display slide 2, and insert the picture file 35Earthpic in the content placeholder.

7. Format the picture as follows:
   - Adjust brightness to make the picture 15% brighter.
   - Adjust contrast to 25%.

     ✓ *You will need to use the Format Picture dialog box to set these adjustments.*

   - Crop about half an inch from the bottom of the picture.
   - Apply the Drop Shadow Rectangle picture style. Your slide should look similar to Illustration A.

8. Save your changes, close the presentation, and exit PowerPoint.

Illustration A

The Gathering Storm

ON YOUR OWN

1. Open **OPP09_xx** or 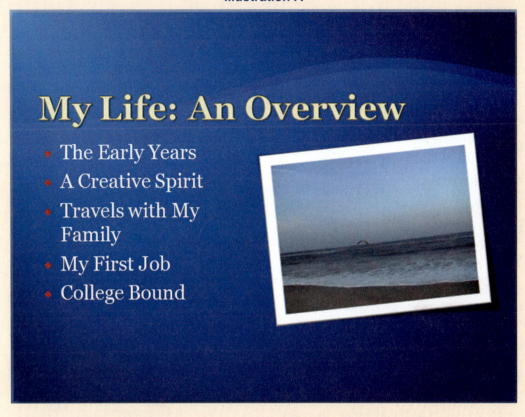**OPP35**.
2. Save the presentation as **OPP35_xx**.
3. Replace the clip art picture on slide 2 with a picture of you or your family or a family event.

4. Format the picture as desired by adjusting settings and applying a style or effect. Illustration A shows one idea.
5. Save your changes, close the presentation, and exit PowerPoint.

Illustration A

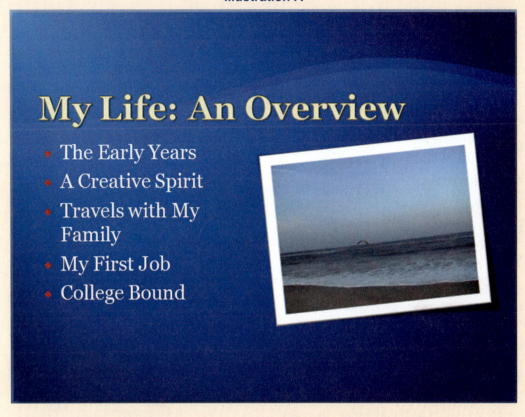

Skills Covered

- **Insert a Movie**
- **Insert Sounds and Music**

Software Skills   For a really dynamic presentation, add media clips such as movies and sounds. Media clips can add considerable impact to a presentation as well as convey information in ways that other graphic objects cannot.

Application Skills   You complete the Planet Earth presentation by inserting movie and sound files.

TERMS

No new terms in this exercise.

NOTES

Insert a Movie

- In PowerPoint, a *movie* can mean one of two things: an animated clip art graphic or an existing movie file saved in a standard multimedia format.

- Use one of these options to insert a movie on a slide:
  - Click the Insert Media Clip icon in any content placeholder to insert an existing movie file.
  - Click the Movie button on the Insert tab to insert a movie file.
  - Click the Movie button's down arrow to display a menu and choose either Movie from File or Movie from Clip Organizer.

- Choosing the Movie from Clip Organizer option opens the Clip Art task pane with available animated graphic movie files displayed in the results area and Movies already selected as the media type.

- You can search for movies using keywords just as when searching for other types of clip art. A search for movies related to the keyword *space* returns the files shown in the following illustration.

Locate an animated graphic movie in the Clip Art task pane

- Note the small star symbol at the lower-right corner of each thumbnail. This symbol signifies the file is animated.

- Insert an animated graphic movie the same way as any other clip art object, by clicking it in the task pane. Most animated graphic movies are fairly small and some cannot be enlarged without loss of quality.

- To see the animation in motion, display the slide in Slide Show view.

- If you choose to insert an existing movie file, the Insert Movie dialog box shown in the following illustration opens to allow you to navigate to the location of the file.

Insert Movie dialog box

- Note the Files of type box in the Insert Movie dialog box, which shows the types of movie files PowerPoint can handle: ASF, WMD, AVI, and MPEG, among others.

- As soon as you insert the file, PowerPoint displays the dialog box shown in the following illustration to allow you to choose how to play the movie during the presentation.

Choose how to control the movie

- The default choice, Automatically, starts the movie as soon as the slide displays on the screen. Use When Clicked if you want to control exactly when to play the movie.

- Use the tools on the Movie Tools Options tab, shown in the illustration at the bottom of this page, to work with a movie.

- Use the Preview button in the Play group to preview the movie while in Normal view.

- The Movie Options group gives you more control over how the movie plays during the presentation.
  - Use the Slide Show Volume option to control the movie's volume if it includes sound.
  - Change the play setting using the Play Movie list. You can play the movie automatically, when clicked, or set the movie to continue playing as you continue to display later slides.
  - You can choose to hide the movie during the show, play it at full screen size, loop it (play it over and over) until you stop it by pressing Esc, or return the movie to its first frame after it has finished playing.

- Use the Arrange tools to adjust the order or alignment of the movie object relative to other objects on the slide.

- Use the Size controls to adjust the height and width of the movie object. Be careful when doing so that you don't distort the movie images.

- Note from the previous illustration that the Picture Tools Format tab is also active when a movie object is selected. You can apply picture formats such as borders and effects to a movie object to further enhance it.

- When you insert a movie file on a slide, you establish a link from the file to the presentation. For this reason, you should store movie files in the same folder as the presentation and insert the file from that folder so PowerPoint will know where to find the file during the presentation.

  ✓ *If you find that a movie will not play or does not appear on a slide during a presentation, the link has probably been broken by moving the presentation or the movie file from its previous location. To reestablish it, reinsert the movie object from a known file location.*

Movie Tools Options tab

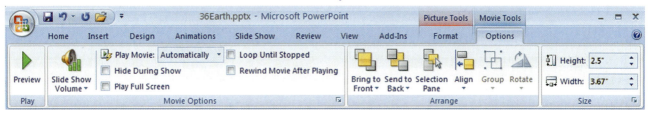

Insert Sounds and Music

- You can add sound and music clips to your presentation to make it more interesting or to emphasize a slide. Your computer must have speakers and a sound card to play music or sounds during a presentation.

- Use the Sound button on the Insert tab to choose what kind of sound to insert:

  - Sound from File allows you to select an existing sound file using the Insert Sound dialog box. This process is similar to inserting an existing movie file. The sound file can be in any of a number of formats, including AIFF, AU, MIDI, MP3, WAV, and WMA.

  - Sound from Clip Organizer opens the Clip Art task pane with all available sound files displayed and the Sounds media type selected. You can search for a sound by keyword just as you search for clip art or movies.

  - Play CD Audio Track lets you play one or more tracks from a CD in your computer's CD or DVD drive. Choosing this option opens the Insert CD Audio dialog box shown in the following illustration, where you can choose the track to start and end with and set the amount of time to play the track. You can also choose to loop the audio, adjust its volume, and hide the sound icon if desired.

  - Use the Record Sound option to record your own sound or music for the slide.

Insert CD Audio dialog box

- When you insert any sound file, a sound icon displays in the center of the slide and you are prompted to choose whether the sound will play automatically when the slide displays or when you click the sound icon.

- You can move the sound icon to any location on the slide just as you move any object. If you have chosen to play the sound automatically, you can even move the sound icon off the edge of the slide so it will not display during the show.

  ✓ *The sound icon must appear on the slide if you intend to control a sound by clicking it during the presentation.*

- You can preview a sound file by double-clicking it on the slide in Normal view. Stop the sound by clicking anywhere else on the slide.

- Use the Sound Tools Options tab, shown in the illustration at the bottom of this page, to control sound options.

- Many of these options look similar to those on the Movie Tools Options tab and operate in the same way. You can use Preview to listen to the sound in Normal view, for example, and use the Sound Options group tools to hide the sound icon, loop the sound, or adjust the play setting.

- The Max Sound File Size setting in the Sound Options group determines whether a sound file will be embedded or linked to the slide. By default, only WAV files smaller than the maximum sound file size will be embedded on the slide. All other file formats, and WAV files larger than the maximum file size, will be linked to the slide.

- To avoid a situation where a sound does not play because the linked file is elsewhere, store sound files in the same folder with the presentation and insert them from that folder.

  ✓ *To reestablish a link to a sound file, move the sound file to the same folder with the presentation and reinsert the sound file from that location.*

- You can adjust the maximum sound file size if you have a good reason for wanting to embed a WAV file on a slide rather than link it.

Sound Tools Options tab

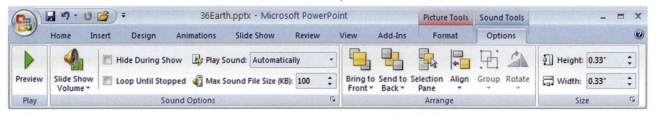

■ Note that if you use the Package for CD feature to prepare a presentation for use elsewhere, the feature will automatically locate and store files such as movies and sounds with the presentation so you will have all necessary materials on one disk or in one folder.

✓ *You learn more about packaging a presentation in Lesson 5, Exercise 49.*

■ If you choose to play a CD track on a slide, you use the CD Audio Tools Options tab to control how the track plays. You can have the track play across a series of slides, for example, rather than on a single slide.

PROCEDURES

Insert a Movie

To insert an animated graphic movie:

1. Click **Insert** tab .... `Alt`+`N`

   Media Clips Group

2. Click **Movie** button 🎬 .... `V`
3. Click **Movie from Clip Organizer** .... `M`
4. In the Clip Art task pane, type a keyword in the Search for box.
5. Click the Search in down arrow and select collections to search.
6. Click `Go` .... `↵Enter` to begin search.
7. Click animated graphic file from the search results to insert the movie on the slide.

To insert an existing movie file:

1. Click **Insert Media Clip** button 🎬 in any content placeholder.

   OR

   a. Click **Insert** tab .... `Alt`+`N`

   Media Clips Group

   b. Click **Movie** button 🎬 .... `V`
   c. Click **Movie from File** .... `F`
2. Navigate to the location where the file is stored and select the file.

3. Click `OK` .... `↵Enter`
4. Choose how to play the movie:
   ■ Click `Automatically` `A` to start the movie when the slide displays.
   ■ Click `When Clicked` `C` to start the movie when you click it.

To preview a movie in Normal view:

1. Click the movie object to select it.
2. Click **Movie Tools Options** tab .... `Alt`+`J`, `N`

   Play Group

3. Click **Preview** button ▶ .... `P`

Insert Sounds and Music

To insert a sound from the Clip Organizer:

1. Click **Insert** tab .... `Alt`+`N`

   Media Clips Group

2. Click **Sound** button 🔊 .... `O`
3. Click **Sound from the Clip Organizer** .... `S`
4. In the Clip Art task pane, type a keyword in the Search for box.
5. Click the Search in down arrow and select collections to search.
6. Click `Go` .... `↵Enter` to begin search.

7. Click sound file from the search results to insert the sound icon on the slide.
8. Choose how to play the sound:
   ■ Click `Automatically` `A` to play the sound when the slide displays.
   ■ Click `When Clicked` `C` to play the sound when you click the sound icon.

To insert an existing sound file:

1. Click **Insert** tab .... `Alt`+`N`

   Media Clips Group

2. Click **Sound** button 🔊 .... `O`
3. Click **Sound from File** .... `F`
4. Navigate to the location where the file is stored and select the file.
5. Click `OK` .... `↵Enter`
6. Choose how to play the sound:
   ■ Click `Automatically` `A` to start the movie when the slide displays.
   ■ Click `When Clicked` `C` to start the movie when you click it.

To control sound options:

1. Click sound object to select it.
2. Click **Sound Tools Options** tab .... `Alt`+`J`, `N`
3. Select options on this tab to control the sound as desired.

EXERCISE DIRECTIONS

1. Start PowerPoint and open **35Earth_xx** or open **36Earth**.

2. Save the presentation as **36Earth_xx**.

3. On slide 1, insert the movie file **36Earthmovie.mpeg** in the content placeholder. Choose to play the movie automatically.

4. Format the movie as follows:
   - Move the movie upwards so that the top of its selection box is more or less aligned with the top of the text in the placeholder to the left of the movie.
   - Change the height of the movie object to 2.7 inches.
   - Preview the movie in Normal view. The slide should look like Illustration A after the movie finishes playing.

5. Add a sound clip to slide 2 as follows:
   - Choose to insert a sound from the Clip Organizer.
   - Search using the keyword *thunder* to locate a thunder sound.
   - Insert one of the resulting sound files and choose to have it play automatically.
   - Move the sound icon off the slide so it will not display when you show the slides.

6. View the slides in Slide Show view to see the movie and hear the sound.

7. Save your changes, close the presentation, and exit PowerPoint.

Illustration A

ON YOUR OWN

1. Open **OPP35_xx** or 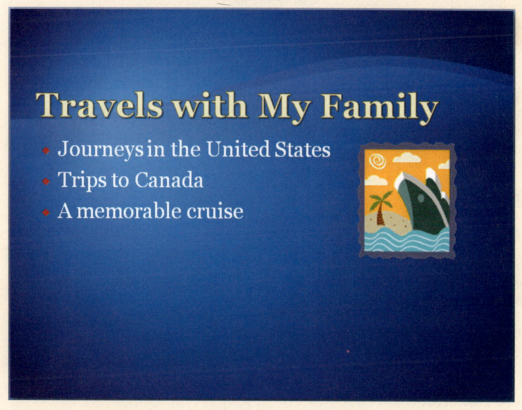**OPP36**.

2. Save the presentation as **OPP36_xx**.

3. Locate a sound or music file that complements the information in your presentation. You may use a sound effect or a music file. If you choose a music file, decide whether you want the music to play on a single slide or across multiple slides.

4. If you have video footage of you or your family in a suitable format (AVI or MPEG), insert it on one of the slides. Otherwise, locate a clip art animated graphic movie and insert it on a slide. Illustration A shows an appropriate animated graphic movie file on a slide.

5. View your slides in Slide Show view to check sound and movie settings.

6. Save your changes, close the presentation, and exit PowerPoint.

Illustration A

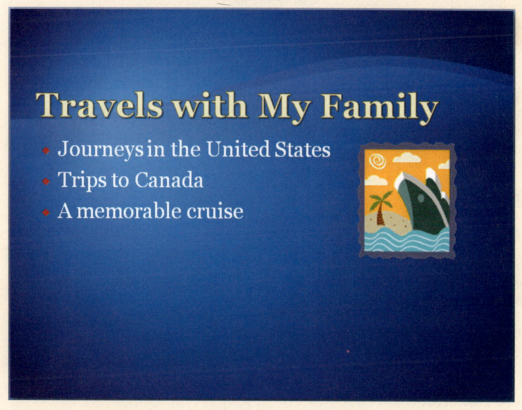

Skills Covered

■ **Create a Photo Album**　　　　　■ **Compress Pictures**

Software Skills　PowerPoint's Photo Album feature makes it easy to create a presentation that consists of illustrations and their captions. You can arrange the photos in a number of layouts and apply enhancements such as frames and other effects. To reduce file size of a presentation, you can compress pictures.

Application Skills　Voyager Adventure Travel is setting up a new hiking adventure to Glacier National Park and wants you to create a photo album of Glacier Park images to present at a travel show.

TERMS

Resolution　The number of dots or pixels per linear unit of output. For example, a computer monitor's resolution is usually 72 pixels per inch.

NOTES

Create a Photo Album

- PowerPoint's Photo Album feature allows you to collect pictures and then create a new presentation to display those pictures as an album.

- A PowerPoint photo album is just like a physical photo album in that it is designed primarily to show-case images. You can add text in the form of captions or text boxes, but the focus of a photo album is on the pictures.

- Use the Photo Album button on the Insert tab to begin creating a new photo album.

- The Photo Album dialog box, shown in the illustration at right, is where you choose pictures for the album and select settings for the way the pictures will display.

Photo Album dialog box

- Selected picture file names display in the Pictures in album list in the center of the dialog box. The currently selected picture displays in the Preview area.

- You can choose to add a text box to the list of pictures. Text boxes display according to the current picture layout, at the same size as the pictures. If you have chosen to lay out the album with two pictures per page, for example, you can insert a text box in the place of one of those images so that you have a picture and a text box on the same slide.

- You can adjust the order of pictures or remove a selected picture. You can use the buttons below the preview to flip the picture horizontally or vertically, adjust its contrast, or adjust its brightness.

- The Picture Options check boxes allow you to add a caption to each picture or transform all pictures to black and white. By default, the captions that display use the picture's file name, but you can replace these captions with more descriptive ones on the slides.

- The Album Layout area gives you a number of options for formatting the album.

  - Select from seven different picture layout options, including the Fit to slide option that displays each picture the full size of the slide; options to display one, two, and four pictures per slide; and options to display varying numbers of pictures with slide titles. As you select one of these layout options, the small preview at the right shows your choice.

  - Choose from seven different frame options, from a simple black frame to shadow and soft edge effects.

  - Select one of PowerPoint's default themes, or another available theme, to format the album.

- Once you are satisfied with the list of pictures and the settings, you create the album. PowerPoint places the chosen pictures in a new presentation that includes a title slide with a default title and the current user name in the subtitle.

- You save the photo album like any other PowerPoint presentation.

- The following illustration shows how a new photo album looks in Slide Sorter view.

A photo album in Slide Sorter view

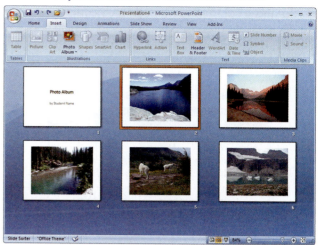

- You can edit an existing photo album by displaying it in Normal view and then clicking the down arrow on the Photo Album button. Choosing Edit Photo Album opens the Photo Album dialog box. After you make changes, click the Update button to apply your changes to the album.

- If you did not choose a theme in the Photo Album dialog box, you can apply one at any time to the presentation.

Compress Pictures

- A photo album—or any presentation that contains pictures, movies, or sounds—can turn into a large file that may be a challenge to store or take extra time to open.

- To streamline a presentation's file size, use the Compress Pictures option on the Picture Tools Format tab.

- Clicking this button opens the Compress Pictures dialog box shown in the following illustration.

Compress Pictures dialog box

- By default, PowerPoint will compress all pictures in the presentation. If you want to compress only a selected picture or pictures, click the Apply to selected pictures only check box.

- For more control over the compression settings, click the Options button to display the Compression Settings dialog box shown in the following illustration.

Compression Settings dialog box

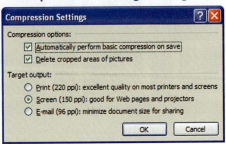

- Note that by default PowerPoint compresses pictures automatically when the file is saved.

- If you have cropped pictures to hide areas you don't want to see, you can choose to delete the cropped portions of the pictures. Once you do this, of course, you cannot go back and uncrop a picture.

- The Target output settings allow you to choose a **resolution** appropriate for the way the pictures will be viewed. Measurements for the resolution are given in ppi, pixels per inch.

- If the slides will eventually be printed, use the Print setting for the best quality. Slides that will be viewed on a screen will look fine at the Screen setting. Use the E-mail setting to reduce file size so a presentation will transmit quickly.

  ✓ *You will learn about sending a presentation via e-mail for review in the next lesson.*

PROCEDURES

Create a Photo Album

1. Click **Insert** tab...................... Alt+N

   Illustrations Group

2. Click **Photo Album** button .... A

3. Click **New Photo Album**............... A

4. Click [File/Disk...] .... Alt+F

5. Navigate to the location of the pictures you want to use in the album and select one or more pictures.

6. Click [Insert ▾] .... ↵Enter

   ✓ *Repeat step 6 until all pictures are inserted.*

7. Click [Create] .... Alt+C

To change the order of pictures in the album:

In Photo Album dialog box

1. Select a picture in the **Pictures in album** list........... Alt+R, ↓ or ↑

2. Click [↑] to move picture up in the list.

   OR

   Click [↓] to move picture down in the list.

To remove a picture from the album list:

In Photo Album dialog box

1. Select a picture in the **Pictures in album** list.......... Alt+R, ↓ or ↑

2. Click [Remove] .... Alt+V

To specify picture options:

In Photo Album dialog box

- Click **Captions below ALL pictures** check box.................. Alt+A

  ✓ *This option is not available for the Fit to slide picture layout.*

- Click **ALL pictures black and white** .... Alt+K

To specify a layout for the album:

In Photo Album dialog box

1. Click the **Picture layout** down arrow .... Alt+P, ↓

2. Select the desired layout .... ↓, ↵Enter

To specify frame options:

In Photo Album dialog box

1. Click the **Frame shape** down arrow .... Alt+M, ↓

2. Select the desired frame option......................... ↓, ↵Enter

To specify a theme:

In Photo Album dialog box

1. Click [Browse...] .... Alt+B

2. Choose a theme ...... ←→↑↓

3. Click [Select] .... ↵Enter

Edit a Photo Album

1. Click **Insert** tab............... Alt+N

   Illustrations Group

2. Click **Photo Album** button .... A

3. Click **Edit Photo Album**............... E

4. Modify settings in Photo Album dialog box as desired.

5. Click [Update] .... Alt+U

Compress Pictures

1. Select any picture in a presentation, or select only the pictures you want to compress.
2. Click **Picture Tools Format** tab .... Alt + J , P

   Adjust Group

3. Click **Compress Pictures** button 🔳 .... M
4. Click [OK] .... ↵Enter to compress all pictures in the presentation.

   OR

   a. Click **Apply to selected pictures only** .... Alt + A
   b. Click [OK] .... ↵Enter

To specify compression settings:

In Compress Pictures dialog box

1. Click [Options...] .... Alt + O
2. Select compression options:
   - **Automatically perform basic compression on save** .... Alt + A
   - **Delete cropped areas of pictures** .... Alt + D
3. Select target output settings:
   - **Print (300 ppi)** .... Alt + P for slides that will printed.
   - **Screen (150 ppi)** .... Alt + S for slides that will be viewed on a monitor or other screen.
   - **E-mail (96 ppi)** .... Alt + E for slides that will be sent via e-mail.
4. Click [OK] .... ↵Enter

EXERCISE DIRECTIONS

1. Start PowerPoint and choose to begin a new photo album.
2. Select the following picture files for the album: 🔘**37Glacier1**, 🔘**37Glacier2**, 🔘**37Glacier3**, 🔘**37Glacier4**, and 🔘**37Glacier5**.
3. Make the following changes in the dialog box:
   - Make sure the pictures are listed from 1 to 5, and then move 37Glacier2 below 37Glacier3 in the picture list.
   - Choose the 1 picture layout.
   - Choose any frame option.
   - Choose to set captions below all pictures.
4. Create the album.
5. On the title slide, change the title to **Voyager Travel Adventures Presents**. Change the subtitle to **Glacier National Park**.

6. View the slides in Slide Show view to see the pictures in the album.
7. The captions do not add much to the album. Choose to edit the album and turn off captions for all slides. Then select the Centered Shadow Rectangle frame option and update the photo album.
8. Apply the Concourse theme to the title slide only.
9. View your album again in Slide Show view to check your final settings. Your first picture slide should look similar to Illustration A.
10. Compress all pictures in the presentation for screen output.
11. Save the presentation as **37Glacier_xx**, close the presentation, and exit PowerPoint.

ON YOUR OWN

Create a photo album of places in your city, town, or neighborhood. Before you begin this exercise, take pictures using a digital camera, scan existing pictures, or locate pictures on the Internet that you can save to your computer. Try to find or create at least five pictures.

1. Start PowerPoint and begin a new photo album.
2. Insert your pictures in the album and arrange them in an attractive way.
3. Select the number of pictures per slide and decide whether or not to add captions. You may also want to add text boxes to allow you to insert explanatory text.
4. View the completed album and change captions if desired.
5. Edit the photo album to choose a different frame style.
6. Edit the title slide to use your name and an appropriate title. Apply a theme if desired. Illustration A shows a sample layout for one slide.
7. Save the presentation as **OPP37_xx**.
8. View your slides in Slide Show view to check your pictures.
9. Save your changes, close the presentation, and exit PowerPoint.

Illustration A

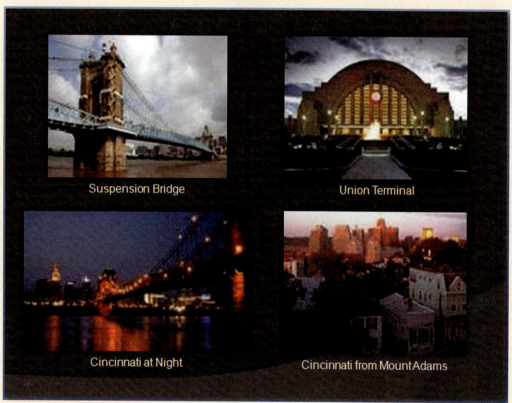

Skills Covered

■ **About the Slide Master**

■ **Customize Slide Master Elements**

■ **Create a Custom Layout**

Software Skills   A presentation's slide master controls the appearance and layout of all slides in the presentation. Use the master to easily adjust elements for an entire presentation. Create a new layout to further customize a presentation.

Application Skills   Natural Light has asked you to fine-tune a presentation they are preparing for a home décor trade show. They have asked you to make some changes that will apply to a number of slides, so you will customize the slide master by applying a theme, changing bullets, colors, and the background, and by adding a new layout for a specific kind of content.

TERMS

Slide master   A slide that controls the appearance of all slides in a presentation. If you make a change to the master, all slides based on that master will display those changes.

NOTES

About the Slide Master

■ A **slide master** controls the appearance of slides in a presentation by storing information about background, fonts, colors, and the placement of place-holders on a slide. PowerPoint supplies a slide master for each theme.

■ If you wish to make global changes throughout a presentation—for example, specifying a new font for all titles or adding a logo to all slides—you can make the change once on the slide master and then see that change on all slides based on that master.

■ You work with slide masters in Slide Master view. Use the Slide Master button on the View tab to switch to Slide Master view, shown in the following illustration.

Slide master and the Slide Master tab

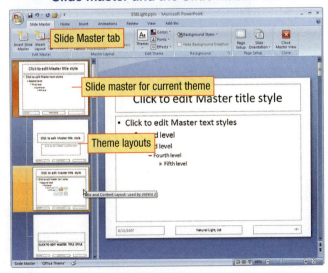

- The slide master displays at the top of the left pane, and the layouts for the theme display below the slide master. These are the same layouts you choose among when you add a new slide or change a slide layout.

- Rest the mouse pointer on any layout in the list to see a ScreenTip giving the layout name and the number of slides in the presentation that use that layout.

- You can select any of these layouts to make changes that will apply only to slides based on that layout.

- Some changes you make to the slide master will also appear on other layouts. For example, if you change the title font on the slide master, the same change will be made to the title font on some of the other layouts.

Customize Slide Master Elements

- One easy way to customize a slide master is to move or resize placeholders. You do this by simply dragging a placeholder or sizing handle, just as you would when modifying a placeholder in Normal view.

- You can also delete placeholders on any master layout if you know you will not use them. This includes the title and content placeholders as well as those for the date, footer, and slide number.

- You can modify text formats such as font, font style, font size, color, alignment, and so on by clicking the object you want to format on the slide master in the Slide pane and then applying the desired text formats using the tools on the Home tab.

- Applying bold or a different font color to the slide number placeholder on the slide master, for example, quickly formats all slide numbers in the presentation. Applying center alignment to a slide master title centers titles on all slides.

- Modify bullet symbols and colors on the master by clicking in a bullet level and then selecting new formats in the Bullets and Numbering dialog box, accessed from the Home tab.

- The Slide Master tab, shown in the following illustration, provides additional tools for customizing slide master elements.

- The Edit Master group gives you several options for editing masters.
  - Use the Insert Slide Master button to insert another slide master with its accompanying layouts. You can format additional slide masters with formats different from those of your default slide master. Using more than one slide master gives you the freedom to pick and choose among layouts when creating slides.
  - Click the Insert Layout button to add a new layout to the slide master list. You can customize this layout for a specific purpose, as described in the next section.
  - You can use the Delete option to delete any new layout or slide master you have added to the list, but you cannot delete any of the default slide master layouts, or the default slide master itself.
  - Use the Rename button to give a layout a new name that will display in the New Slide and Slide Layout palettes.
  - The Preserve button allows you to keep a slide master stored with a presentation even if no slides in the presentation use that master.

- The Master Layout group contains tools for controlling default placeholders and adding new placeholders.
  - Clicking the Master Layout button when the slide master is selected displays a list of the default placeholders. If you have deleted one of the default placeholders, you can use this dialog box to select the placeholder and restore it to the slide master, as shown in the following illustration.

Master layout dialog box lets you restore a placeholder

Slide Master tab

- When creating your own layout, you use the Insert Placeholder palette to add placeholders to the layout.
  - Use the Title and/or Footers check box to quickly turn off these placeholders on any layout.
- Use the familiar tools in the Edit Theme group to apply a theme to a slide master or select new theme colors, fonts, or effects.
- The Background group tools are identical to the background tools on the Design tab. They allow you to modify a background or hide background graphics on any slide master layout.
- Use the Page Setup group tools to modify slide master size and orientation just as you would in Normal view.

Create a Custom Layout

- Although PowerPoint provides a number of useful and versatile layouts, you may discover that you need to create your own layout for a specific type of content.
- If you need only one such special slide, you can easily create it by positioning objects on a blank or title only slide. If you will need a number of slides with the same arrangement, you can save yourself a lot of time by creating a custom layout.
- Use the Insert Layout button in the Edit Master group on the Slide Master tab to add a new layout to the list in the left pane. When you add a layout, a new master displays in the slide pane.
- You can then use the Insert Placeholder palette, shown in the following illustration, to add any of the typical placeholders to the slide.

Insert Placeholder palette

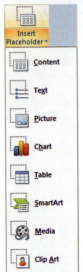

- You draw and position the placeholders just as if they were shapes.
- If you insert a Text placeholder, you can format the text as desired so it will always display those formats on slides created from the layout.
- The following illustration shows two clip art placeholders added to a new layout, along with two text placeholders that are formatted to display text in 20-point Arial italic.

Two clip art placeholders and two text placeholders on a new layout

- When creating your own layout, you may wish to display the grid to help you arrange placeholders so that they align attractively with each other and other placeholders on the slide.
- Rename a custom layout if desired to describe it. Custom layouts display on the layout gallery along with the other default layouts.

PROCEDURES

View the Slide Master

1. Click **View** tab............... Alt+W

   Presentation Views Group

2. Click **Slide Master**
   button 🖻 .... M

To close Slide Master view:

- Click **Close Master
  View** button ❌.

Customize Slide Master Elements

To modify existing placeholders:

- Drag a placeholder to a new
  position.
- Resize a placeholder by dragging a sizing handle.
- Delete a placeholder by
  selecting its outside border
  and pressing Del.

To modify slide master text:

- Click in the text to modify and
  use Font or Paragraph tools on
  the Home tab to make
  changes.

To modify bullets on the slide master:

1. In Slide Master view, click in
   the bulleted text you want to
   modify. (For example, to modify the bullet formats of the
   first-level bulleted text, click
   *Click to edit Master text
   styles.*)
2. Click **Home** tab .... Alt+H

3. Click **Bullets** button ☰ ▾ down
   arrow .... U
4. Select a different standard bullet character.

   OR

   a. Click **Bullets and
      Numbering** .... N

   b. Click a standard bullet
      character or choose your
      own **Picture** to use art or
      Customize to change the bul-
      let character.

   c. Click **Size** .... Alt+S
      and type the desired per-
      centage of text size.

   d. Click **Color** .... Alt+C
      and select a new color for
      the bullet from the palette.

   e. Click [OK] .... ↵Enter

Create a Custom Layout in Slide Master View

1. Click **View** tab .... Alt+W

   Presentation Views Group

2. Click **Slide Master**
   button 🖻 .... M

   Edit Master Group

3. Click **Insert Layout**
   button 🖻 .... Alt+M, I
4. Choose to display master
   elements:

   - Click **Title** .... E
     to show or hide the Title
     placeholder.

   - Click **Footers** .... F
     to show or hide the footer
     placeholders.

To insert placeholders:

   Master Layout Group

1. Click **Insert Placeholder**
   button 🖩 .... Alt+M, A
2. Select the type of placeholder
   to insert.
3. Draw the placeholder on the
   slide.
4. Format the placeholder as
   desired.

To rename a layout in Slide Master view:

1. Select the layout to rename.

   Edit Master Group

2. Click **Rename**
   button 🖻 .... Alt+M, R
3. Type the new name for the
   layout.
4. Click [Rename] .... ↵Enter

EXERCISE DIRECTIONS

1. Start PowerPoint and open 🔵 **38Light**.

2. Save the presentation as **38Light_xx**.

3. Your client has asked you to apply a new theme or modify the background to give the presentation more interest. You will apply a new theme in Slide Master view:
   - Display Slide Master view and select the Office Theme Slide Master at the top of the list in the left pane.
   - Apply the Apex theme. Close Slide Master view to see how this theme looks with the current presentation.

4. You chose the Apex theme because the shafts of light seemed appropriate, but the result is a bit subdued. Next you will try creating a custom background for all slides:
   - Return to Slide Master view and select the Apex Slide Master at the top of the left pane if necessary.
   - Open the Format Background dialog box and specify a gradient fill.
   - Choose the Ocean preset and the Rectangular type. Do not change direction.
   - Remove Stop 1. (Make sure Stop 1 shows below Gradient stops and then click the Remove button.) The gradient now has only three stops, rather than four.
   - For the new Stop 1, change the color to the Light Blue under Standard Colors. The gradient is now a more subtle blend of blues. Apply the background to all layouts and close the dialog box.

5. Change the theme colors to those for the Module theme.

6. Modify the bullet symbols and colors as follows:
   - Change the first-level bullet symbol to a five-pointed star (choose Customize in the Bullets and Numbering dialog box and select the star from the displayed symbols). Change the size to 70% and the color to 40% lighter Gold.
   - Change the second-level bullet symbol to 90% of text size and change the color to 25% darker Orange.

7. Change the color of the text in the date, footer, and slide number placeholders to white.

8. Add a graphic that will appear on all slides as follows:
   - Draw a four-pointed star about 0.75 inches tall by 0.5 inches wide.
   - Remove the outline, fill with white, and add a white glow effect. (Apply the glow effect, then change the glow color to white using More Glow Colors on the Glow gallery.)
   - Position the star in the upper-right corner. It should display on all slides in that location.

9. Display the Title Slide Layout (just below the Slide Master in the left pane) and change the color of the title to the lightest gold theme color (Bold, Accent 1, Lighter 80%). Note that making this change does not affect the title colors on other layouts.

10. Display the Comparison Layout in the left pane and make the following changes to the two placeholders directly under the title placeholder:
    - Fill each placeholder with 25% darker Orange and apply a shadow effect.
    - Change the text case to Sentence and center the text.

11. Create a custom layout to display featured products as follows:
    - Insert a layout at the bottom of the layout list.
    - Change the size of the title to 32 points and left align the title.
    - Draw a Clip Art placeholder that is about 3.75 inches high by 3 inches wide and position it as shown in Illustration A. (Don't worry if the text in the placeholder displays a bullet.)
    - Draw a Text placeholder that is about 1.5 inches high by 4 inches wide and position it as shown in Illustration A.
    - Delete all the text in the Text placeholder. On the Home tab, turn off bullet formatting and launch the Paragraph dialog box. Remove any indents and spacing above the text.
    - Change the text size to 20 points.
    - Rename the custom layout as **Featured Item**.

12. Exit Slide Master view. Navigate through the slides to see how your changes have affected the look of the presentation.

13. Add a new slide at the end of the presentation with the new Featured Item layout. Add content as follows:

- Insert the title **Featured Item**.
- Click the Clip Art placeholder and in the Clip Art task pane search for photos with the keyword *chandelier* and insert the picture of the red room with the crystal chandelier.

- Type the following text in the text box:

  Chandeliers are in! We have an amazing variety, from rustic wrought iron to brass to glittering crystal.

14. Save your changes, close the presentation, and exit PowerPoint.

Illustration A

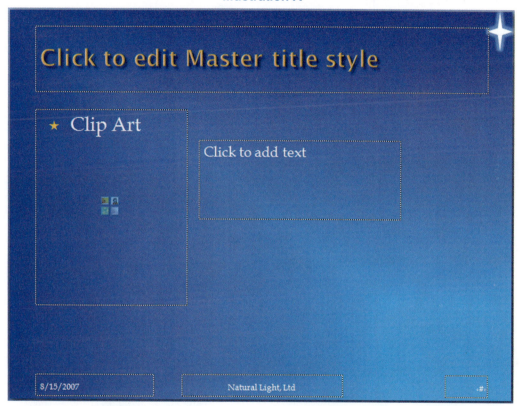

ON YOUR OWN

1. Open **OPP34_xx** or ⊙**OPP38**.
2. Save the presentation as **OPP38_xx**.
3. On the slide master, create a new background for the slides. You may adjust the gradient that forms the slide background or modify the rounded-corner rectangle on top of the background with a new fill, border, or effect, or make any other change to the background that improves the appearance of the slides.
4. Change the bullet symbol and color for first-level and second-level bullets. You may also want to adjust the indents for the second-level bullets.
5. Change the color of the slide number and apply bold formatting.
6. Change the color and position of the footer and date placeholders. Adjust text alignment in the placeholders if desired.
7. Make any other adjustments you think improve the look of the presentation's slides. Illustration A shows one slide after the slide master changes.
8. Save your changes, close the presentation, and exit PowerPoint.

Illustration A

How to Get Involved

- Volunteer your services
  - ✓ Newspapers list volunteer opportunities on a weekly basis
- Find a local chapter or organization
  - ✓ Try Web sites for lists of local chapters
- Attend an event such as a walkathon or other benefit
  - ✓ MS Walk coming up in September
  - ✓ AIDS Awareness Week in November

The Power of Giving   8/17/2007   6

Skills Covered

■ **Work with the Notes Master**　　■ **Work with the Handout Master**

Software Skills　You learned in the previous exercise how to make changes to the slide master that modify formats throughout a presentation. You can also work with the masters for notes pages and handouts to adjust the appearance of slides shown in these views.

Application Skills　In this exercise, you will return to an earlier presentation for Holmes Medical Center to customize the notes and handouts masters.

TERMS

No new terms in this exercise.

NOTES

Work with the Notes Master

■ As the appearance of slides is controlled by the slide master, the appearance of notes pages and handouts are controlled by their own masters.

■ The notes master controls the placeholders used to display information in Notes Page view, as shown in the following illustration.

Notes Master view

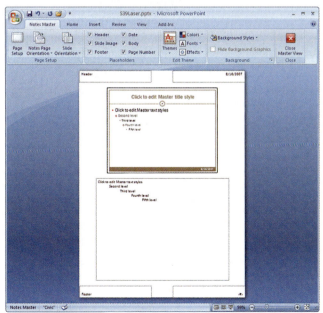

■ By default, the notes master displays placeholders for the header, date, slide image, body (the area where you insert notes), footer, and page number. You can adjust the size or position of any of these placeholders.

■ As for the slide masters, you can modify text formats for any placeholder that contains text. For example, you can apply bold formatting to the header placeholder or change the alignment in the body placeholder to center align all notes in this placeholder.

■ You can also add content to the placeholder, such as a new text box or a graphic that will then display on all notes pages.

■ For a special look on notes pages you print, you can apply graphic formats such as Quick Styles or fills, borders, and effects to any placeholder on the notes master.

■ The Notes Master tab, shown in the illustration at the top of the next page, gives you a number of options for customizing the notes master.

■ The Page Setup group options let you change size or orientation of the notes page itself and the slide image on the master.

- Use the Page Setup button to open the Page Setup dialog box, where you can specify the size you intend to use for display or output. The slide image on the master adjusts accordingly.

- If you have a great many notes to organize, you can allow more room for the body placeholder by changing the notes page orientation to landscape.

  ✓ *Note that if you change the notes master orientation to landscape, the handout master will also be displayed in landscape orientation.*

- You can also change the slide image placeholder from the default landscape to portrait if desired.

▪ The Placeholders group contains check boxes you can use to show or hide the standard notes master placeholders.

▪ Note that even though the Themes button appears on the Notes Master tab, you cannot use it to apply a theme. You can, however, use the Colors, Fonts, and Effects buttons to apply theme formatting.

▪ By default, a notes master uses the Office theme colors, fonts, and effects, no matter what theme is applied to the slides in the presentation. Changing fonts and colors to match the current theme can give your notes pages consistency with the slides.

▪ Use the Background Styles option in the Background group to apply a background that will fill the entire notes page.

▪ When you have completed your work on the notes master, you can switch to Notes Page view to see your changes on all pages.

Work with the Handout Master

▪ Display the handout master to adjust the size, position, and text formats for any of the text placeholders on any of the handout options.

▪ The handout master, shown in the following illustration, displays text placeholders and a varying number of placeholders for the slide images.

Handout Master view

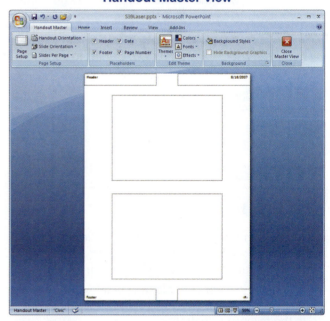

▪ By default, the handout master displays placeholders for the header, date, footer, and page number.

▪ You can adjust the size or position of any of these placeholders, and you can format the text in them using any desired font and alignment options.

▪ You cannot move or resize the placeholders for the slides, but you can add content such as a text box or a graphic.

▪ When adding content such as a text box to the handout master, consider that your added content must be positioned so it doesn't interfere with the slide image placeholders for layouts other than the one you are currently working with.

▪ If you insert a text box above the slide image on the one-slide-per-page layout, for example, it will obscure the slide images for other handout layouts.

▪ Use tools on the Handout Master tab, shown in illustration at the top of the next page, to customize the handout master.

Handout Master tab

- Use the Page Setup group options in the same way you use them for the notes master. Changes you make to slide size are reflected in the slide image placeholders. Change the handout or slide orientation to adjust from the default orientations in special situations, such as when you want to allow plenty of room for your audience to write notes.
- Use the Slides Per Page list in the Page Setup group to choose the number of slides to display on the master. As you customize the master, use this option to make sure your changes work well with all slide layouts.

- Use the Placeholders group check boxes to show or hide default placeholders.
- As for the notes master, you can apply theme colors, fonts, and effects and background styles to your handout master.
- After you have customized the handout master, you must preview your presentation as handouts to see your changes.

Curriculum Connection: Language Arts

To Be or Not to Be

William Shakespeare is considered one of the world's greatest poets and playwrights. He lived and worked in Elizabethan England at the end of the 16th century, but his works are so full of human truths that they are still widely performed today on stage and in films.

Shakespeare on Film

Create a PowerPoint presentation to list successful film adaptations of Shakespearian plays. Using a source such as the Internet Movie Database, locate information on several recent comedies, tragedies, and histories that have been filmed. Save an image from each film or of one of the film's actors and use it to illustrate the information on the slide. Supply information on principal cast members, director, and year released. If the film won any major awards, list them in a shape such as a banner or star.

PROCEDURES

View the Notes Master

1. Click **View** tab............... Alt + W

   ### Presentation Views Group

2. Click **Notes Master** button 🔲 .... K

To modify existing placeholders:

- Drag a placeholder to a new position.
- Resize a placeholder by dragging a sizing handle.
- Delete a placeholder by selecting its outside border and pressing Del.

OR

Placeholders Group

- Click the check box of any placeholder to turn it off.

To modify notes master text:

- Click in the text to modify and use Font or Paragraph tools on the Home tab to make changes.

To close Notes Master view:

- Click **Close Master View** button ❌.

View the Handout Master

1. Click **View** tab............... Alt , W

   ### Presentation Views Group

2. Click **Handout Master** button 🔳 .... H

To close Handout Master view:

- Click **Close Master View** button ❌.

EXERCISE DIRECTIONS

1. Start PowerPoint and open 39Laser.
2. Save the presentation as 39Laser_xx.
3. Display the notes master and make the following changes:
   - Apply the Equity theme colors and the Trek theme fonts.
   - Change the font size for all placeholders to 14 point.
   - Boldface the text in the header, date, footer, and slide number placeholders, and change vertical alignment to middle for these placeholders.
     - ✓ You can select all placeholders and then apply the formats only once to save time.
   - Change the notes master to landscape orientation to see how information displays, then change back to portrait orientation.
   - Apply a new background style of your choice to the page.
4. Exit Notes Master view and change to Notes Page view to see how your changes look. Illustration A shows a sample.
5. Now customize handouts for your audience:
   - Display the handout master and change the display to 4 slides per page.
   - Apply the Equity theme colors and the Trek theme fonts.
   - Reduce the width of the header and the date placeholders to free up space at the upper middle area of the handout master.
   - Draw a text box in the free area between the header and date placeholders and insert the text **WELCOME TO HOLMES!**.
   - Format the text box with a Quick Style and adjust text formats as desired.
   - Move the text box down so its top border is below the header and date placeholders.
   - Display all other slides-per-page layouts and make sure your text box does not obscure any slide image placeholders.
   - Change the text formatting for all other placeholders as desired.
   - Create a new background for the handout master using one of the background styles or a fill or gradient background you create yourself.
   - Make any other changes you think will improve the look of the handouts.
6. Exit Handout Master view and preview the slides to see your changes.
7. Print a notes page and a handout page to see your custom master changes.
8. Save your changes, close the presentation, and exit PowerPoint.

Illustration A

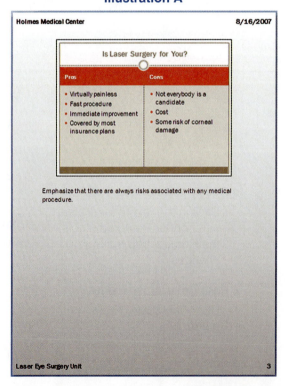

ON YOUR OWN

1. Open **OPP38_xx** or 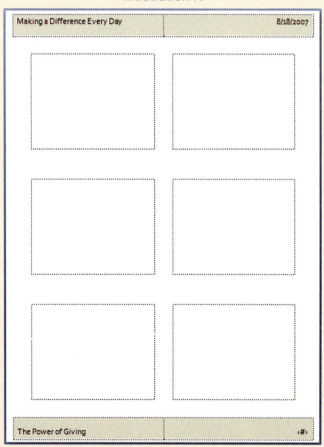**OPP39**.
2. Save the presentation as **OPP39_xx**.
3. Display the notes master:
   - Change the theme colors and fonts to match those of the slides. (Use the Foundry colors and the custom theme fonts you created for this presentation.)
   - Change the size of the text in the notes placeholder to 14 point and center the notes text.
4. Display the handout master:
   - Select 6 slides per page if necessary.
   - Change the theme colors and fonts to match those of the slides.
5. Select the header placeholder and move it down and to the right to provide more margin between the placeholder and the edge of the page. Change the text size to 14. Move the date placeholder down and to the left and change text size.

6. Move the bottom placeholders up and to the right or left as for the top placeholders, and change text size to match.
7. Expand the top placeholders so they meet in the center of the page, and then apply a fill of your choice to both placeholders so it creates a band of color across the top of the handout.
8. Repeat this process to format the bottom placeholders. Illustration A shows an example.
9. Preview notes pages and handouts to see your changes to the masters, then print one notes page and one handout page.
10. Save your changes, close the presentation, and exit PowerPoint.

Illustration A

Making a Difference Every Day		8/18/2007

The Power of Giving		‹#›

■ **Create a Theme or Template**

■ **Apply Custom Themes and Templates**

Software Skills Create custom themes and templates to create your own unique presentations. You can apply a custom theme to any presentation. Custom templates display in the New Presentation dialog box for easy access.

Application Skills Michigan Avenue Athletic Club wants you to create a custom template that can be used for several presentations as part of a special public relations campaign. In this exercise, you will create a theme you can use for future presentations and also save the presentation as a template.

TERMS

No new terms in this exercise.

NOTES

Create a Theme or Template

■ As you learned in Exercise 6, a theme is a collection of formatting options that includes colors, fonts, and special effects. If you consult PowerPoint's help system about the definition of a theme, you learn that a theme is "a set of unified design elements that provides a look for your presentation by using colors, fonts, and graphics."

■ If you use PowerPoint's default themes as an example, however, you can understand that a theme is much more than a collection of colors, fonts, and graphic effects. Each of PowerPoint's themes also supplies a unique background, slide layouts, and graphic elements in some instances.

■ In the illustrations at right, for example, note the differences between the two title slides, one formatted with the default Office theme and the other with the Solstice theme.

Title slides formatted with different themes

■ The Office theme has a plain white background, plain text formatting, and simple center alignment. The Solstice theme displays a complex graphic background, attractive text formatting, and a more sophisticated alignment scheme.

■ If you want to create a theme that, when applied, will completely change the appearance of the current presentation, as PowerPoint's themes do, you must make changes not only to colors but also to background and layouts—the kinds of changes you learned to make in Exercise 38 in Slide Master view.

■ To save a theme, you use the Save Current Theme command on the Themes gallery to open the Save Current Theme dialog box, shown in the following illustration.

Save Current Theme dialog box

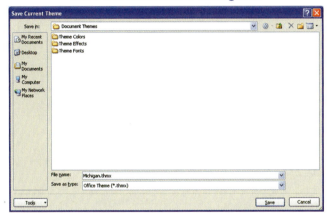

■ Your custom theme is saved in the Document Themes folder to make it available for use with any presentation.

■ You also have the option of saving a presentation that you have customized as a template.

■ The only difference between a theme and a template in practical terms is how the two options are used. A theme is applied to an existing presentation. A template is used to start a new presentation.

■ Save a presentation as a template using the Save As dialog box.

■ As soon as you specify that you want to save a template, the file location in the Save As dialog box changes to the Templates folder where all PowerPoint templates are stored, as shown in the following illustration.

Save As dialog box

■ To create either a theme or a template, you can customize an existing theme and then save your version with a new name. Or, you can start from scratch to create a unique design using Slide Master view to format the background and layout as you wish and then save the new theme.

Apply Custom Themes and Templates

■ A custom theme displays in the Themes group on the Design tab along with PowerPoint's built-in themes. The following illustration shows two custom themes added to the Themes gallery.

Custom themes display in the Themes gallery

- To apply a custom theme, simply click the thumbnail in the theme gallery. If you no longer want to use a custom theme, you can delete it from the Themes gallery.
- Display custom templates by clicking the My Templates link in the New Presentation dialog box. Another New Presentation dialog box opens, as shown in the illustrations at right, with custom templates shown in the My Templates tab.

My Templates in the New Presentation dialog box

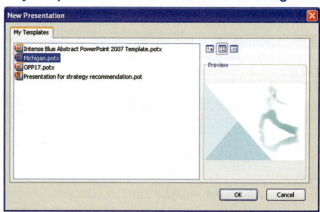

PROCEDURES

Customize and Save a Theme or Template

To choose theme colors:
1. Click **Design** tab .... Alt+G

   Themes Group

2. Click **Theme Colors** button .... T, C
3. Click **Create New Theme Colors** C
4. Click the down arrow of the color to be changed.
5. Select a new color from the palette.

   OR

   Click one of the Standard colors.

   OR

   a. Click **More colors** .... M
   b. Mix a color on the **Custom** tab or click **Standard** tab and select a color.
   c. Click OK .... Enter
6. Click **Name** .... N and type a name for the theme colors.
7. Click Save .... Enter

To choose theme fonts:
1. Click **Design** tab .... Alt+G

   Themes Group

2. Click **Theme Fonts** button .... T, F
3. Click a different theme's font combination to apply it.

   OR

   a. Click in any title or text placeholder.
   b. Click **Home** tab .... Alt+H

   Font Group

   c. Click **Font** down arrow .... F, F
   d. Select a new font from the font list .... ↓, Enter

To choose theme effects:
1. Click **Design** tab .... Alt+G

   Themes Group

2. Click **Theme Effects** button .... T, E
3. Select one of the default theme effects options .... ←→↑↓, Enter

To save a theme:
1. Click **Design** tab .... Alt+G
2. Click **More** button .... H
3. Click **Save Current Theme** .... S
4. Type a name for the theme.
5. Click Save .... Enter

To save a template:
1. Click **Office Button** .... Alt+F
2. Click **Save As** .... A
3. Click **Save as type** .... Alt+T
4. On the drop-down list, click **PowerPoint Template (*.potx)**.
5. Click **File name** .... Alt+N
6. Type a name for the template.
7. Click Save .... Enter

Apply a Custom Template
1. Click **Office Button** .... Alt+F
2. Click **New** .... N
3. Click **My templates**.
4. Select the desired template.
5. Click OK .... Enter

EXERCISE DIRECTIONS

1. Start PowerPoint to open a new, blank presentation. You will create your theme based on the default Office theme.

2. First modify the theme colors as follows:
   - Change the Text/Background – Dark 2 color to Background 2, Lighter 60%.
   - Change the Accent 3 color to a teal color (such as the RGB color 0, 153, 153).
   - Save the current color settings as **Michigan**.

3. Create new theme fonts using Cambria for headings and Calibri for text. Save the theme fonts as **Michigan**.

4. Now you are ready to create the custom backgrounds:
   - Switch to Slide Master view and select the Slide Master in the left pane.
   - Display the Format Background dialog box and choose to insert a picture fill. Use the File button to insert ⊚ **40Background** from the data files.
   - The picture does not need to be stretched over the entire slide background. In the Format Background dialog box, change the offsets to: Left, 39%; Right, 2%; Top, -6%; Bottom, 8%.
   - Change the Transparency to 20%.
   - Still in the Format Background dialog box, click Picture in the left pane. Choose to Recolor the picture and select the Accent color 3 Light variation. Apply the changes to all layouts and close the dialog box.
   - Now add another graphic for interest: Use the Right Triangle drawing shape to draw a triangle from the upper-left corner of the slide to the bottom of the slide. The lower-right corner of the triangle should be below the right edge of the footer placeholder, as shown in Illustration A.
   - Remove the outline of the shape and fill it with Aqua, Accent 5, Lighter 80%. Use the Format Shape dialog box to change transparency to 10%.
   - Send the shape to the back to be behind all text.
   - On the Title Slide layout only, add an additional triangle that intersects in some way with the right triangle and make it a darker shade of aqua.

5. Now customize text and layout options:
   - On the Slide Master, left-align the title and choose new bullet characters and colors. Change the color of the date, footer, and slide number placeholder text to Dark Teal, Accent 3, Darker 50%.
   - On the Title Slide layout, left align both the title and the subtitle, and change the color of the subtitle to Dark Teal, Accent 3, Darker 25%.
   - Choose one of the other layouts, such as Comparison or Picture with Caption, and customize it with color and an effect.

6. Save the current presentation as a theme with the name **Michigan**. Then save it again as a template with the same name.

7. Close the current template presentation and create a new presentation based on your new template. Save the file as **40Michigan_xx**.

8. Insert the title **Michigan Avenue Athletic Club** and the subtitle **Fitness First!**.

9. Add a Title and Content slide and insert the text shown in Illustration B.

10. Add another slide using the layout you customized and add appropriate content.

11. Display the date, slide numbers, and a footer on all slides except the title slide. Print the presentation as handouts with 4 slides per page.

12. Save your changes, close the presentation, and exit PowerPoint.

Click to edit Master title style

▶ Click to edit Master text styles
- Second level
  - Third level
    - Fourth level
      » Fifth level

8/16/2007   Footer

Experience the Finest

▶ State-of-the-art equipment

▶ Attractive facilities

▶ Experienced staff

▶ Personalized training
- Individual coaching
- Group classes also available

ON YOUR OWN

1. Create a new presentation theme for an animal shelter organization for which you volunteer. You can base the theme on a blank presentation or any other default theme.

2. Choose new colors and fonts, if desired, for the theme.

3. On the slide master, create a background, apply colors, make layout choices, and insert graphics as desired to customize the template. Format some of the graphics with Quick Styles if desired. Illustration A shows a design you might use on the title layout.

4. Save the presentation as a template with the name **OPP40_xx**.

5. Create a new presentation based on the new template.

6. Save the presentation as **OPP40-2_xx**.

7. Add slide content to at least three slides.

8. Save your changes, close the presentation, and exit PowerPoint.

Illustration A

Critical Thinking

Application Skills In this exercise, you will complete a presentation you began in Exercise 30 to customize a theme and add graphics to a presentation for Restoration Architecture.

DIRECTIONS

1. Start PowerPoint to display a new, blank presentation.

2. Your first task is to create a new theme to apply to the previous presentation you created for the client and future presentations.

   - Switch to Slide Master view.

   - Apply the Technic theme and then change the theme colors to the Solstice theme.

   - Display the Title Slide layout. Note that the shape that forms the right-hand side of the slide background and the shape along the bottom of the slide can be selected. Change the fill of either or both of these shapes as desired by adding a picture, a texture, or a new color.

   - Display the Slide Master and change the fill of the same shape(s), but using different fill options.

   - Change the bullet symbols for first- and second-level bullets.

   - Change theme fonts if desired and choose a different font color for the title on the title slide.

   - Change the color and size of the date, footer, and slide number text. (Make sure the color you choose shows up on all slide layouts.)

   - Make any changes you think necessary on other slide layouts.

3. Create a small drawing of a house using basic shapes as shown in Illustration A. You may rotate, flip, and size the shapes as necessary to create the graphic. Group the shapes and choose a fill (solid color or gradient) and apply an effect such as shadow. Resize the graphic to fit neatly in the upper-right corner of the slide master.

4. Insert a text box on top of the house graphic and add the text **Restoration Architecture**. Change font, font size, font style, and font color as desired to contrast well with the house graphic. Use alignment tools to center the two objects with each other, and then group to create one object.

5. Save the current theme as **Restoration**.

6. Open **30Architecture_xx**, the previous presentation you created for the client, or open ⊙**41Architecture**.

7. Save the presentation as **41Architecture_xx**.

8. Apply the Restoration theme to the presentation. Close the presentation you used to create the theme without saving.

9. Scroll through the slides and adjust any formats that need to be changed because of the new theme. You may, for example, need to change background colors in tables and worksheet objects, fonts, and font sizes. You may also need to adjust the position of some objects such as tables on the slides.

   ✓ *Use the drawing guides to help you line up objects. You can move the drawing guides to the position of the top and left border of a content placeholder to make sure all objects align at those same coordinates.*

10. Add a slide with the Picture and Caption layout at the end of the presentation. Insert a picture of a historic-looking house in the picture placeholder. Adjust picture settings as necessary to make the picture look good.

✓ *If you do not have a suitable picture, use the Clip Art task pane to locate a photo of a period house such as a Victorian and insert it on the slide. Right-click the picture, select Save as Picture, and save the picture in a suitable location. Delete the picture from the slide. Then click the Picture placeholder and navigate to the saved picture to insert it in the placeholder.*

11. Insert the title text **Take Care of Your Most Important Investment** and then insert the following text in two columns in the text box below the title:

Odds are, you have spent more on your house than on any other single item in your investment portfolio. Your home is not merely a roof over your head, it is long-term security.

Safeguard your investment by taking care of the fabric of your house. We can help you renovate and upgrade systems to ensure your home shelters you now and in the future.

12. Adjust the width of the placeholder and the space between columns to avoid crowding the text.

13. Compress all pictures in the presentation to screen resolution.

14. Insert a music clip on slide 1 that will play across all slides.

15. Display a date, footer, and number for slides and handouts, and create an appropriate header for the handouts.

16. View the slides in Slide Show view. Then preview handouts with 6 slides per page.

17. Print the handouts in grayscale.

18. Save your changes, close the presentation, and exit PowerPoint.

Illustration A

Exercise | 42

Curriculum Integration

Application Skills   Many of us have heard of the equation $E = mc^2$, but not so many of us can explain what it means or why it is important. You have been asked to prepare a presentation to explain Einstein's theories of relativity and how they relate to the famous equation. Before you begin this exercise, do some research to locate:

- One or more pictures of Albert Einstein that you can download and save to your computer.

- Explanations (simple!) of both the special theory of relativity and the general theory of relativity. (Wikipedia has a good explanation.)

DIRECTIONS

Begin a new presentation. You may use a blank presentation or use one of PowerPoint's online presentation templates. Save the presentation with an appropriate name, such as **42Relativity_xx**. Insert an appropriate title and subtitle on the first slide.

Apply the Metro theme. In Slide Master view, adjust the background to eliminate the white border at the left side of the slide and the strips of pink, gold, and black. Your slides should have a simple space-like black to blue gradient. You may want to move placeholders to the left to compensate for the removal of the white strip.

Select a different set of theme fonts, and customize bullets for the first two levels. Customize the appearance of the date, footer, and slide number placeholders.

Add a slide with the Blank background and use this to insert the famous equation on the slide. Use shapes that contain text and equation shapes to create the equation. Illustration A shows one way you might set this equation on the slide. (The superscript *2* is set in a shape with a black fill.)

Align and distribute the shapes appropriately, and adjust order if necessary to allow for close overlap. Then group the shapes and center align the group both horizontally and vertically to the slide.

Insert text boxes below the equation to explain what the symbols mean: *E* stands for Energy, for example, and *m* for mass.

Add a slide to explain the bare bones of special relativity. Use one of the pictures of Einstein you downloaded and modify and format the picture as required to improve its appearance.

Add a slide that explains the consequences of special relativity, one of which is the mass-energy equivalence (the famous equation).

Add a slide to explain the bare bones of general relativity. Insert a second picture of Einstein if you have one and format it attractively.

Add slide numbers and a date that updates automatically to all slides except the title slide. Add a header and footer for notes and handouts.

Customize the handout master using the 4 slides per page layout. Add a text box or other object to the master and adjust the position and formats of text placeholders. You may also want to add a background to the handouts.

View the slides in Slide Show view, and then preview the handouts you will need to provide to the class. Print the slides as handouts with four slides per page.

Save changes to the presentation and close it. Exit PowerPoint.

Illustration A
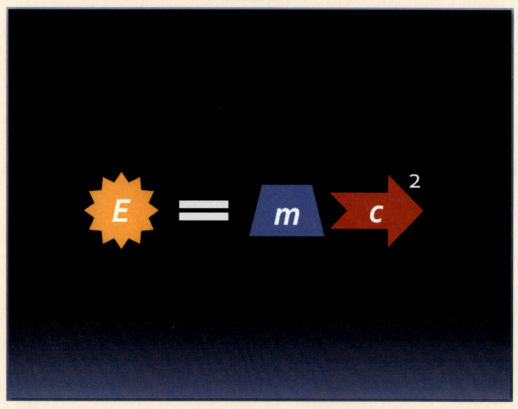

Lesson | 5

Prepare and Present a Slide Show

Skills Covered

- **Add Slide Transitions**
- **Control Slide Advance**

Software Skills   Transitions play as one slide is replaced by another and provide visual interest for the audience. After you choose a transition, you can make further decisions on how slides advance during the presentation.

Application Skills   The public relations director at Holmes Medical Center has informed you that she will present the laser surgery unit slide show to a large audience. She wants to advance slides automatically but also wants to be able to control slides manually. She also wants transitions between slides. In this exercise, you will add transitions and adjust the slide advance.

TERMS

Advance slide timing A setting that controls the amount of time a slide displays on the screen.

Transitions The visual effects used when one slide moves off of the screen and another moves onto the screen.

NOTES

Add Slide Transitions

- PowerPoint provides **transitions** that you can use to make the slide show more interesting. Transitions are visual effects that display when you replace one slide with another during a presentation.

- You can apply transitions in either Normal view or Slide Sorter view using tools on the Animations tab.

- The Transition gallery offers almost 60 different transitions. A portion of the gallery is shown in the illustration at right. The transition applied to the current slide is highlighted.

Transitions gallery

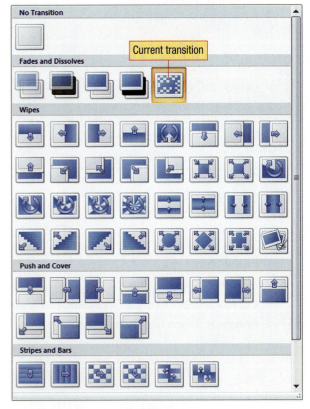

- If you are in Normal view, resting the pointer on a transition previews the transition on the current slide. In Slide Sorter view, select a transition from the gallery to apply it and see a preview of the effect.

- To remove a transition from a slide, select the No Transition option.

- The Transition to This Slide group on the Animations tab, shown in the following illustration, offers several other important options related to transitions.

**Transition to This Slide group
on the Animations tab**

- You can:
  - Select a sound effect or sound clip to accompany the transition. PowerPoint offers 19 default sound effects such as Chime and Applause. You can also insert any other sound file using the Other Sound option to open the Add Sound dialog box. You can also choose to loop a sound continuously until the next slide that contains a sound.

    ✓ *Be careful when adding sound effects to transitions (or animations). Too many sound effects in a presentation can become very distracting.*

  - Choose a speed for the transition: Slow, Medium, or Fast. Try to adjust this setting to the speed of the computer on which you are presenting the slides. On a fast computer, the Fast setting may be too quick to appreciate the transition effect, but on a slower computer the Fast setting may be ideal.

  - Apply settings to all slides at the same time.

  - Choose how to advance slides: by clicking the mouse or automatically based on a specific time lapse. This option is discussed further in the next section.

- After you have applied a transition or animation, you can use the Preview button on the Animations tab to review all effects you have applied to the slides.

- A slide to which you have applied a transition has a star symbol below the slide in Slide Sorter view, as shown in the following illustration. You can click this symbol to preview the transition effect.

  ✓ *The star symbol also displays under the slide number in the Slides tab.*

Symbols indicate transitions and timings

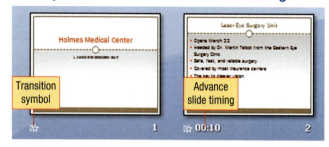

Control Slide Advance

- By default, you advance slides in a presentation manually by clicking the mouse button or a keyboard key. If you do not want to advance slides manually, you can have PowerPoint advance each slide automatically.

- **Advance slide timing** defines the amount of time a slide is on the screen before PowerPoint automatically advances to the next slide.

- You can set advance slide timing on the Animations tab for individual slides or for all slides in a presentation. Set advance slide timing in seconds or minutes and seconds.

- Even if you set automatic advance timings for your slides, you can also choose to advance a slide manually. Click any time before the timing elapses to move to the next slide.

- The advance slide timing for each slide is indicated in Slide Sorter view by a number below the slide, as shown in the previous illustration.

PROCEDURES

Add Slide Transitions

1. Select the slide(s) to which you want to add a transition in Slide Sorter view or the Slides tab.
2. Click **Animations** tab .... Alt + A

   Transition to This Slide Group

3. Click **More** button ▼ .... T
4. Select desired transition from the gallery .... ← → ↑ ↓ , ↵Enter

To add a sound effect to a transition:

1. Click **Transition Sound** button 🔊 .... Alt + A , U
2. Select the desired sound .... ↓ , ↵Enter

To change the transition speed:

1. Click **Transition Speed** button 🔲 .... Alt + A , E
2. Select the desired speed .... ↑ or ↓ , ↵Enter

To apply current transition settings to all slides:

- Click **Apply To All** button 🔲 .... Alt + A , L

To remove a transition:

1. Select the slide(s) that contains the transition to remove.
2. Click **Animations** tab .... Alt + A

   Transition to This Slide Group

3. Click **No Transition** at the left end of the Transition To This Slide gallery.

Control Slide Advance

1. Select the slide(s) for which you want to apply slide timings.
2. Click **Animations** tab .... Alt + A

   Transition to This Slide Group

3. Click **On Mouse Click** .... M if necessary to select option.

   OR

   a. Click **Automatically After** ..... F
   b. Click spin box .... Alt + I and enter desired timing.

EXERCISE DIRECTIONS

1. Start PowerPoint and open 💿**43Laser**.
2. Save the presentation as **43Laser_xx**.
3. Apply several different slide transitions to the slides using a medium speed. View the slides in Slide Show view to see the transitions.
4. Choose to advance the slides automatically with a setting of 10 seconds, and view the presentation again without clicking the mouse button to advance each slide.
5. Save your changes, close the presentation, and exit PowerPoint.

ON YOUR OWN

1. Start PowerPoint and open 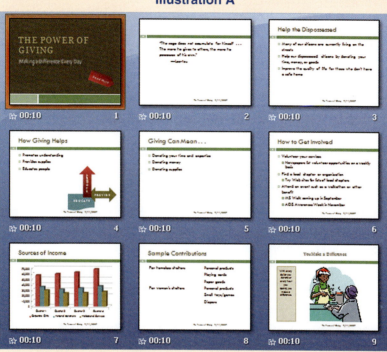OPP43. This is a familiar presentation given a new look with a new theme.

2. Save the presentation as **OPP43_xx**.

3. Add a dissolve transition to all slides at a medium speed.

4. Add the sound effect of a chime to the title slide.

5. Apply an automatic slide advance to all slides. Your slides should look similar to Illustration A in Slide Sorter view.

6. Save your changes, close the presentation, and exit PowerPoint.

Illustration A

Skills Covered

- **About Animating Objects**
- **Apply a Built-In Animation**
- **Create Custom Animation Effects**
- **Rehearse Timings**

Software Skills PowerPoint allows you to add animations to make your slides more visually interesting during a presentation. After you set up animations, you can rehearse the show to make sure you have allowed enough time for the audience to view slide content.

Application Skills   In this exercise, you will animate both text and objects in the Holmes Medical Center presentation. Then you will rehearse the presentation to check your timings.

TERMS

Animate To apply movement to text or an object to control its display during the presentation.

NOTES

About Animating Objects

- You can **animate** objects on slides to add interest to your presentation or to emphasize special points.

- For example, you can animate text so that it appears one word or one paragraph at a time or animate objects such as pictures or charts so they fade into view or display one section at a time. You can even animate an object so that it moves along a set path on the slide.

- You have two options for applying animation: built-in animations supplied by PowerPoint and custom animations that you create yourself.

Apply a Built-In Animation

- If you want to add a simple animation effect without having to choose among a lot of options, use the Animate drop-down list on the Animations tab (see the following illustration) to apply one of PowerPoint's built-in animation effects.

Built-in animation options

- This menu gives you only a few animation effects to choose among. For each effect, you can choose from All At Once (all the content of a placeholder displays at one time) or By 1st Level Paragraphs (bullet items in a placeholder appear one by one).

- The built-in animation menu in the previous illustration is the one that displays if you choose a bulleted list placeholder. If you choose a different kind of object, such as a title placeholder or a picture, you have fewer animation options available.

- Because you must select a placeholder or object before the Animate list becomes active, you must be in Normal view to apply these animations.

- To start a built-in animation in Slide Show view, you click the mouse button, and you must continue to click the button to display items such as each bullet in a bulleted list.

- This procedure does not hold true, however, if you have established advance slide timings.

- If you have applied a slide timing, the built-in animation will start and play automatically in the amount of time you have allotted for that slide. If you intend to run a presentation automatically, make sure to allow enough time for all animations to play.

Create Custom Animation Effects

- If you want more control over animation effects, use the Custom Animation task pane.

- Using the Custom Animation task pane, you can choose the effect to add, indicate when the effect starts, select a property for the effect such as what direction the animated object will come from, and set a speed for the effect.

- You can use the Custom Animation task pane to build animation effects from scratch or to modify a built-in animation.

- To begin the process of creating an animation effect, select an object such as a placeholder or picture on a slide. Then display the Custom Animation task pane and click the Add Effect button.

- The Add Effect menu offers four options for when effects will occur:

  - Entrance effects occur as an object displays on the slide. For example, you can have an object fly into place on the slide as soon as the slide displays on the screen.

  - Emphasis effects are applied to objects that are already displayed on the slide. Use these effects to draw attention to an object.

  - Exit effects are used to remove an object from a slide in an interesting way. You may want to use an exit effect to fade a picture off a slide while other slide content remains in view.

  - Motion Path effects are used to guide an object along a path on the slide that you specify. These effects add emphasis to objects and allow you to redistribute objects on a slide during the presentation.

- Each of these categories has a submenu on which you can select from among a list of effects, as shown in the following illustration.

Effect options

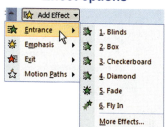

- If you do not find an effect you like on the submenu, click the More Effects command to open a dialog box where you can find many more effects for the particular category.

- After you select an effect, you can specify how the animation starts, a property for the effect, and the effect's speed.

- You have three choices when starting an effect:

  - On Mouse Click, the default, starts the animation when you click the mouse during the presentation.

  - With Previous starts the animation at the same time the previous effect (either an animation or a transition) is taking place. Using this option prevents delays between animations.

  - After Previous starts the animation after the previous effect has finished.

- Properties for animations differ depending on the animation. For a Fly In animation, for example, you can specify that the object fly in from left, right, top, bottom, and so on. Some effects will not offer a property.

- All animations offer a choice of speeds, but some animations offer more options than others. Be sure to view your animations in Slide Show view to make sure your animations are neither too fast nor too slow.

- As you select effects for objects, the object name and an effect symbol display in the Custom Animation task pane, shown in the following illustration. This list represents the order in which the effects take place when the slide is viewed.

Effects display in the Custom Animation task pane

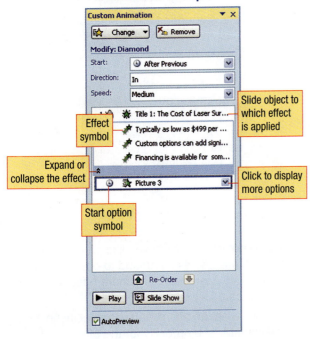

- Numbers display on the slide in the Slide pane that correspond to the numbers in the effects list so you can easily see the order in which content will be animated.

- Note the symbols to the left of the animation effect symbol that indicate the start option. On Mouse Click displays a mouse symbol, no symbol is displayed for With Previous, and a clock symbol indicates After Previous.

- If the object you are animating is a text placeholder with more than one line, you can expand the effect, as shown in the previous illustration, to animate each line separately.

- You can adjust the order in which effects take place using the Re-Order arrows at the bottom of the task pane.

- The Play button allows you to preview the animations to make sure they display as you want them to. You can also use the Slide Show button to display the slide in Slide Show view.

- Built-in animation effects also display in the effect list in the Custom Animation task pane. You can modify those effects if desired in the Custom Animation task pane.

- If you decide you do not like an animation, you can select it in the list and click the Change button to start over, or you can click the Remove button to delete the effect.

- To see more options for controlling an effect, click the drop-down arrow to the right of the effect item to display the drop-down menu shown in the following illustration.

Set details for an animation

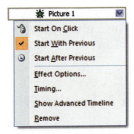

- Choosing Effect Options from this menu opens a dialog box specific to the current effect where you can specify options such as accompanying sound effects and additional timing control.

- The following illustration shows an options dialog box for the Fly In effect.

Fly In effect options dialog box

■ Options and tabs in this dialog box depend on the type of effect and the object that has been animated. If you are animating text, for example, you will see a Text Animation tab. If you are animating a chart, the dialog box includes a Chart Animation tab. Use these tabs to define how multiple items (such as the columns of a chart) are grouped in the animation.

■ All effect options dialog boxes include a Timing tab. You can adjust timing of objects to create delays between animations to better control the flow of information on the slide. You can also specify a *trigger* for an animation—an object on the slide that you click to start the animation.

Rehearse Timings

■ To make sure you have allowed enough time for your audience to view your slides and the transitions and animations you have applied, you can rehearse the presentation.

■ Use the Rehearse Timings command on the Slide Show tab to start the presentation and display a toolbar like the one shown in the following illustration.

Rehearsal toolbar

■ As you view each slide, the timers show how much time you have spent on that slide as well as the total time elapsed for the show.

■ You can use buttons on the Rehearsal toolbar to pause and restart the show, and you can also repeat a slide if you find you need to start again.

■ After you have finished viewing all slides, PowerPoint asks if you want to keep the slide timings. If you click Yes, these timings replace any other advance timings you have set.

PROCEDURES

Apply Built-In Animations

1. Click in text or object to be animated.
2. Click **Animations** tab .... Alt + A

   Animations Group

3. Click **Animate** list .... A
4. Select desired animation from list .... ↓ , ↵Enter

Create Custom Animations

1. Click in text or object to be animated.
2. Click **Animations** tab .... Alt + A

   Animations Group

3. Click **Custom Animation** button 🎨 .... C to open Custom Animation task pane.
4. Click 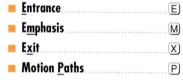 .

5. Choose category:
   ■ **Entrance** .... E
   ■ **Emphasis** .... M
   ■ **Exit** X
   ■ **Motion Paths** .... P
6. Choose effect you want to apply .... ↓ , ↵Enter
7. Click **Start** drop-down arrow and choose appropriate option:
   ■ **On Click** starts the effect when you click the mouse button.
   ■ **With Previous** starts the effect at the same time as another effect.
   ■ **After Previous** starts the effect after the previous effect has ended.
8. Click the property drop-down arrow and choose appropriate option.

   ✓ *The property will change depending on which effect you have selected.*

9. Click **Speed** and choose appropriate option:
   ■ **Very Slow**
   ■ **Slow**
   ■ **Medium**
   ■ **Fast**
   ■ **Very Fast**

To set effect options:

1. In the Custom Animation task pane, click the drop-down arrow of an effect in the effects list.
2. Click **Effect Options** .... E
3. Click the appropriate tab.

   ✓ *Tabs will vary according to the effect.*

4. Set the appropriate details.
5. Click [OK] .... ↵Enter

To change an animation effect:

1. Select effect to be changed in effects list.
2. In the Custom Animation task pane, click ⭐ **Change** ▾.
3. Select a new effect and adjust it as desired.

To remove an animation effect:

1. Select text or object from which to remove animation.
2. In the Custom Animation task pane, click ✖ **Remove**.

Rehearse Slide Timings

1. Display presentation to rehearse.
2. Click **Slide Show** tab .... Alt + S

   Set Up Group

3. Click **Rehearse Timings** button 🖱 .... T

4. Advance from slide to slide, reading slide contents and any comments you intend to make in the presentation.
5. At the end of the show, click [Yes] .... ↵Enter to keep slide timings.

   OR

   Click [No] to discard slide timings .... Alt + N

EXERCISE DIRECTIONS

1. Start PowerPoint and open 💿 **44Laser**.

   ✓ *This is a version of the presentation you worked with in the last exercise without the transitions you added. The transitions have been removed to make it easier to work with animations.*

2. Save the presentation as **44Laser_xx**.

3. Apply built-in animations as follows:

   - On slide 1, apply the Fade animation to the title and the Wipe (All At Once) animation to the subtitle.
   - Apply the Fade animation to titles on all other slides.

4. Display the Custom Animation task pane and make the following changes:

   - For each of the Fade animations on all slides, change the start setting to With Previous.
   - On slide 1, change the start setting for the subtitle to After Previous, the Direction setting to From Top, and speed to Medium.

5. Insert the following custom animations:

   - On slide 2, apply a Fly In entrance effect for the text placeholder. Set Start to After Previous, the Direction to From Right, and the Speed to Medium.
   - On slide 3, apply any custom Emphasis effect to the Pros and Cons text boxes.

   - On slide 4, animate the text placeholder items as desired.
   - On slide 5, apply entrance effects so that the text in the left-hand placeholder displays after the title and then the clip art graphic displays. You may want to specify that the placeholder enter as one object using the effect options dialog box.
   - On slide 6, change the title effect to Fly In, and set the title and the text placeholder below it to fly in from the left at the same time the photo at the right is fading into view.
   - On slide 7, animate the text placeholder items as desired.
   - On slide 8, apply any exit effect to the WordArt graphic.

6. You have decided not to animate the title on the title slide. Remove the animation from this object.

7. Rehearse timings for all slides and then choose to keep the timings.

8. View the presentation again without clicking the mouse button to advance each slide and let PowerPoint display the slides according to your timings.

9. Save your changes, close the presentation, and exit PowerPoint.

ON YOUR OWN

1. Start PowerPoint and open **OPP43_xx** or open ⊙ **OPP44**.

2. Save the presentation as **OPP44_xx**.

3. Apply a built-in animation to the title and subtitle on slide 1.

4. Apply a custom animation to the shapes on slide 1 and slide 4.

5. Animate the slide text for all slides with lists.

6. Animate the chart on slide 7 and the picture on slide 9.

7. Rehearse slide timings and save the timings. Your slides should look similar to Illustration A in Slide Sorter view.

8. View the slides, allowing PowerPoint to control the advance.

9. Save your changes, close the presentation, and exit PowerPoint.

Illustration A

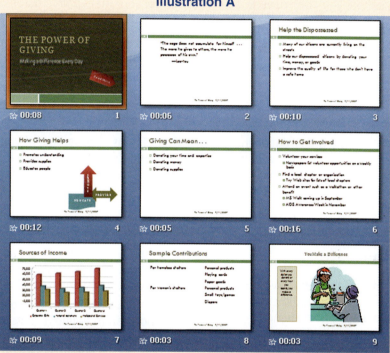

Skills Covered

- **Create a Custom Show**
- **Add Narration to a Presentation**

Software Skills   Create a custom show to organize related slides that you can then show separately from the rest of the presentation. Add narration to a presentation so that you don't have to be present to get your main points across.

Application Skills   You are working on the Aquatics Center campaign for the Campus Recreation Center. In this exercise, you will organize some of the slides into a custom show and learn how you can add narration to the presentation.

TERMS

Custom show A show within a presentation in which you specify the slides and the order in which the slides appear during the presentation.

Narration A recording of your voice that describes or enhances the message in each slide.

NOTES

Create a Custom Show

- As you build longer, more comprehensive presentations, you may find yourself wanting to show only a portion of the slides to a specific audience.

- For example, a corporate presentation may include slides on sales data of considerable interest to the sales staff and slides on customer surveys of great interest to the marketing department, while the entire presentation is of interest to the board of directors.

- You can create **custom shows** to organize groups of slides that you want to be able to show separately from the other slides in the presentation.

- In the example above, you could create a custom show for the sales staff containing only the slides relating to sales data and a custom show for the marketing department containing the customer survey slides.

- All slides used in custom shows remain in the comprehensive presentation, so that they are available for viewing by any audience.

- Use the Custom Slide Show button on the Slide Show tab to define a custom show. The Custom Shows dialog box, shown in the following illustration, allows you to work with existing shows or create a new one.

Create a new custom show

- Clicking the New button opens the Define Custom Show dialog box, shown in the following illustration. Here you name the show and select the slides that will be part of the custom show.

Select the slides for a custom show

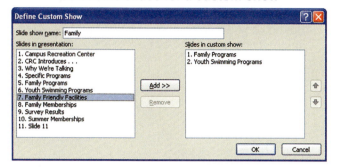

- The Slides in presentation list shows the slide numbers and titles of the slides in the current presentation. Select a slide and use the Add button to add the slide to the custom show. If you have added a slide by mistake, use the Remove button to delete it from the custom show list.

- Slides are renumbered consecutively in the Slides in custom show list, but they retain their original slide numbers when you view the show.

- If you rearrange slides in the main presentation so that their slide numbers change, custom shows in the presentation do not have to be changed because they are stored according to slide title.

- You have several options for displaying a custom show.

  - You can use the Custom Shows dialog box, shown previously, to run the show.

  - You can select the show from the Custom Slide Show menu on the Slide Show tab.

  - You can create a link to the show so that you can easily jump to it when presenting your slides. You will learn about this option in the next exercise.

  - You can also specify the custom show when running a presentation unattended. You will learn how to do this in Exercise 47.

- If you need to edit a custom show, select it in the Custom Shows dialog box and use the Edit button to return to the Define Custom Show dialog box, where you can add slides to or remove slides from the custom show.

- You can also use the Custom Shows dialog box to remove a custom show or copy it. Copying a show can save time if you want to use a substantial number of the same slides in another custom show.

Add Narration to a Presentation

- You might want to record voice **narration** for a self-running slide show to explain or emphasize your points to the audience.

  ✓ *To do so, your computer must have a microphone, speakers, and sound card.*

- You can record voice or sound for one slide or for all slides. Narration takes precedence over all other sounds on a slide.

- To record narration, use the Record Narration button on the Slide Show tab to open the Record Narration dialog box, shown in the following illustration.

Record Narration dialog box

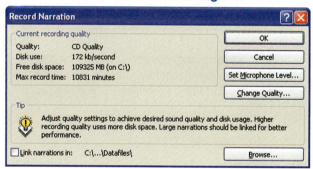

- Before you begin adding narration to slides, you can use the options in this dialog box to specify settings that will optimize your narration sound.

  - Use the Set Microphone Level option to make sure your microphone is working correctly.

  - Use the Change Quality option to open the Sound Selection dialog box, shown in the following illustration. You can choose from three quality settings: CD Quality, Radio Quality, or Telephone Quality. The Attributes list allows you to select further sound quality settings. Keep in mind that the better the quality of the recording, the more disk space the recording takes.

Sound Selection dialog box

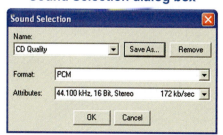

- The Tip in the Record Narration dialog box suggests linking a narration file to the presentation if you are using best sound quality and recording a large amount of narration. You can browse to the location where you want to save the linked sound file, which should be in the same folder as the presentation.

- When you have finished specifying settings, clicking the OK button displays the following dialog box. As indicated, you can start on the current slide or the first slide. Once you make a choice here, the presentation displays in Slide Show view so you can match your narration to each slide.

- When you have finished your narration, PowerPoint lets you know the narration has been stored and gives you the option of saving your slide timings.

- In Normal view, you will see that each slide to which you added narration has a sound icon displayed in the lower-right corner. Viewers can click the icons to hear your narration, or you can use the Sound Tools Options tab to specify that they play automatically.

Choose the first slide to narrate

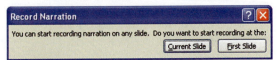

✓ *The dialog box shown in the previous illustration does not display if you have the first slide selected in Normal view.*

Curriculum Connection: Science

Defining Planets

In 2006, an assembly of astronomers refined the definition of what it means to be a planet. As a result, Pluto lost its status as a planet in our solar system and was demoted to the classification of dwarf planet. Not everyone was happy with the change.

What Is Pluto?

Research the decision that led to Pluto's reclassification and create a presentation that gives your opinion about it. Use slides to explain the criteria astronomers use to establish what is and is not a planet, and add pictures of Pluto and other planets. (You may be able to find good graphics on a NASA or JPL site.) Explain why you either agree or disagree with the change, and back your opinion with facts.

PROCEDURES

Create a Custom Show

1. Click **Slide Show** tab .... Alt + S

   Start Slide Show Group

2. Click **Custom Slide Show** button 🖳 .... M
3. Click **Custom Sho_w_s** .... W
4. Click New... .... Alt + N
5. Click **Slide show _n_ame** box .... Alt + N and type a name for the custom show.

6. Select a slide in the **Slides in presentation** box .... Alt + P, ↓
7. Click Add >> to add the slide to the custom show.
8. Continue adding slides as desired.
9. Click OK .
10. Click Close C

Add Narration to a Presentation

1. Click **Slide Show** tab .... Alt + S

   Set Up Group

2. Click **Record Narration** button ▶🎤 .... N
3. Check microphone:

   a. Click Set Microphone Level... .... Alt + M
   b. Speak into the microphone to record levels.
   c. Click OK .... ↵Enter

4. Specify sound quality:

   a. Click

      [Change Quality...] .... Alt + C

   b. In the Name drop-down box, choose one of the following:

- **CD Quality**
- **Radio Quality**
- **Telephone Quality**

   c. Click [OK] .... ↵Enter

5. Specify a location to save linked sound files:

   a. Click **Link narrations in** .... Alt + L check box.

   b. Click [Browse...] .... Alt + B and navigate to the location where you want to save the file.

   c. Click [Select] Alt + E

6. Click [OK] .... ↵Enter

7. Choose the slide to begin narration on:

- Click [Current Slide] .... Alt + C to start the narration with the current slide.

- Click [First Slide] .... Alt + F to start narration on the first slide.

   ✓ *These options are available only if a slide other than slide 1 is displayed in Normal view.*

8. Speak into the microphone to record as you view a slide, and advance each slide as needed.

9. When you have finished going through the slide show:

- Click [Save] .... ↵Enter to save the timings with the narration.

   OR

- Click [Don't Save] to discard slide timings.

EXERCISE DIRECTIONS

1. Start PowerPoint and open 🔘 **45Aquatics**.

2. Save the presentation as **45Aquatics_xx**.

3. Create a custom show of slides aimed at families so it will be easy to display them when the presentation is delivered to campus families:

- Name the custom show **Family**.

- Add slides 7–10 to the custom show, then close it.

4. In the Custom Shows dialog box, choose to show the Family show.

5. If you have a microphone available, record the following narration for slide 1:

The Campus Recreation Center staff welcome you to the Aquatics Center campaign.

6. Save slide timings after you record the narration.

7. Play the slide show to hear your narration.

8. Save your changes, close the presentation, and exit PowerPoint.

ON YOUR OWN

1. Start PowerPoint and open OPP45.

2. Save the presentation as **OPP45_xx**.

3. Create a custom show named **Gallery** that includes slides 11–14. Illustration A shows the slides for the Gallery custom show.

4. Create a custom show named **Sample Fees** that includes slides 8 and 9. Illustration B shows the slides for the Sample Fees custom show.

5. Use the Custom Slide Show menu to view both shows.

6. If you have a microphone available, record narration for one or more slides in the presentation.

7. Save your changes, close the presentation, and exit PowerPoint.

Illustration A

Illustration B

Skills Covered

- **Insert Links on Slides**
- **Add Action Settings**

Software Skills   Links and action settings allow you to move quickly from one slide to a distant one, connect to the Internet, or open other documents or applications.

Application Skills   In this exercise, you will add links and action buttons to the Aquatics Center presentation so that the presenter can move to specific slides and an Excel file while showing the presentation.

TERMS

Action   A setting that performs a specific action, such as running an application or jumping to a specific slide.

Target   The slide, show, file, or page that will display when you click a link on a slide.

NOTES

Insert Links on Slides

- Adding links to slides can make a presentation more interactive. Use a link to jump instantly from one slide to another in the current presentation or to jump to a different presentation.

- You can also set up a link whose target is a custom show, allowing you to jump directly to the first slide of the custom show.

- You can use links to move from a presentation to another application to view data in that application. This is an easy way to view Microsoft Excel data during a presentation, for example, if you do not want to insert the Excel data on a slide.

- If the computer on which you are presenting the slides has an active Internet connection, you can also use a link to jump from a slide to any site on the Web.

- You can set up a link using text from a text placeholder or any object on the slide, such as a shape or picture. After you select the object for the link, you use the Hyperlink button on the Insert tab to open the Insert Hyperlink dialog box.

- The Insert Hyperlink dialog box, shown in the following illustration, allows you to select the **target** of the link—the slide, show, file, or page that will display when the link is clicked.

Choose the target of the link

- You have four target options to choose from.

- Existing File or Web Page lets you locate a file on your system or network. After you select the file, its path displays in the Address box near the bottom of the dialog box.

- You can also use the Browse the Web button to open your browser. After you navigate to the page you want to use as your target, return to PowerPoint. The Web page address will automatically appear in the Address box.

- Place in This Document lets you select a slide or custom show from the current presentation. As you click a slide for the target, it displays in the Slide preview area.

- If the presentation contains custom shows, you can select the custom show, as shown in the following illustration.

Select a custom show as the target of a link

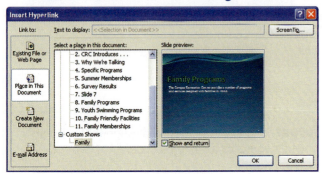

- When linking to a custom show, you can click the Show and return check box below the Slide preview. This option will automatically return you to the slide on which the link appears after the custom show's last slide.

- Create New Document allows you to specify the name of a new document and link to it at the same time. PowerPoint creates the document according to the file extension you use when you specify the file name. If you create a file with the name Results.xlsx, for example, Excel opens so you can enter data in the Results workbook.

- The E-mail Address option lets you link to an e-mail address. You might use this option when setting up a presentation to be viewed by an individual on his or her own computer. Clicking the link opens the default e-mail program to send a message to the specified e-mail address.

- If you want to provide a little extra help to a viewer about what will happen when a link is clicked, you can provide a ScreenTip such as the one shown in the following illustration.

Specify a ScreenTip for a link

- Links are displayed in a different color with an underline, as on a Web page. Links are active only in Slide Show view.

- You can edit a link by right-clicking the link and choosing Edit Hyperlink from the shortcut menu. Remove a link by right-clicking it and choosing Remove Hyperlink.

Add Action Settings

- Another way to control what happens during a presentation is to create **actions** that perform specific chores.

- Like links, actions allow you to link to a slide in the current presentation, a custom show, another presentation, a Web page URL, or another file.

- You can also use actions to run programs or macros, specify the Edit or Open command for an object you have inserted on the slide from another application, or play a sound effect or sound file.

- Actions can be applied to text or to any other object such as a shape or picture.

- Click the Action button in the Links group on the Insert tab to open the Action Settings dialog box shown in the following illustration.

Action Settings dialog box

- Click the action option, such as Hyperlink to, Run program, or Play sound. You can then provide additional information to carry out the action, such as what target to link to or what sound file to play.

- Note that the Action Settings dialog box contains two tabs, Mouse Click and Mouse Over. By default, you set actions on the Mouse Click tab, which means that the action takes place when you click on the action object during the presentation.

- The Mouse Over tab contains the same options as the Mouse Click tab. Actions you set on this tab will take place when you hover the mouse pointer over the action object.

- This means that you can actually set up two actions with the same object: one that will take place if you click and one that will take place if you hover the mouse pointer.

- Although, as mentioned earlier, you can apply an action to any object on a slide, a popular way to use action settings is to create action buttons.

- Action buttons are programmed to perform specific tasks, such as return to the previous slide or jump directly to the first slide in the presentation. You can also apply any other action setting to an action button, such as running a program or a macro or playing a sound.

- Action buttons appear at the bottom of the shape gallery, as shown in the following illustration.

Action button shapes

- Each action button has a specific function that is indicated by the graphic on the button. The button with the question mark on it, for example, can be used to link to a slide or document that provides help.

  ✓ *To see exactly what each action button is designed to do, hover the mouse pointer over the button.*

- The Custom action button, which is blank, allows you to add your own text to tell viewers what the button will do when clicked.

- Draw the button on the slide like any shape. As soon as you release the mouse button after drawing the shape, the Action Settings dialog box opens, as shown in the following illustration.

Draw an action button to open the Action Settings dialog box

- The Action Settings dialog box displays a default action that matches the button. You can apply any other setting, though if you intend to choose an action that doesn't match up with the button's graphic, you may want to use the Custom button.

- The button can be formatted like any other shape with fill, outline, and effect formats. It can also be resized or moved anywhere on the slide.

- You can quickly add the same action button to a number of slides by copying and pasting it as you would any shape. Pasted buttons appear in the same place on each slide and contain the same action settings as the button you copied.

PROCEDURES

Insert a Link on a Slide

1. Select the text or object that will become the link.
2. Click **Insert** tab .... Alt+N

   Links Group

3. Click **Hyperlink** button  I

4. Choose what to link to:
   - **Existing File or Web Page** .... Alt+X
   - **Place in This Document** .... Alt+A

   ✓ *Use this option to see slides and custom shows in the current presentation.*

   - **Create New Document** ...... Alt+N
   - **E-mail Address** .... Alt+M

5. Navigate to the page, slide, custom show, or other target of the link and select it.
6. Click OK .... ↵Enter

To show a custom show and then return:

1. Select the text or object that will become the link.
2. Click **Insert** tab .... Alt+N

   ### Links Group

3. Click **Hyperlink** button 🔗 I
4. Click **Place in This Document** .... Alt+A
5. Choose the custom show in the list of slides and custom shows.
6. Click **Show and return** .... Alt+S below the preview of the first slide of the custom show.
7. Click [OK] .... ↵Enter

Insert an Action Button

1. Display the slide on which the button should appear.
2. Click **Home** tab .... Alt+H

   ### Drawing Group

3. Click **More** button ▼ .... S, H
4. Select action button from group at bottom of gallery .... ←→↑↓, ↵Enter
5. Draw the button shape on the slide.
6. Click **Hyperlink to** .... Alt+H
7. Select the slide to jump to .... ↓, ↵Enter
8. Click [OK] .... ↵Enter

   ✓ You can also access the Shapes gallery on the Insert tab.

EXERCISE DIRECTIONS

1. Start PowerPoint and open **45Aquatics_xx** or open ⊙**46Aquatics**.
2. Save the presentation as **46Aquatics_xx**.
3. In a program such as My Computer, copy the ⊙**46Survey.xlsx** Excel file to the folder in which you saved the presentation.
4. Display slide 3. Create links that will display either a chart or the raw Excel data:
   - In the text box at the bottom of the slide, select the words *View the chart*.
   - Choose to link to a place in this presentation, and then select slide 11.
   - In the text box at the bottom of the slide, select the words *View the raw data*.
   - Choose to link to an existing file and select the **46Survey.xlsx** file in the current folder.
5. Display slide 4. Create a link to the custom show you created:
   - Select the text of the second bullet item, *Families*.
   - Link to the Family custom show.
   - Under the preview of the first slide of the custom show, select the *Show and return* check box.

6. Display slide 6 and insert an action button that will return to the first slide of the presentation:
   - Choose the Beginning action button.
   - Draw the button at the lower-center of slide 6.
   - Accept the default link in the Action Settings dialog box and close it.
   - Apply a different Quick Style to the button. Illustration A shows one option.
7. Display slide 11 and insert an action button that will return to slide 3:
   - Choose the Back or Previous action button.
   - Draw the button at the lower-center of slide 11.
   - In the Action Settings dialog box, hyperlink to the Last Slide Viewed.
8. Apply the same Quick Style you used for the button on slide 6 and insert a text box next to it with the text **Return to slide 3**.
9. Play the presentation in Slide Show view. Try the link on slide 3, then use the action button to return to slide 3.

   ✓ If you rest the pointer for any amount of time on the links on slide 3, PowerPoint may move automatically to the next slide. Be sure to click immediately on the links.

10. Use the second link on slide 3 to open the Excel data file. Close Excel after you have viewed the data to return to the slide show and continue to the next slide.

11. Use the link on slide 4 to show the Family custom show. When you reach the end of this show, you will return automatically to slide 4.

12. Continue to slide 6 and use the action button to return to the first slide.

13. Save your changes, close the presentation, and exit PowerPoint.

Illustration A

ON YOUR OWN

1. Start PowerPoint and open **OPP45_xx** or open **OPP46**.
2. Save the presentation as **OPP46_xx**.
3. On slide 3, create the following links:
   - Link the text *Client diversity* to slide 6.
   - Link the text *Reasonable fees* to the Sample Fees custom show. Select *Show and return* for this link.
   - Link the text *architectural styles* to the Gallery custom show. Select *Show and return* for this link.
   - Link the text *Client/designer interaction* to slide 7. Your slide should look like Illustration A.

4. Insert Back or Previous action buttons on slides 6 and 7 to return to slide 3. Insert the Home action button on slide 10 to allow the presenter to return to slide 1. Format buttons as desired.
5. View the slides in Slide Show view, checking all links and action buttons.
6. Save your changes, close the presentation, and exit PowerPoint.

Illustration A

- Hide Slides
- Set Slide Show Options
- Control Slides During a Presentation
- Annotate Slides During a Presentation

Software Skills   Hide slides that you don't want to show during a particular presentation. You can specify how a slide show runs for different kinds of presentations. When presenting slides, you have a number of options for controlling slide display. You can annotate slides during the presentation and save annotations if desired.

Application Skills   You are ready to set up the Holmes Medical Center show and run through it a final time before handing it over to the client. The client wants two versions of the show: one for the Vice President to present and one to run unattended at a kiosk in the Medical Center lobby.

TERMS

No new terms in this exercise.

NOTES

Hide Slides

- You can hide slides in your presentation so they do not show when you run the slide show. For example, you might hide some slides to shorten the presentation, or hide slides that don't apply to a specific audience.

- Use the Hide Slide button on the Slide Show tab to hide the currently selected slide. Click the button again to unhide the slide.

- PowerPoint indicates a hidden slide in Slide Sorter view or the Slides tab by positioning a box and a diagonal line behind the slide number, as shown in the following illustration. In the Slides tab, the hidden slide may also be highlighted.

- Hidden slides remain in the file and appear in all views except Slide Show view. You can also print hidden slides if desired.

- If you find you want to refer to a hidden slide while in Slide Show view, you can use the Go to Slide command on the Slide Show shortcut menu to go to the hidden slide.

  ✓ *You learn more about controlling slides during a presentation later in this exercise.*

Set Slide Show Options

- Before finalizing a presentation, you must decide how it will be presented. If you plan to run the presentation unattended, without a speaker to control the slides, you need to set up the show accordingly.

Hidden slide in Slide Sorter view

- Use the Set Up Show dialog box, shown in the following illustration, to specify options for the slide show.

Set Up Show dialog box

- You have three options for show type:
  - Use *Presented by a speaker (full screen)* if your presentation will be delivered by a moderator to a live audience. Slides are displayed at full screen size, the way they are when you view them in Slide Show view.
  - Select *Browsed by an individual (window)* if you intend for the presentation to be viewed by an individual on his or her own computer. Slides display within a window that includes a title bar and window sizing controls, as shown in the following illustration. If you select the Show scrollbar check box, a vertical scrollbar displays to make it easy for the viewer to navigate the presentation.

Browsed by an individual (window) slide show option

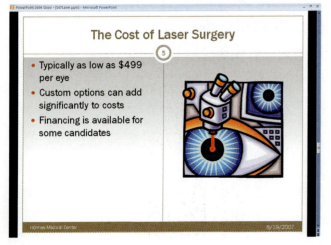

- Choose *Browsed at a kiosk (full screen)* when you want the presentation to run unattended, without a speaker to introduce the slides. This option is typically used when you prepare a presentation to run at a show where the slides loop over and over so that viewers can watch as much of the presentation as they want.

- Once you have decided what type of show to set up, you have additional decisions to make. You can select which slides to show, or specify a custom show if your presentation includes any.

- The Show options section of the dialog box lets you select other options for the presentation. You can choose to loop the slides continuously until the Esc key is pressed, show the presentation without narration, or show it without animations.

- If you intend to mark on slides—that is, annotate them—during the presentation, you can choose the color of the pen you will use at this point, so you don't have to interrupt the presentation to do so. (Annotating slides is covered later in this exercise.)

- You can specify how to advance slides. If you plan to run the slide show unattended, you must provide slide timings to advance slides because a speaker will not be present to do so.

- PowerPoint allows you to run a presentation on multiple monitors, if your projection system offers that option. Using Presenter view, you can display the presentation for the audience on one monitor while you view the presentation on another monitor that gives you access to notes and other computer resources that can help you with your presentation.

- Use options in the Performance area of the dialog box to control your system's performance.
  - If your system has a video graphics accelerator, select the Use hardware graphics acceleration option to prompt PowerPoint to take advantage of this device to boost performance.
  - Choose a resolution option from the Slide show resolution drop-down list to adjust the speed/quality ratio. The faster you want the slides to display, the poorer the quality will be, and vice versa.

Control Slides During a Presentation

■ You learned earlier to advance through slides during a slide show by clicking the mouse button. There are a number of other ways to control slide advance using keys or on-screen prompts.

■ During a presentation, a set of tools displays faintly in the lower-left corner of each slide. As you move the mouse pointer over the tools, they display in color, as shown in the following illustration.

Presentation tools in Slide Show view

■ Use these tools to go to the next slide (shown in the previous illustration), go to the previous slide, display annotation tool options, or display a menu.

■ This menu, which you can also display by right-clicking any slide, provides a number of ways to control slides, as shown in the following illustration.

Control menu in Slide Show view

■ Use this menu to navigate from slide to slide, go to the last-viewed slide or a specific slide (even a hidden slide, as indicated in the previous illustration), or go to a custom show.

■ The Screen command gives you options to replace the current slide with a black screen or a white screen, which is useful if you want to suspend the slide show without leaving the current screen content in view. You can also access the Switch Programs command, which displays the Windows taskbar at the bottom of the screen so you can switch to another program you have running.

■ If you are using slide timings, you can use the Pause command to stop the automatic advance and then Resume to continue.

■ PowerPoint also offers many keyboard options for quickly navigating the slides during a presentation. The following table lists some of these options.

Action	Keystroke
Show the next slide or animation	N ↵Enter Spacebar PgDn → ↓
Show the previous slide or animation	P PgUp ←Backspace ← ↑
Go to specific slide	Type slide number, press ↵Enter
End show	Esc

■ If you have set up the show for an individual to browse in a window, control options differ from those available when you set up the show for a speaker.

   • The presentation tools do not display at the lower-left corner of the window.

   • You cannot advance slides using the mouse button.

   • Right-clicking on a slide displays a shortcut menu different from the one that displays when you set up the show for a speaker.

■ You can advance slides in this kind of show using the scrollbar, or you can use the keystroke shortcuts shown previously. You can also use the Advance and Reverse commands on the shortcut menu.

Annotate Slides During a Presentation

- You can add annotations, such as writing or drawing, to a slide during a slide show. You may want to annotate to emphasize a specific point on a slide or add a comment to the slide.

- When you use the annotation feature, the mouse becomes a pen. You can choose different pen colors and pen styles, such as ballpoint or highlighter, as shown in the following illustration.

Choose an annotation pen style

- PowerPoint suspends automatic timings while you use the annotation feature.

- Use the erase options to remove any annotations you have made on a slide. The Eraser option allows you to remove any single annotation. Click Erase All Ink on Slide to remove all annotations on a slide.

- When you have finished annotating a slide, press Esc to change the pointer from a pen pointer back to the arrow pointer so you can click to advance to the next slide.

- When you close the slide show, PowerPoint offers you the option of saving your annotations or discarding them. If you save them, you will see them in Normal view and they can be printed.

  ✓ *Delete an annotation in Normal view by clicking on it and deleting it like any shape.*

PROCEDURES

Hide Slides

1. Select the slide or slides to hide.

2. Click **Slide Show** tab .... Alt + S

   Set Up Group

3. Click **Hide Slide** button 🔲 ...... H

To unhide a slide:

- Repeat the process above.

Set Slide Show Options

1. Click **Slide Show** tab .... Alt + S

   Set Up Group

2. Click **Set Up Slide Show** button 🔲 .... S

3. Choose one of the following show types:
   - **Presented by a speaker** .... Alt + P
   - **Browsed by an individual** .... Alt + B
   - **Browsed at a kiosk** ..... Alt + K

4. Choose any of the following show options:
   - **Loop continuously until 'Esc'** .... Alt + L
   - **Show without narration** .... Alt + N
   - **Show without animation** .... Alt + S

5. Choose how to advance slides:
   - **Manually** .... Alt + M
   - **Using timings, if present** .... Alt + U

6. Set performance options:
   - Click **Use hardware graphics acceleration** .... Alt + G if you have a video graphics accelerator.
   - Click **Slide show resolution** .... Alt + R, ↓ and select a resolution.

7. Click [OK] .... ↵Enter

Control Slides During a Presentation

- In Slide Show view, use the follow options to control slides:

To go to the next slide:

- Click (N), (→), (↓), (PgDn), (↵Enter), or (Spacebar).
- Click ➡ at lower-left corner of screen.

  OR

1. Right-click the screen.
2. Click **Next** .... (N)

To return to the previous slide:

- Click (P), (←), (↑), (PgUp), or (↵Backspace).
- Click ⬅ at lower-left corner of screen.

  OR

1. Right-click the screen.
2. Click **Previous** .... (P)

   OR

   Click **Last Viewed** .... (V)

To go to a specific slide:

- Type the slide number and press (↵Enter).

  OR

1. Right-click the screen.
2. Click **Go to Slide** .... (G)
3. Select slide to view .... (↓), (↵Enter)

To pause the show:

1. Right-click the screen.
2. Click **Pause** .... (S)

To resume the show:

1. Right-click the screen.
2. Click **Resume** .... (S)

Annotate During a Presentation

1. Right-click the screen.
2. Click **Pointer Options** .... (O)
3. Select a pen style:
   - **Ballpoint Pen** .... (B)
   - **Felt Tip Pen** .... (F)
   - **Highlighter** .... (H)
4. Hold down the mouse button and drag to write annotations.

To choose a pen color:

1. Right-click the screen.
2. Click **Pointer Options** .... (O)
3. Click **Ink Color** .... (C)
4. Select a color from the color palette.

To erase annotations:

- Press (E).

  OR

1. Right-click the screen.
2. Click **Pointer Options** .... (O)
3. Click **Eraser** .... (R)
4. Move the eraser over the annotation and click to erase.

   OR

1. Right-click the screen.
2. Click **Pointer Options** .... (O)
3. Click **Erase All Ink on Slide** .... (E)

To keep or discard annotations:

1. End the slide show.
2. Click [Keep] .... (↵Enter)

   OR

   Click [Discard] .... (D)

EXERCISE DIRECTIONS

1. Start PowerPoint and open 🔘**47Laser**.
2. Save the presentation as **47Laser_xx**.
3. Hide slide 8.
4. Run the show in Slide Show view and let automatic timings display the first two slides. Then go to slide 7 and pause the show long enough to read the text.
5. Resume the show and return to the last slide viewed (slide 2).
6. Choose the felt tip pen option and draw an arrow to point to *Opens March 22*. Erase the annotation you just created.
7. Advance to slide 4 and use the highlighter to highlight the *Almost immediate results* bullet item. Then finish viewing the slides by advancing them manually. Notice that slide 8 does not display. Discard the annotation at the end of the show.

8. Now set up the show for unattended use:
   - Save the current presentation, and then save it as **47Laser-2_xx**.
   - Unhide slide 8.
   - Set up the show to be browsed at a kiosk. Note that this option also automatically selects the Loop continuously option.
   - Set the resolution to the 640x480 (Fastest, Lowest Fidelity) setting.
9. Start the show and allow it to run all the way through once. The quality is indeed pretty low, so adjust the show setting to use the current resolution and start the show again.
10. When you reach slide 2 again, stop the show.
11. Save your changes, close the presentation, and exit PowerPoint.

ON YOUR OWN

1. Start PowerPoint and open ⊙ **OPP47**.
2. Save the presentation as **OPP47_*xx***.
3. Hide slide 3.
4. Set up transitions and slide timings for all slides.
5. Run the slide show. Stop the show to annotate several of the slides. For example, circle or highlight one of the topics on a slide.
6. When exiting the presentation, save the annotations and then view them in Normal view, as shown in Illustration A.
7. Print the presentation as handouts with 4 slides per page, choosing to print comments and ink markup and to print hidden slides.
8. Save your changes, close the presentation, and exit PowerPoint.

Illustration A

Staff Training

▶ All staff members are trained in
  ■ Fitness and nutrition
  ■ Equipment safety and use
  ■ Exercise regime planning
▶ Ratio of staff to members: 1 to 10

Skills Covered

- **Protect a Presentation**
- **Work with Comments and Markup**
- **Send a Presentation for Review**

Software Skills   If you need to share a presentation with others, you can take steps to make sure the presentation will not be altered by anyone unauthorized to edit the slides. Use comments to share information or request changes and control the display of comments by showing or hiding markup on the slides. You can use your e-mail program to send a presentation for review.

Application Skills   In this exercise, you will learn how to protect a presentation by setting permissions and applying a digital signature and passwords. Add comments to the Campus Recreation Center presentation and then send it for review via e-mail.

TERMS

Comment A note you add to a slide to provide corrections or input to the slide content.

Digital signature A feature that provides a way to authenticate a presentation's author and ensure that the presentation has not been changed.

Encryption The process of transforming data into a form that cannot be read or decoded without a key (password).

Information Rights Management (IRM) A feature that lets an author or administrator control who has *permission* to use a file.

Permissions Rights to read or modify a file.

NOTES

Protect a Presentation

- If you regularly share presentations with others, such as team members or other colleagues, you need to know how to protect your work so that it is not changed without your permission.

- PowerPoint 2007 offers more security features than previous versions of the program, reflecting the heightened awareness in the work world of the damage that can be done by hackers or those in the workplace who might tamper with your files.

- You can set passwords, encrypt a presentation, apply a digital signature, or set permissions for a presentation. These options are discussed in depth in the following sections.

Apply Passwords to a Presentation

- Passwords are familiar security devices that require a user to enter a word or phrase specified by the author of a file before that file can be opened or edited.

- In PowerPoint 2007, you can set passwords when saving a presentation. In the Save As dialog box, click the Tools button and select General Options to open the dialog box shown in the following illustration.

General Options dialog box

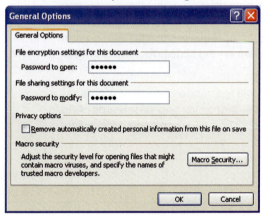

- Note that you can set two different passwords in this dialog box: one that is required to open the file and another that is required if you want to modify the file.

- When you open a presentation to which a password has been applied, a dialog box displays to allow you to enter the password. If you have requested passwords for both opening and modifying, you must supply both before you can work with the presentation.

- If a password has been specified for opening a presentation, you must have it to display the slides. If a password has been specified for modifying a presentation, you do not need it to display the slides. You can choose to open a Read Only copy of the presentation that you can review but not change.

- Remove password protection by displaying the General Options dialog box and clearing the passwords you entered.

Encrypt a Presentation

- Another way to protect a presentation is to apply **encryption**. When you encrypt any document, you convert it into a form that cannot be read. Decoding an encrypted file requires a *key*, or password.

- To encrypt a presentation, point to the Prepare command on the Office menu and then select Encrypt Document on the submenu.

- PowerPoint requires you to enter a password, as shown in the following illustration. You must then confirm the password.

Encrypt Document dialog box

- Encrypt Document actually provides the same level of protection as specifying a password to open a file in the General Options dialog box, and you can use either method to apply encryption. Use the Save As method when you are saving the file; use the Encrypt Document method at any time while working with the presentation.

- Remove encryption as discussed above for removing passwords, or display the Encrypt Document dialog box again and clear the password from it.

Add a Digital Signature

- A **digital signature** provides a different form of security for a presentation. Rather than preventing someone from tampering with the file, it provides the assurance that the file was created by a specific person and has not been changed since that person applied the signature.

- A digital signature requires an author to acquire a certificate that is issued by some trusted authority. A person who receives a presentation with a digital signature knows that the author's identity has been confirmed by that trusted authority and the file is safe to open.

- Commercial certificates can cost quite a bit of money, but you can create one for the purposes of testing this feature using Microsoft Office tools.

- You become your own "trusted authority," so such a digital signature is not worth much as a form of security, but it can give you an idea how digital signatures work.

- You apply a digital signature using the Add a Digital Signature command on the Office menu's Prepare submenu. If you have a signature "on file" on your computer, the Sign dialog box shown in the following illustration displays.

Sign dialog box

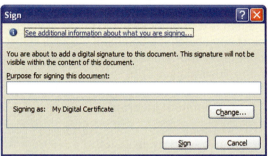

- You can supply a purpose for the signature, or simply click the Sign button to apply the signature. After informing you that the presentation has been signed, PowerPoint displays the Signature task pane and a certificate icon, as shown in the following illustration.

Presentation file after a digital signature has been applied

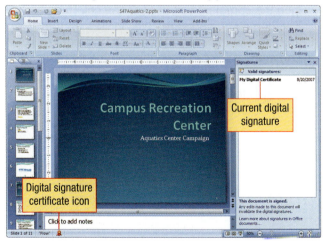

- A presentation to which a digital signature has been applied is "locked" so that you cannot edit it, because editing would invalidate the signature.

- Some commands on the Office menu are still active, however, and if you issue one of these commands, you are informed that it will invalidate the current signature. An invalid signature displays in red, as shown in the following illustration.

Invalid digital signature

- You can revalidate the signature by pointing to the signature to display a down arrow and then selecting Sign Again.

- You can also use this list menu to remove a signature so that you can continue to edit a presentation.

Restrict Permission Using Information Rights Management

- The final security option you can apply to prevent unauthorized persons from opening or changing your presentations is to set **permissions** using Information Rights Management (IRM).

- **Information Rights Management** is a feature that allows an author or administrator to control who has access to a file.

- You use the Protect Presentation button on the Review tab or the Restrict Permission command on the Office menu's Prepare submenu to start the process of specifying permissions. If you have a valid IRM certificate, you will then see a Permission dialog box like the one in the following illustration.

Permission dialog box

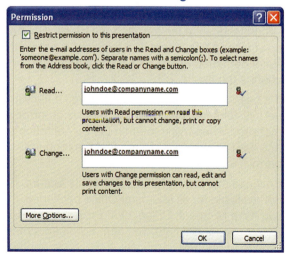

- To permit users to read or change a presentation, you insert their e-mail addresses in the appropriate boxes.

- After you have set permissions, a message bar displays below the Ribbon to indicate that permission has been restricted for this presentation.

- The More Options button opens the version of the Permission dialog box shown in the following illustration. Here you can work with the list of users to add or remove a user; specify a date on which a permission expires; select additional permissions for a user, such as the right to copy or print material; and provide an e-mail address so a user can request further information about permissions.

Additional permission options

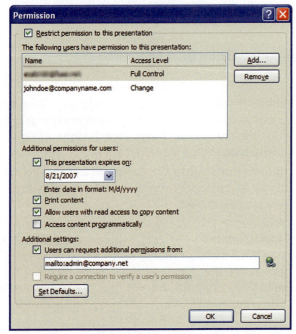

- Information Rights Management is a robust form of security because the permissions travel with the file as you send it to others. If a recipient is not on the list of permitted users, he or she cannot read or change the file.

- If a user who is not on the list receives a file with permissions set, he or she will receive an error message when trying to open the presentation and then be prompted to request the required permission.

- Because this is a higher-level security feature, it is not available for all Microsoft Office packages. If you have Microsoft Office 2007 Professional Plus, Enterprise, or Ultimate, you can download a trial version of the IRM certificate. If you have another Office package, you may not be able to use this feature.

Work with Comments and Markup

- As you work with a presentation, you may want to insert notes for yourself about information you need to add or work that needs to be done on a slide. If you have been asked to review a presentation, you might want to give the author your views on specific points.

- It is inappropriate to use the Notes pane for such information. Instead, you can use **comments** to supply information for yourself or someone else.

- You can add a comment to an entire slide or to selected text or other selected object. If you do not select any object, the comment displays in the upper-left corner of the slide, as shown in the following illustration.

Comment inserted on a slide

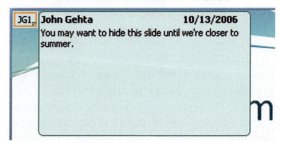

- The name and initials that display on each comment are those of the current user.

- When you are done creating a comment, click outside the comment box to close the comment box. The comment marker remains in view on the slide. To read a comment that is not open, point to the comment marker to open the comment box.

- You use the Comments group on the Review tab, shown in the following illustration, to work with comments.

Comments group options

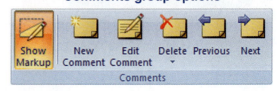

- Use the New Comment button to insert a comment. The Edit Comment button opens a selected comment so you can modify it. The Delete button allows you to remove a single comment, all comments on a slide, or all comments throughout a presentation.

- If you have a number of comments in a presentation, the Previous and Next buttons allow you to move quickly from comment to comment, opening each so you can read it.

- When you open a presentation that contains comments, the comment markers display on the slides by default, and the Show Markup button is active on the Review tab.

- If you want to hide comments as you review a presentation, click the Show Markup button to deactivate it. The comment markers then disappear from the slides.

Send a Presentation for Review

- Presentations are often created in collaborative environments, such as companies and organizations. PowerPoint makes it easy for you to send a presentation to your colleagues for review.

- Use the Send command to choose whether to e-mail or fax the presentation.

- You must have an Internet fax provider to fax a presentation.

- If you choose to send a presentation by e-mail, a new message displays such as the one shown in the following illustration.

Send a presentation via e-mail

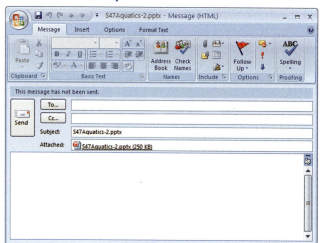

- Note that the name of presentation is automatically included in the message as the subject and the file is supplied as an attachment. You need only supply the recipient's e-mail address and a message.

- Sending a presentation this way from PowerPoint can save time that you would spend opening your e-mail program, composing a message, and then locating and attaching the file.

- If you have applied a digital signature to a presentation, e-mailing it will invalidate the signature.

PROCEDURES

Apply Passwords to a Presentation

1. Click **Office Button** ..... Alt + F
2. Click **Save As** ..... A
3. Click Tools ..... Alt + L, ↓
4. Click **General Options** ..... G
5. Click **Password to open** ..... Alt + O
6. Type password to be used to open file.
7. Click **Password to modify** ..... Alt + M
8. Type password to be used to modify file.
9. Click OK ..... ↵Enter
10. Confirm password to open by reentering the password.
11. Click OK ..... ↵Enter
12. Confirm password to modify by reentering the password.
13. Click OK ..... ↵Enter
14. Click Save ..... Alt + S

To remove a password:

1. Click **Office Button** ..... Alt + F
2. Click **Save As** ..... A
3. Click Tools ..... Alt + L, ↓
4. Click **General Options** ..... G
5. Click **Password to open** ..... Alt + O
6. Delete the password in the box.
7. Click **Password to modify** ..... Alt + M
8. Delete the password in the box.
9. Click OK ..... ↵Enter
10. Click Save ..... Alt + S

Encrypt a Presentation

1. Click **Office Button** ..... Alt + F
2. Point to **Prepare** ..... E
3. Click **Encrypt Document** ..... E
4. Click **Password** ..... Alt + R
5. Type the desired password.
6. Click OK ..... ↵Enter
7. Confirm password to open by reentering the password.
8. Click OK ..... ↵Enter

To remove encryption:

1. Click **Office Button** 📇 ...... `Alt`+`F`
2. Point to **Pre̲pare** .... `E`
3. Click **E̲ncrypt Document** .... `E`
4. Click **Password̲** .... `Alt`+`R`
5. Delete the password from the box.
6. Click `    OK    ` .... `↵Enter`

Create a Digital Signature

Use the instructions below to create a self-signing digital signature you can use to test this feature.

1. Click the Windows **Start** button
   ` start ` / 📇 .... `Ctrl`+`Esc`
2. Point to **All Programs̲** .... `P`, `↵Enter`
3. Point to **Microsoft Office**.
4. Point to **Microsoft Office Tools**.
5. Click **Digital Certificate for VBA Projects**.
6. Click **Y̲our certificate's name** .... `Alt`+`Y`
7. Type the name you want to use on your certificate.
8. Click `    OK    ` .... `↵Enter`
9. Click `    OK    ` again .... `↵Enter`

Apply a Digital Signature

1. Click **Office Button** 📇 ...... `Alt`+`F`
2. Point to **Pre̲pare** .... `E`
3. Click **Add a Digital S̲ignature** ...... `S`
4. Click **OK**.
5. Type a purpose for the signature if desired.
6. If the signature is not the one you created:
   a. Click ` Change... ` .... `Alt`+`H`
   b. Click your signature.
   c. Click `    OK    ` .... `↵Enter`
7. Click ` Sign ` .... `Alt`+`S`
8. Click `   OK   `.

To remove a digital signature:

1. Click 🧑 if necessary to display Signatures task pane.
2. Point to signature you want to remove in Signatures task pane.
3. Click down arrow at right side of signature.
4. Click **Remove Sig̲nature** .... `N`
5. Click ` Yes ` .... `Alt`+`Y` to remove signature.

   OR

   Click ` No ` .... `Alt`+`N` to retain the signature.
6. If you clicked ` Yes `, click `   OK   ` to complete the process.

Set Permissions Using Information Rights Management

Instructions below assume you have an IRM certificate installed. If you do not, see your instructor for further help.

1. Click **Office Button** 📇 ...... `Alt`+`F`
2. Point to **Pre̲pare** .... `E`
3. Point to **R̲estrict Permission** ...... `R`
4. Click **R̲estricted Access** .... `R`

   OR

1. Click **Review** tab .... `Alt`+`R`

   Protect Group

2. Click **Protect Presentation** button 🔒 .... `P`
3. Click **R̲estricted Access** .... `R`

To specify permitted users:

In the Permission dialog box

1. Click **R̲estrict permission to this presentation** .... `Alt`+`R`
2. Click in **Read** box and type e-mail address(es) of permitted user(s).
3. Click in **Change** box and type e-mail address(es) of permitted user(s).
4. Click `    OK    ` .... `↵Enter`

To remove permissions:

1. Display Permission dialog box.
2. Click **R̲estrict permission to this presentation** .... `Alt`+`R`

Work with Comments and Markup

Insert a comment:

1. Display the slide on which you want to comment, or select text or an object to which the comment should be attached.
2. Click **Review** tab .... `Alt`+`R`

   Comments Group

3. Click **New Comment** button 📒 .... `C`
4. Type the comment text in the comment box.
5. Click outside the box to close the comment box.

View a comment:

- Point to the comment marker to open the comment box.

Modify a comment:

1. Click a comment marker to select it.
2. Click **Review** tab .... `Alt`+`R`

   Comments Group

3. Click **Edit Comment** button 📝 .... `T`
4. Modify the comment text as desired.

Delete a comment:

1. Display the slide on which the comment appears.
2. Click **Review** tab .... Alt + R

   Comments Group

3. Click **Delete** button 🖼 .... D

   OR

   a. Click **Delete** button down arrow.
   b. Choose what to delete:
      - Click **D̲elete** .... D
        to remove a single or selected comment.
      - Click **Delete A̲ll Markup on the Current Slide** .... A
      - Click **Delete All Markup in this P̲resentation** .... P

To show or hide markup:

1. Click **Review** tab .... Alt + R

   Comments Group

2. Click **Show Markup** button 🖊 .... H
   to show or hide markup.

Send a Presentation for Review

1. Click **Office Button** 🅱 ...... Alt + F
2. Point to **Send̲** .... D
3. Select option for sending:
   - **E-mail** .... E
   - **Internet Fax̲** X

To send via e-mail:

1. When the e-mail header opens in the PowerPoint window, type the e-mail address of the person to whom you are sending the presentation.
2. Add a message in the message area if desired.
3. Click 📧 .... S

EXERCISE DIRECTIONS

1. Start PowerPoint and open 💿 **48Aquatics**.
2. Save the presentation as **48Aquatics_xx**.
3. On slide 1, insert a comment to remind yourself to check all links in the presentation.
4. Display slide 3 and add the comment **Should we pull the raw data into the presentation?** .
5. Display slide 5 and add the comment **Check membership rates.**
6. Modify the comment on slide 3 to read **Carol, should we create a slide that contains the raw data?** .
7. Run the presentation to check the links and action buttons, and then delete the comment on slide 1.
8. Assume you have checked the membership rates on slide 5 and delete that comment.
9. Save the presentation, and then apply encryption with the password **Campus**.
10. Send the presentation to your instructor if you have e-mail capability.
11. Save your changes and close the presentation.
12. Open the presentation and supply the correct password. Then remove the password.
13. Save and close the presentation, and exit PowerPoint.

ON YOUR OWN

1. Start PowerPoint and open **OPP48**.

2. Save the presentation as **OPP48_xx**.

3. Add a comment on slide 1 to the president of the company, Jim, informing him that this is the next draft of the presentation and you need comments by the end of the week.

4. If you have the ability to protect the presentation using information rights management, set permissions for your instructor or a classmate to read the presentation only.

5. If you have a digital signature available, sign the presentation with your signature.

6. Try editing the comment you inserted. You should not be able to make any changes in the presentation, though you can read all slides.

7. E-mail the presentation to your instructor. Click OK when you are informed the action will invalidate the digital signature.

8. If you were able to set permissions, remove the permission at this point.

9. Re-sign the presentation.

10. Save and close the presentation, and exit PowerPoint.

Skills Covered

- The Prepare Submenu
- Run the Compatibility Checker
- Use the Document Inspector

- Mark a Presentation as Final
- Package for CD
- Other Output Options

Software Skills   Use options on the Prepare submenu to check compatibility with earlier versions of PowerPoint, remove document properties, and mark a presentation as final. You can easily package the presentation materials on a CD or use other output options such as saving the presentation as a PowerPoint Show or as slide images.

Application Skills   In this exercise, you will check compatibility of the Holmes Medical Center presentation, inspect the presentation, and package it for distribution. Then you will mark the presentation as final.

TERMS

No new terms in this exercise.

NOTES

The Prepare Submenu

- You have already used the Prepare submenu to perform some chores for a presentation, such as encrypting the file and adding a digital signature.
- This submenu, shown in the following illustration, offers several other tools and options you can use to finalize a presentation.

Prepare submenu

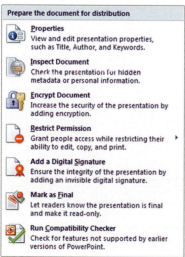

- Options on this submenu are among the last you will perform when completing work on a presentation.
- In the following sections, you will learn about the options you have not yet used: Run Compatibility Checker, Inspect Document, and Mark as Final.

Run the Compatibility Checker

- The Compatibility Checker is a feature designed to flag features in your current presentation that are not supported in previous PowerPoint versions.
- It is especially important to use this feature before saving to an earlier version of PowerPoint, because some of PowerPoint 2007's effects cannot be edited in previous versions of the program.

- When you click Run Compatibility Checker from the Prepare submenu, the Compatibility Checker reviews each slide for compatibility issues and then displays a report such as the one shown in the following illustration.

Compatibility Checker report

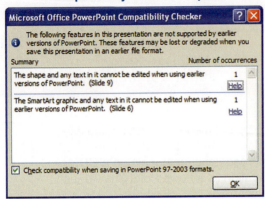

- The Summary tells you the compatibility issue, such as a SmartArt graphic that cannot be edited in earlier versions of PowerPoint, lets you know how many times the issue occurs, and offers a Help link that provides more information about the issue.

- In most cases, the compatibility issues will not compromise the look of the slides when they are shown in other versions of PowerPoint. Though you will not be able to edit a SmartArt graphic, for example, its components are saved as pictures that will display the same way they do in PowerPoint 2007.

- The help files offer advice on how to modify PowerPoint 2007 features if you want to maintain some edibility. For example, you can convert a SmartArt graphic to separate shapes so that you can edit them in any version of PowerPoint.

Use the Document Inspector

- Companies and organizations are increasingly careful about sharing files that contain properties such as those you added to a presentation earlier in the course. Properties can reveal a lot about a file, including who wrote it or reviewed it, when the file was created or edited, and so on.

- The Inspect Document option searches for personal information you may not want to accompany a presentation when you send it to someone else.

- After you issue the Inspect Document command, PowerPoint displays a dialog box like the one in the following illustration to tell you what kinds of hidden and personal information the Document Inspector can locate.

What the Document Inspector looks for

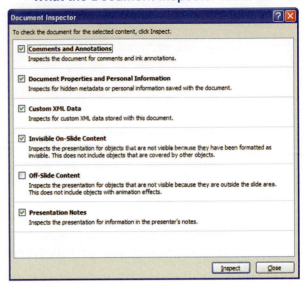

- After you choose the types of content that the Document Inspector will look for, you inspect the presentation.

- The Document Inspector creates a report such as the one shown in the following illustration that shows the types of information the Document Inspector found. Buttons give you the option of removing all sensitive data so that it will not be included with the presentation if you send it elsewhere.

What the Document Inspector finds

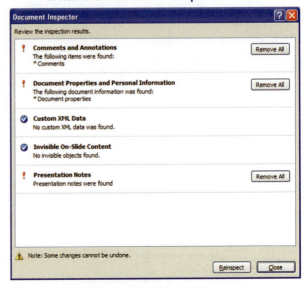

- You can reinspect the presentation after removing inspection results if desired.

Mark a Presentation as Final

- The Mark as Final command locks a presentation so that it cannot be further edited, although you can navigate through the slides and read the slide content.

- Many other options also become unavailable, such as the ability to inspect or encrypt the document.

- You know a presentation has been marked as final if it displays the Marked as Final icon in the status bar.

- You can reverse this command by simply issuing it again to make the presentation once again available for editing.

Package for CD

- Use the Package for CD feature when you want to run a slide show on another computer. This features helps you collect all the files you need for a presentation and then stores them in a folder or on a CD.

- You don't have to worry whether the computer on which you plan to run the packaged show has PowerPoint, because the PowerPoint Viewer can be included in the package. The PowerPoint Viewer lets you run a PowerPoint show without the use of PowerPoint.

- Start the process of packaging a presentation using the Package for CD command on the Office menu's Publish submenu.

- Note that the PowerPoint Viewer requires files to be in the PowerPoint 97-2003 file format, so when you issue the Package for CD command, PowerPoint lets you know your file will be converted to that format if you choose to include the PowerPoint Viewer in the package.

- The Package for CD dialog box, shown in the following illustration, lets you control the process of packaging the presentation files and copying them to a folder or a CD.

Package for CD dialog box

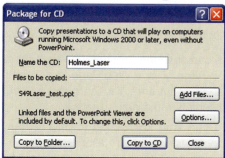

- You first provide a name for the package in the Name the CD box. The presentation that will be stored in the package is shown in the Files to be copied area.

- You can use the Add Files button to select additional presentations to be packaged at the same time. This is a good way to archive or pack up several presentations on a single disk to make the most efficient use of the disk's storage capacity.

- The Options button opens the dialog box shown in the following illustration to give you additional options for packaging the presentation.

Package for CD Options dialog box

- First decide whether you need the PowerPoint Viewer. The Viewer Package is selected by default, but you can choose the Archive Package to pack files without the Viewer.

  ✓ *The Archive Package option produces many fewer files in the package and can thus save space on a disk or in a folder.*

- If you choose the Viewer Package, you can also select how your stored presentations will play in the viewer if you have more than one presentation in the package. For example, you can play all presentations in order, play the first one automatically, let the user choose which presentation to play, or turn off the option that plays the CD automatically.

- By default, linked files are included in the package. This means that if you have inserted a movie or sound file in a presentation, PowerPoint will locate those linked files and add them to the package for you.

- Choose to embed TrueType fonts to use the same fonts during the presentation that you selected when creating the slides. This option will increase the size of your package, but it ensures your presentation's font quality.

- You can set security options in this dialog box, such as requiring a password to open and/or modify presentations in the package. You can also prompt PowerPoint to inspect presentations for hidden or private information.

- When you have finished setting options, you are ready to decide whether to store your package on a CD or in a folder.

- If you have a CD available in a writable drive, click the Copy to CD button to start the process of copying files. You will be asked if you trust the source of all linked files, and then the copying process begins. When the process is complete, you will be asked if you want to copy the files to another CD.

- If you want to store the package in a folder, click the Copy to Folder button. You are then asked to specify a folder in which to store the package, as shown in the following illustration.

Select a folder for the package

- You can use the Browse button to navigate to the location where you want to store the presentation package. The files will then be copied to that location in a folder with the name you provided.

- You can use Windows Explorer or My Computer to navigate to the location where you stored the package.

- If you chose to package with the PowerPoint Viewer, the folder contains a number of files, among them the PPTVIEW.EXE file (the PowerPoint Viewer) and the presentation file itself.

- Start the PowerPoint Viewer by double-clicking the PPTVIEW.EXE file. The presentation displays in the Viewer as shown in the following illustration.

PowerPoint Viewer window

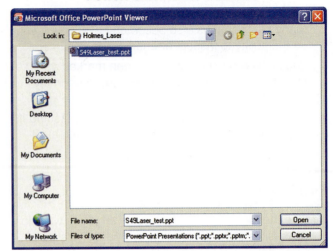

- When you select a file in this window and click Open, the presentation launches immediately in Slide Show view.

- If you chose not to use the PowerPoint Viewer, your package contains only the presentation file. You can open it in PowerPoint and then present it using Slide Show view.

Other Output Options

- You will generally want to output your slides using the Package for CD feature to pack up and organize the presentation. But you do have several other important output options.

- The Page Setup dialog box allows you to size slides for output such as different paper sizes, overhead transparencies, banners, and 35mm slides.

- The Save As dialog box offers some additional output options:

  - You can save the presentation as a PowerPoint Show. A PowerPoint Show opens automatically in Slide Show view, saving time if all you want to do is present the slides.

    ✓ *You can also find this option by pointing to Save As on the Office menu to display the Save As submenu.*

  - You can save the presentation as a Single File Web Page or as a Web Page to publish it on the Web or an intranet. You learn more about Web publishing in the next exercise.

  - You can save the slides in one of four popular graphics formats (GIF, JPG, PNG, TIFF) to export the current slide or all slides in that format. Slides saved as images make excellent illustrations for reports associated with the presentation.

PROCEDURES

Run the Compatibility Checker

1. Click **Office Button** .... Alt + F
2. Point to **Prepare** .... E
3. Click **Run Compatibility Checker** C
4. Read the report on compatibility issues.
5. Click OK .... ↵Enter

Use the Document Inspector

1. Click **Office Button** .... Alt + F
2. Point to **Prepare** .... E
3. Click **Inspect Document** I
4. Select content that Document Inspector will inspect.
5. Click Inspect .... ↵Enter
6. Review results and if desired click Remove All to remove information.
7. Click Close .... ↵Enter

Mark a Presentation as Final

1. Click **Office Button** .... Alt + F
2. Point to **Prepare** .... E
3. Click **Mark as Final** .... F
4. Click OK .... ↵Enter
5. Click OK again .... ↵Enter

Package for CD

1. Open the presentation to pack.
2. Click **Office Button** .... Alt + F
3. Point to **Publish** .... U
4. Click **Package for CD** .... K
5. Click **OK** .... ↵Enter when asked if you want to update files for the Viewer.
6. Enter a title in the **Name the CD** box .... Alt + N

7. Click Options... .... Alt + O to specify options:
   - Click **Viewer Package** Alt + V to include the PowerPoint Viewer in the package.
   - Click **Select how presentations will play in the viewer** .... Alt + S, ↓, ↵Enter to select play option for Viewer.
   - Click **Archive Package** Alt + A to package without the Viewer.
   - Click **Linked files** .... Alt + L to include all files linked to slides.
   - Click **Embedded TrueType fonts** .... Alt + E to include fonts used on slides.
   - Click **Password to open each presentation** .... Alt + O and type a password.
   - Click **Password to modify each presentation** .... Alt + M and type a password.
   - Click **Inspect each presentation for inappropriate or private information** .... Alt + I
8. Click OK .... ↵Enter
9. Click Copy to CD .... Alt + C
10. When asked if you want to use linked files, click Yes .... ↵Enter
11. When asked if you want to copy the files to another CD, click No .... N
12. Click Close .

To copy to a folder rather than a CD:

1. In the Package for CD dialog box, select all options.
2. Click Copy to Folder... .... Alt + F
3. Type the name of the folder.
4. Type the location of the folder.
   OR
   a. Click Browse... and navigate to the folder location.
   b. Click Select .... Alt + E

5. Click OK .... ↵Enter
6. Click Close .

To unpack and run presentation:

1. Insert CD in computer and navigate in My Computer to CD drive to see files on CD.
   OR
   Navigate to location of folder in which you saved files.
2. Double-click **PPTVIEW.EXE**.
3. Click name of show and then click Open ▼ .... ↵Enter

Save a Presentation as a Show

1. Open the presentation to save as a show.
2. Click **Office Button** .... Alt + F
3. Point to **Save As** right-pointing arrow .... F
4. Click **PowerPoint Show** .... S
5. Type a different name for the file if desired.
6. Click Save .... ↵Enter

Save a Slide or Slides as an Image

1. Open the presentation to save in image format.
2. Click **Office Button** .... Alt + F
3. Click **Save As** .... A
4. Click **Save as type** down arrow .... Alt + T
5. Select desired image format .... ↓, ↵Enter
6. Type a new name for the image file.
7. Click Save .... ↵Enter
8. Click Every Slide .... ↵Enter
   OR
   Click Current Slide Only .
9. Click OK if you chose to save every slide.

EXERCISE DIRECTIONS

1. Start PowerPoint and open 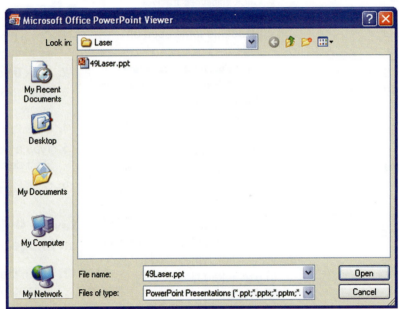49Laser.

2. Save the presentation as **49Laser_xx**.

3. Run the Compatibility Checker and read the resulting report, which lets you know you will not be able to edit the WordArt graphic in previous versions of PowerPoint.

4. Run the Document Inspector. Remove document properties and the comment, but do not remove the presentation notes.

5. Package the presentation as follows:

   - Name the CD folder in which to store the files **Laser**.

   - Display Options and choose to embed TrueType fonts.

   - If you have the ability to copy to a CD, do so and then close the Package for CD dialog box.

   - If you cannot copy to a CD, browse to a known location on your hard drive, such as the Documents and Settings folder, select the location, and copy the files to the Laser folder at that location.

6. Display the PowerPoint Viewer at the location where you saved the show. It should look similar to Illustration A. run the show, then close the show and the Viewer.

7. Mark the **49Laser_xx** presentation as final, close the presentation, and exit PowerPoint.

Illustration A

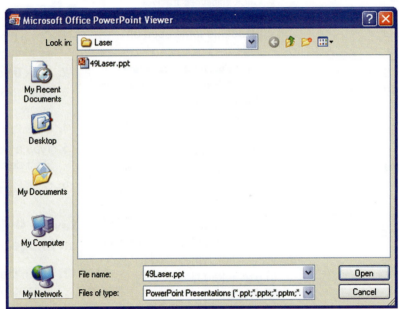

ON YOUR OWN

1. Start PowerPoint and open ⊙OPP49.

2. Save the presentation as **OPP49_xx**.

3. Run the Compatibility Checker to see what kinds of issues might arise if you save to a previous version of PowerPoint. (The theme itself will result in a number of slides being flagged, as shown in Illustration A.)

4. Run the Document Inspector and then remove comments and properties.

5. Package the presentation using the Archive Package option in a folder named **Restoration**. Embed TrueType fonts.

6. Save the presentation as a show with the name **OPP49-2_xx**.

7. Choose to save slide 4 only as a JPG image with the name **OPP49-3_xx**, then close the presentation.

8. In My Computer, navigate to the location where you saved the show file and double-click it to open it. Note that the presentation opens in Slide Show view.

9. Run the slide show. Then exit PowerPoint.

Illustration A

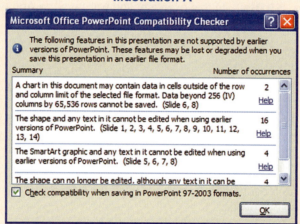

Skills Covered

- **Save a Presentation as a Web Site**
- **View a Web Presentation**
- **Set Publishing Options**

Software Skills Save your presentation as a Web site and publish it to the Web so that a larger audience can view it. You might, for example, already have a Web site established for customers to view your products or services. Add a presentation to the site to interest more customers and provide an additional resource.

Application Skills In this exercise, you will save the Aquatics presentation as a Web site so that those involved in the campaign can easily access it over the campus intranet.

TERMS

HTML (Hypertext Markup Language) A formatting language used to create Web pages. Web browsers can read the HTML language over the Internet.

Publish Set options to make the presentation more suitable for viewing on the Web by specific browsers.

Web site A collection of Web pages; a site usually contains information about a specific topic.

NOTES

Save a Presentation as a Web Site

- Save a presentation as a **Web site** so you can **publish** it to the World Wide Web or an intranet at a company, organization, or school.

- PowerPoint lets you save a presentation in **HTML** (**Hypertext Markup Language**) format so that you can open it in a Web browser such as Internet Explorer.

- In a presentation Web site, each slide becomes a separate page in the site. The title slide is the home page of the site.

- You have two options when saving a presentation for Web use, as shown in the illustration at right.

  - Use the Single File Web Page file type in the Save As dialog box to save the presentation as one file using the MHT file format.

- Use the Web Page file type to save the presentation in HTM format.

Save as Web page options in Save As dialog box

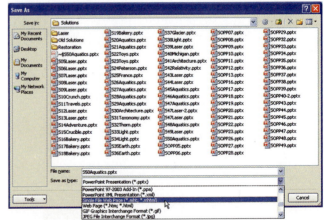

- When you save in MHT format, everything the browser needs to display the Web site is included in one file. Although this is convenient, not all browsers can use the MHT format.

- When you save in HTM format, PowerPoint creates the Web file and also creates a folder with the same name to hold supporting files, such as buttons, images, backgrounds, and so on. You must be sure to upload both the presentation file and the supporting files folder to the Web server that will host your site.

- Links on your presentation Web pages work just as when you show the presentation in Slide Show view. Action buttons may not work quite as well, depending on your browser, and multimedia files such as sounds and movies may not display or play correctly.

  ✓ *Be sure to test your Web site in a number of browsers. For best results, specify Internet Explorer 6.0 or later as the browser of choice.*

Set Publishing Options

- After you select a Web page file format, the Save As dialog box changes to show other files saved in that format (if any) in the current folder, as shown in the following illustration.

Publishing options in Save As dialog box

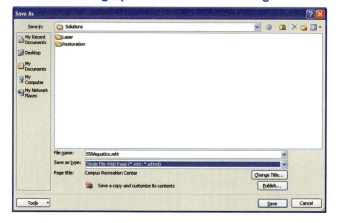

- The default page title is shown below the Save as type box. The page title displays in the browser's title bar (or tab, if you are using a browser that supports tabbed browsing).

- You can change the page title using the Change Title button.

- You can click Save to convert the presentation to a Web site using all slides and default publishing settings.

- For more control over the publishing settings, click the Publish button.

- The Publish button opens the Publish as Web Page dialog box, shown in the following illustration.

Publish as Web Page dialog box

- In the Publish what area, you can choose a range of slides to publish or a custom show. You can also choose whether to display any speaker notes your presentation includes.

- The Browser support area allows you to choose browser versions you want your Web site to support.

- In the Publish a copy as section of the dialog box, you once again have the option to change the page title, and you can check the path for the Web site.

- To save time, select the Open published Web page in browser check box. As soon as you click the Publish button, the presentation is converted and opens in your default browser.

- To further customize a presentation, click the Web Options button in the Publish as Web Page dialog box.

- The Web Options dialog box, shown in the following illustration, has six tabs of options you can select. On the General tab, for example, choose to add navigation controls, specify a color scheme for the outline that accompanies the slides in the Web site, control slide animation, and resize graphics to fit the browser window.

Web Options dialog box

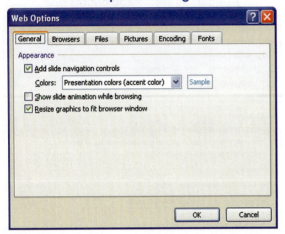

- Other tabs in this dialog box offer additional settings you may need to adjust:
  - On the Browsers tab, you can select the browser and browser version you want to target. If you have Internet Explorer 6.0 or later, you should specify that target browser for best results in testing Web pages. Select other options that relate to the target browser, such as whether PNG graphics are supported.
  - The Files tab allows you to specify how files are organized and named and whether Web pages created in Office applications can be edited in those applications.
  - Use the Pictures tab to set a default screen size for pictures that will work for most site visitors.
  - The Encoding and Fonts tabs define settings for use in the United States. You generally do not need to change these settings.
- When you have adjusted settings as desired, you can close this dialog box and publish the presentation.
- If your ultimate goal in creating a presentation is to publish it as a Web site, you should keep the following tips in mind when creating content.
  - Add action buttons and hyperlinks for easier navigation. You want your audience to access your Web pages easily.
  - Use small graphics and pictures to cut downloading time. If a visitor to your site has to wait a long time for a picture to download, that person will likely move on instead of wait.

- Use one major heading on each page to let readers know where they are. Don't squeeze too much text on one page.
- As a general rule, use the GIF image format for clip art graphics or other pictures with few colors; use JPEG format for photographs; use PNG format for buttons, bullets, and small images.

View a Web Presentation

- You view your presentation on the Web as you would any Web page; simply enter your URL in the Address box of the browser or use the Open command on the browser's File menu to open the presentation.

  ✓ You may need to authorize active content in your browser before the Web page will display.

- A Web presentation generally looks similar to the one shown in the following illustration.

A Web presentation in a browser

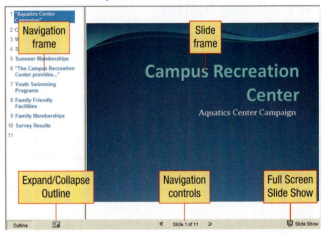

- When you publish your presentation to the Web, the presentation automatically includes a navigation frame, a slide frame, controls for showing or hiding frames, and a full-screen viewing option.
- Click in a slide title in the navigation frame to display that slide, or use the previous slide and next slide arrows to navigate.
- You can hide the slide titles by clicking the Outline button at the bottom of the navigation frame, or expand the outline to show all text on each slide.
- Click the Full Screen Slide Show button to see each slide in the full screen.

Curriculum Connection: Language Arts

Compound Words

When two or more words are combined to make a new word, the new word is called a compound word. There are three types of compound words: A closed compound word is written as single word with no hyphenation, such as doghouse. A hyphenated compound, uses a hyphen between the two words, such as white-collar. The third type, called an open compound, keeps the two words separated by a space, such as school bus or science fiction.

Make Your Own

Think up your own compound word. Create a PowerPoint presentation that could be used to market your new word to for inclusion in a new dictionary. Include the definition of the word, the part of speech, and examples of how to use it in a sentence. Spice up the presentation using enhancements such as transitions, pictures, animations, and varied backgrounds. Publish the presentation as a Web site so that your classmates can easily view the presentation.

PROCEDURES

Save a Presentation as a Web Site

1. Open the presentation to save as a Web site.
2. Click **Office Button** 🔲 ...... Alt + F
3. Click **Save As** .... A
4. Type a different name for the file if desired.
5. Click **Save as type** .... Alt + T
6. Select **Single File Web Page** (*.mht; *.mhtml) or **Web Page** (*.htm; *.html) .... ↓ , ↵Enter
7. Change page title if desired:
   a. Click Change Title... ...... Alt + C
   b. Type new page title.
   c. Click OK .... ↵Enter
8. Click Save .... ↵Enter

Specify Publishing Options

1. Follow steps 1–7 in previous procedure.
2. Click Publish... .... Alt + P
3. Select desired options in the Publish as Web Page dialog box.
4. Specify additional options:
   a. Click Web Options... ...... Alt + W
   b. Click each tab in Web Options dialog box to select options.
   c. Click OK .... ↵Enter
5. Click Publish .... ↵Enter

View a Web Presentation

1. Open the presentation in your browser.
2. Click a slide title in the navigation frame to advance to that slide.
   OR
   Click the **Next Slide** or **Previous Slide** button below the slide frame.
3. Click the **Outline** button to show or hide the navigation frame.
4. Click the **Collapse/Expand Outline** button 🔲 to show or hide bullet items below each slide title in the outline.
5. Click the **Full Screen Slide Show** button 🔲 to display the slides in the full browser screen.

EXERCISE DIRECTIONS

1. Start PowerPoint and open 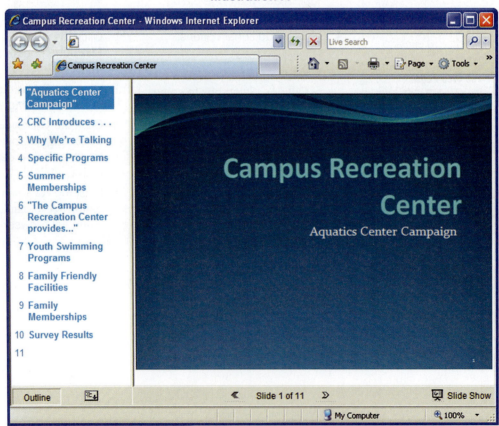50Aquatics.
2. Save the presentation as **50Aquatics_xx**.
3. Save the presentation as a Single File Web Page with the same title in the location where you are saving other PowerPoint presentations. Click Publish in the Save As dialog box to set the following publishing options:
   - Click the Web Options button and display the General tab.
   - In the Colors list, select Presentation colors (accent color).
   - Click the Browsers tab.
   - On the *People who view this web page will be using* list, choose Microsoft® Internet Explorer® 6 or later.
   - Click OK, and then choose to open the published page in the browser.
4. Click the Publish button to convert the file and open it in your browser.
5. If necessary, right-click the message bar in Internet Explorer and click Allow Blocked Content. Click Yes to confirm. Your page should look similar to Illustration A.
6. Navigate through the slides using the outline or navigation buttons, checking the links throughout the presentation.
7. Expand the outline, then hide the outline. Restore the outline and collapse it.
8. View the presentation in the full browser window. Right-click any slide and click End Show to stop the full-screen version.
9. Close the Web site and your browser.
10. Save and close the **50Aquatics_xx** presentation and exit PowerPoint.

Illustration A

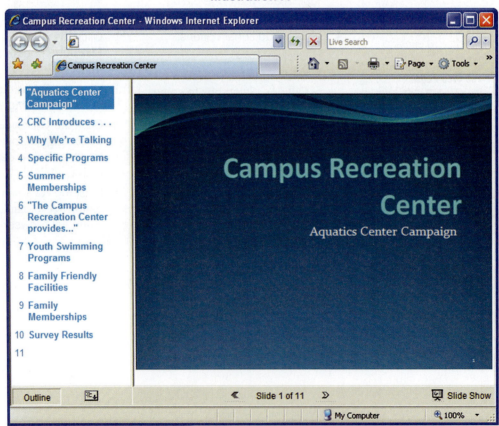

ON YOUR OWN

1. Start PowerPoint and open **OPP49_xx** or open **OPP50**.

2. Save the presentation as **OPP50_xx**.

3. Save the presentation as a single file Web page with the same name, supplying an appropriate page title and using other publishing options of your choice. Your page should look similar to Illustration A.

4. Test the links in the Web presentation. If you find the links to the custom shows do not work, return to the PowerPoint presentation and change the links from links to custom shows to links to the slides that begin each custom show. Then republish the presentation.

5. When you are happy with the look of the Web presentation, close the Web site and the browser.

6. Save any changes you have made to **OPP50_xx** and exit PowerPoint.

Illustration A

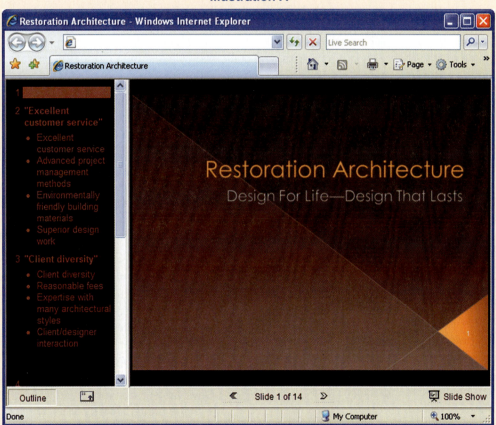

Critical Thinking

Application Skills   Great Grains Bakery has asked you to finalize the slide show you worked on in Lesson 2. The bakery's PR staff wants a slide show that can run unattended in a kiosk or display on a Web site as well as a show that can be presented to prospective catering clients. In this exercise, you will add finishing touches such as transitions, animations, links, and custom shows and then output the presentation in several ways.

DIRECTIONS

1. Start PowerPoint, if necessary. Open 🔘 **51Bakery**
2. Save the presentation as **51Bakery_xx**.
3. Apply transitions of your choice to all slides.
4. Display slide 5 and adjust the timing on the animation of the stars so that each one appears at the same time you begin to read that item. (Hint: Use the Timing command on the effect's drop-down menu to specify a delay.)
5. Display slide 7 and animate the text box below the picture using an entrance effect of your choice.
6. Insert the following comment on slide 4: **Link these items to custom shows**.
7. Create a custom show with the name **Catering** for slides 8–10. Create a second custom show with the name **Rental** for slides 11-12.
8. On slide 7, insert an action button or link that will take the viewer back to slide 1. Format the action button as desired. Illustration A shows one alternative.
9. Link the bullet items on slide 4 to the custom shows you created. Specify Show and return for these custom shows.
10. Delete the comment on slide 4.
11. Rehearse the slide show as it will be presented: On slide 4, jump to the first custom show; then, after the custom show ends and slide 4 appears again, jump to the second custom show. After the second show ends, proceed from slide 4 to slide 7 and then use the action button to return to slide 1.
12. Save slide timings and save your changes so far.
13. Run the Document Inspector and remove all properties.
14. Package this version of the presentation in a folder named **Bakery Presenter**. Include the PowerPoint Viewer and TrueType fonts with the package and specify the password **Grains** to open the presentation.
15. Save the current version as a PowerPoint show with the name **51Bakery Show_xx**.
16. Save the current file as a PowerPoint presentation named **51Bakery Kiosk_xx**.
17. Hide slide 4. Remove the action button (and its label, if you provided one) from slide 7. Set up the show to be browsed at a kiosk using the current slide timings. (Check to make sure all slides have slide timings.)
18. Run the show to make sure it loops properly. Stop after you have seen slide 2 the second time.
19. Mark the presentation as final. Close the presentation, and exit PowerPoint.

Illustration A

Exercise | 52

Curriculum Integration

Application Skills   Your math class is covering a unit on finding areas and volumes of plane and solid figures. You have been asked to create a tutorial presentation that students can use to review area formulas. You can use simple drawings and animations to create a useful review tool. Before you begin this exercise, locate the following information:

- Formulas for the areas of common plane figures such as square, rectangle, parallelogram, trapezoid, circle, and triangle

- Formulas for the volumes of several common three-dimensional figures such as cube, cylinder, pyramid, and sphere

- How to use a trigger with animation to create an interactive show (you can find this information in the PowerPoint Help files)

DIRECTIONS

Begin a new presentation. You may use a blank presentation or use one of PowerPoint's online presentation templates. Save the presentation with an appropriate name, such as **52Math_xx**. Insert an appropriate title and subtitle on the first slide. Apply a theme, if necessary, customizing theme colors and fonts if desired.

Add a slide on which you will create a table of contents to allow viewers to jump to slides that show areas of plane figures, or to slides that show volumes of solid figures.

Set up your first formula slide similar to the one shown in Illustration A. Use a separate text box for the formula itself. You can format numbers as superscripts and subscripts using the Font dialog box. Use the Symbol dialog box to locate fractions or Greek symbols you may need.

Add a hint on the first formula slide to let viewers know they must click the shape to see the formula.

To set up the trigger, select the text box that contains the formula and specify a custom animation entrance effect, such as Fade or Fly In. Then click the effect's down arrow and select Timing from the drop-down menu. Click the Triggers button in the effect option's dialog box, click Start effect on click of, and then choose the shape in the list that displays. When the shape is clicked during the slide show, the formula text box will appear with the effect you have chosen.

Duplicate the slide, delete the existing shape, and draw the next shape you want to illustrate. Modify the formula as necessary, and then reset the trigger for the new shape.

Continue in this fashion until you have illustrated all the formulas you want to show. Give each figure a different color and apply effects as necessary. You can find both two-dimensional and three-dimensional shapes in the Shapes gallery. You can use a gradient to give the illusion of three dimensions for a sphere. You will need to construct the pyramid shape using two triangles.

Insert two Section Header slides to introduce each section of figures. Create custom shows for the two groups of figures, and then link the items on slide 2 to the custom shows.

Set up the show to be browsed by an individual, and display the scrollbar.

View the slides in Slide Show view and test all your animations and links.

You may have to save this presentation for previous versions of PowerPoint. Use the Compatibility Checker to see what issues might occur.

Save changes to the presentation and close it. Exit PowerPoint.

Illustration A

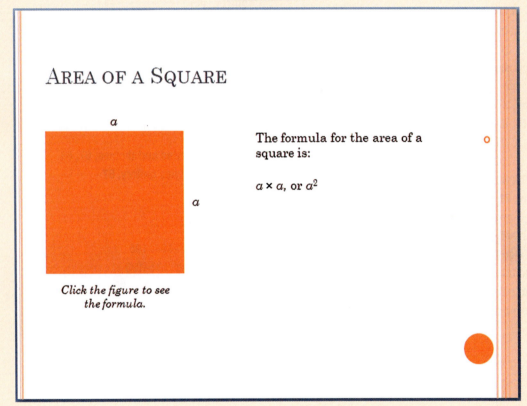

Index

notes, 53, 71
opening, 46, 49
outline format, 53
passwords, 284, 287
permissions, 285–286, 288
personal information attached, 292
previewing, 46, 93
printing, 91, 93
printing as notes pages, 85–86
properties, 40, 41
protecting, 283–286
publishing, 298–300
rehearsing, 263, 264
reusing slides, 80, 82
reviewing, 287, 289
saving, 39, 41
saving as Web site, 298–299, 301
source, 136
spell checking, 54, 55
starting, 41
tables, 154–155
templates, 70–71, 73
text from other programs, 79
themes, 47–48, 49
thumbnails, 53
Web sites, 271
XML format, 39
Presenter view, 278
previewing
animation, 262
handouts, 86, 87
movies, 221, 223
notes pages, 91
presentations, 46, 93
slides, 46, 91
sound, 223
transitions, 257
Previous Slide button, 86
Print dialog box, 91
Print (Ctrl+P) keyboard shortcut, 93
Print Preview, 86, 91
printing
notes pages, 85–86
presentations, 91, 93

Program Close button, 7
program icon, 24
program shortcut icon, 5
program windows
arranging on-screen, 26
default settings, 22
programs
control menu, 22
starting multiple, 25
properties, 36, 40, 46
Properties dialog box, 40
protecting presentations
digital signatures, 284–285
encrypting, 284
passwords, 284
permissions, 285–286
Publish as Web Page dialog box, 299
Publisher, 3
publishing, 298
default page title, 299
options, 301
presentations, 298–300
range of slides, 299
setting options, 299–300
slide shows, 299

Q

Quick Access Toolbar, 7, 9, 12, 15, 17, 61
Quick Style gallery, 128
Quick Styles
charts, 173, 174
pictures, 216
placeholders, 122, 123
shapes, 181
SmartArt graphics, 181
tables, 156, 160
WordArt, 134
Quick Styles gallery, 181

SINGLE PC LICENSE AGREEMENT AND LIMITED WARRANTY